Missouri '49er

Missouri '49er

The Journal of William W. Hunter on the Southern Gold Trail

Edited and annotated
by David P. Robrock

*Published in cooperation with
the Historical Society of New Mexico*

University of New Mexico Press
Albuquerque

Library of Congress Cataloging-in-Publication Data
Hunter, William W., fl. 1844–1852.
Missouri '49er : the journal of William W. Hunter on the southern
gold trail / edited and annotated by David P. Robrock. — 1st ed.
p.   cm. — (Historical Society of New Mexico publications
series)
"Published in cooperation with the Historical Society of New
Mexico."
ISBN 0-8263-1337-X (cloth).
1. Southwest, New—Description and travel.   2. Hunter, William W.,
fl. 1844–1852—Diaries.   3. Hunter, William W., fl. 1844–1852—
Journeys—Southwest, New.   4. Overland journeys to the Pacific.
5. Pioneers—Southwest, New—Diaries.   I. Robrock, David P.
II. Title.   III. Title: Missouri Forty-niner.   IV. Series.
F786.H96   1992
979'.02—dc20   91-40563
                                                    CIP

In memory of my father,
Paul A. Robrock
1917–1987

Contents

Contents

Foreword

The journal of William W. Hunter was discovered by David P. Robrock in the special collections at the University of Arizona library. Robrock recognized the journal as an important addition to the accounts left by gold seekers as the Forty-niners rushed to California. This account is of special value because of the literary abilities of Hunter and the route he took—"the Southern Gold Trail".

This southern trail to California was often preferred by the gold seekers because it avoided the mountains encountered on more northerly routes. Of course, the southern trail was noted for the difficult desert crossings of southern New Mexico and Arizona, which were relatively easy compared to the ninety miles from the Colorado River to San Diego. Hunter vividly describes those crossings.

Hunter was a well-educated man for his time. He recorded clear descriptions of the land and the people of the southwest, including invaluable eyewitness accounts of camp life and the customs of the Indians and Mexicans they encountered. He described the spirit of adventure and the lure of presumed wealth that dominated their thoughts when they left Missouri, only to fall victim to fatigue and, later on, despair. The trials and tribulations of the journey

sapped the travellers' energy and enthusiasm as they strug-
gled along the trail.

The Hunter party left Missouri, passed over the Santa
Fe Trail, took the Cimarron cut-off, and camped near Galisteo, a few miles outside Santa Fe. The party then travelled
south, on the east side of the Sandia and Manzano mountains, to Abo Pass. After a rest, they continued south along
the Rio Grande following the southern trail to California.
Hunter's account provides much new information, in particular the detailed descriptions of the area east of the mountains and of the Rio Grande valley south from modern
Bernardo. The publication of this journal adds to the growing collection of trail books. The Historical Society of New
Mexico is proud to cosponsor this book with the University
of New Mexico Press.

The current officers and members of the board of direc-
tors of the Society are: Robert R. White, President; John W.
Grassham, First Vice President; Darlis A. Miller, Second
Vice President; Andres J. Segura, Secretary; Spencer Wil-
son, Treasurer. Members of the board are: Susan Berry,
Maurice M. Bloom, Jr., Thomas E. Chavez, John P. Con-
ron, Richard N. Ellis, Elvis E. Fleming, Austin Hoover,
Myra Ellen Jenkins, William J. Lock, Riley Parker, Agnesa
Reeve, Albert H. Schroeder, Carl D. Sheppard, Robert J.
Torrez, David Townsend, and John P. Wilson.

Spencer Wilson
October 25, 1991

Acknowledgments

The journal of William W. Hunter presented many problems and challenges in editing for publication. Along the way I met many people whose knowledge and encouragement assisted my editorial efforts. In particular, I am grateful to the following people at the University of Arizona: Dr. James L. Officer and Dr. Kieren McCarty, who provided much useful information on the southwest portion of Hunter's journey. Dr. Harwood P. Hinton, former editor of *Arizona and the West,* offered many practical suggestions on the preparation of the journal for publication. Dr. Bernard L. Fontana, Field Historian, read the text and notes, and provided many useful comments and criticisms. Dr. Louis Hieb, head of Special Collections, brought to my attention the possibility of editing Hunter's journal for publication.

Patricia Etter, Manuscripts Librarian, Arizona State University Library, shared with me her extensive knowledge and research materials on the southern overland trails. Randy Roberts, State Historical Society of Missouri, Columbia, helped me search through the Society's massive collections for materials relating to Missouri during the gold rush. William H. Hunter, of Grand Island, Nebraska, located genealogical background material on Hunter's contemporaries.

Acknowledgments

I am indebted to the members of the editorial committee of the New Mexico Historical Society, Spencer Wilson, Myra Ellen Jenkins, and John P. Conron, for their many useful comments and criticisms. David V. Holtby, University of New Mexico Press, did an outstanding job in the final editing of the manuscript.

And to my wife Janice, I am grateful for her patience and advice during the long course of this project.

David P. Robrock
University of Nevada, Las Vegas

Introduction

*"We do not wish to add to the excitement already
existing upon the subject, but we would certainly
encourage men . . . to strike for 'Eldorado' as quickly
as possible . . . to get a few hundred thousands to
help Missouri!"*
—Fulton (Mo.) Telegraph,
January 26, 1849

Gold mania swept the American continent in early 1849.
The editor of the *Fulton Telegraph*, the major newspaper in
Callaway County, Missouri, was not unusual in his exuber-
ance. While a trickle of emigrants had already made the
arduous trip overland to the West Coast, in 1849 a veritable
flood tide of gold seekers surged across wide deserts and over
rugged mountains to reach California. The beckoning goldfields appeared to offer wealth to anyone intrepid enough to
go out there and bring it back home. This was a heady vision
in pre-industrial America, and one which led to much suffering, hardship, and loss before it became evident that for
most, the gold of California was an illusion. The beginning
of disillusionment came with the exhausting overland trek,
during which many argonauts lost their livestock and property, and arrived in the land of gold in rags and in poor
health.

The huge 1849 migration included a group from Callaway County, who christened their train the "Callaway County, Missouri Pioneers." William W. Hunter chronicled their experiences in a lengthy manuscript he entitled "Diary-Journal of Events, &c., On A Journey From Missouri To California, 1849." He provided a vivid picture of their nine-month journey across the continent over a lesser-used southern route, by way of Santa Fe and Tucson. Although he disappeared from the historical record soon after his arrival in California, Hunter left an interesting, well-written account of one of the great epics in American history, the overland journey of the Forty-Niners.

The series of events that led to the Callaway County Pioneers' departure began in January 1848, when John Marshall discovered gold at Sutter's Mill, on the western slopes of the Sierra Nevada. Rumors of the fabulous discovery raced eastward but did not immediately inspire great enthusiasm. Much skepticism was expressed and it was not put to rest until President James K. Polk included a monumental endorsement in his annual message to Congress in December 1848. He stated that the stories of the gold discovery were "of such extraordinary character as would scarcely command belief were they not corroborated by the authentic report of officers in the public service."[1]

Within a month of Polk's official confirmation, newspapers across the nation began to feature "gold news" columns on their front pages which extolled the wealth available in California. At first skeptical, the editor of the *Fulton Telegraph* became caught up in the frenzy and printed stories, from what he termed "reliable sources," which told of easily acquired riches. Such a letter appeared in the March 30, 1849 issue, wherein a California correspondent wrote: "Frequent instances are known of single men obtaining one thousand dollars a day. A Clergyman, unused to labor, washed in from five to six hours upwards of fifty dollars. A gentleman with one companion, in the dry diggings, picked up in two days upwards of three thousand dollars." The writer added tantalizingly that he "could go on for pages enumerating such facts." The same day, farther west, the Columbia, Missouri *Statesman* published a letter in which a California correspondent claimed that "Parties can easily obtain as high as 300 dollars per day."[2] To people in rural Callaway County, where most endeavors offered only hard work and meager returns, stories such as these made the goldfields an alluring prospect.

Dreams of gold fired the nation, but getting to California in 1849 presented a major problem as overland travel to the West Coast was a new phenomenon. Although wagons traveling westward had been a familiar sight since colonial days, those pioneers moved only a few hundred miles across forests and meadowlands. Emigrant trains traveling across the continent did not appear until the early 1840s, and it was not until 1844 that a party succeeded in bringing wagons through to California. Prior to 1849, California-bound travelers took a northern route down the Platte Valley, through the South Pass, in Wyoming, west to the Humboldt Valley and the rugged Sierra Nevada. This trail was over 2,000 miles long from Independence, Missouri, to Sutter's Fort (in present day Sacramento), and required four to five months to travel. It was not until the great surge of emigration in 1849 that a southern route was considered or needed.[3]

Hunter and his partners started out with the intention of following the northern route, but fear of cholera then raging along the road caused them to consider alternate routes. Other argonauts worried that the unprecedented size of that year's emigration would overload the available water and grazing resources. Where one had traveled on the northern route in 1848, there would be fifty in 1849, and a southern route offered a means of alleviating the congestion.[4]

Several trails constituted the southern route in 1849. Today these routes have names such as the Santa Fe Trail, the Chihuahua Trail, and the Gila Trail. The Callaway County Pioneers followed the main road from Independence to Santa Fe and then traveled down the Rio Grande Valley over roads long used by merchant caravans. Hunter's group did not move over a new trail until they turned west, near present-day Hatch, New Mexico, to pick up Cooke's road.

Lieutenant Colonel Philip St. George Cooke established a wagon road to California in the winter of 1846–1847 during the Mexican War. After occupying New Mexico, Colonel (later General) Stephen Watts Kearny started for California with a small force. He had planned to follow the Gila River from its headwaters in New Mexico to the Colorado River, but learned that the upper Gila Valley was impassable for wagons. Kearny proceeded along the Gila with pack mules and ordered Cooke to blaze a wagon road to California. Cooke's command laid out a road which curved southwest from the Rio Grande, crossed the broad tableland of New Mexico to Guadalupe Pass in southeastern Arizona, and then turned northward along the San Pedro River. Cooke marched through Tucson and north to the Pima Villages on the Gila River. There Cooke's road intersected with Kearny's route and both groups followed the Gila to its junction with the Colorado River. Once across the Colorado the soldiers faced a grueling ninety-mile crossing of the Colorado Desert before they reached the Laguna Mountains and descended to the coastal plain at San Diego. Thus

Cooke and Kearny established the main routes from the Rio Grande to California.

There were several trails which led to the starting points on the Rio Grande. In addition to Independence, Missouri, emigrants could also set out from Fort Smith, Arkansas, on the Arkansas River. This town was easy to reach by riverboat for travelers from the Ohio and the Mississippi valleys. From Fort Smith, the argonauts headed across present-day Oklahoma and the Texas panhandle to Santa Fe.

Gold seekers from the eastern seaboard could sail to a Texas seaport and then travel overland to San Antonio and El Paso. From El Paso, travelers headed northwest to Cooke's road or crossed northern Chihuahua and joined Cooke's road at Guadalupe Pass.

Although they started at various points, from Missouri River towns to ports on the Texas seacoast, all roads converged in the lower Gila Valley and followed the routes explored by Cooke and Kearny to the Colorado River and across the Colorado Desert to the Laguna Mountains in California. Once across the Colorado Desert, the road divided; Forty-Niners who intended to retain their wagons traveled to Los Angeles and then along coastal roads to San Jose and the goldfields. Those who hoped to sell their wagons and obtain ship passage to San Francisco headed for San Diego.[5]

One of the advantages of the southern route was the absence of major mountain ranges. The Laguna Mountains and Guadalupe Pass presented difficult terrain but were much easier to cross than the rugged Sierra Nevada, which travelers had to negotiate on the northern route. Emigrants on the southern route could obtain food and supplies from settlements in New Mexico, Sonora, and at the Pima Villages on the Gila River, while resupply was difficult on the northern route as the region was largely unsettled. The weather along the southern route was generally mild and the road open most of the year, while travelers on the northern route had to cross the Sierra Nevada by late October to avoid snow storms which blocked the mountain passes.

The major disadvantage of the southern route was the deserts. This problem was not immediately apparent; Hunter's party traveled almost two-thirds of the way to California with little difficulty. The journey did not become arduous until they rode out from Tucson. North of that village lay the first of the three major dry portions of road which the Forty Niners referred to as *jornadas,* a Spanish word denoting a day's travel. In the arid southwest, though, the word took on the additional meaning of a long stretch of road on which there was no dependable source of water. The absence of water for long periods was disastrous for livestock, the emigrant's source of locomotion, and the strain of traveling through these jornadas weakened the emigrants.

The first of the major jornadas was the ninety miles from Tucson to the Gila River. The Forty Niners then traveled along the Gila for approximately thirty miles until the river turned abruptly northward. Most travelers left the river at this point and began the second jornada, the fifty-mile crossing of the Gila Bend region. Then followed a 150-mile trek down the barren Gila Valley to the Colorado River. While water from the Gila River was always available, good forage was not. Once across the Colorado, they faced the most desolate jornada of the route, the ninety-mile crossing of the Colorado Desert.

Together these three jornadas presented almost 230 miles of enervating struggle. On Hunter's route, there were also minor jornadas in southwest Kansas (the Cimarron Desert) and in New Mexico, which added another 100 miles for a total of at least 330 miles of extremely difficult travel. In contrast, on the northern route there was only one jornada of any consequence, the fifty-mile crossing of the Carson Desert in Nevada. Hence, on the southern route, emigrants faced six times the waterless travel as on the northern route. These jornadas would not have presented great obstacles to travelers just starting out, in good health, and with strong, well-fed livestock. But coming after several months of strenuous effort and poor diet, the jornadas of the southwest proved fatal to thousands of oxen, mules, and horses, and to many emigrants as well.

A second major disadvantage of the southern route was its length. While it was approximately the same distance from Independence to Los Angeles as from Independence to Sacramento, travelers on the southern route faced an additional 400 miles travel north to the goldfields. Mitigating the extra distance was the fact that the southern route was more accessible to groups starting out from the southern states or from the eastern seaboard.

Although the two routes from the Rio Grande to the Pacific had not been used previously by emigrants, they had been explored and mapped by Cooke and Kearny and these published reports were available to serve as guidebooks. Many diarists took grim delight in finding errors and oversights in these reports, which emphasized the newness of the routes and how imperfectly the southwest was known in 1849. Cooke and Kearny's route saw little use by overland emigrants after 1849 as negative opinions and stories by the argonauts became widely known. In 1850, the editor of the *Fulton Telegraph* advised readers desiring to set out for California to take the northern route, observing that while the

" . . . route of the Gila river . . . [is] capable of being traveled, all things that are possible are not *expedient.*"[6]

Precise figures on the number of people who used the southern route in 1849 are difficult to estimate because of the lack of documentation. Ralph P. Bieber, in an early study, estimated that approximately 9,000 Forty Niners used the southern route. This figure included 3,000 people starting out from each of the major staging areas in Missouri, Arkansas, and Texas. Patricia A. Etter, in her recent study estimated that 12,000 people started out from the United States over the route. They were joined in the Santa Cruz and Gila valleys by perhaps as many as 6,000 Mexican gold seekers, for a total of perhaps 18,000 emigrants on the southern route in 1849. In contrast, approximately 25,000 to 40,000 people traveled to California over the northern route in 1849.[7]

The largest number of Forty-Niners using the northern route is a major reason it has overshadowed the southern route historically. Merrill J. Mattes has identified 375 diaries and journals relating to the northern route in 1849. In contrast, Etter found only 57 diaries and journals relating to the southern route. Several of these southern route journals have been published, among which the best are the accounts of William H. Chamberlin and H. M. T. Powell. Chamberlin traveled with a party from Pennsylvania by way of Fort Smith. From Socorro, they followed Kearny's route using a mule pack train and reached the goldfields in July. Powell was a member of an Illinois party that followed the same general route as Hunter's company. Both accounts offer detailed descriptions and provide a graphic record of the journey. Unfortunately, they are not readily available. Chamberlin's account appeared in four numbers of the 1945 *New Mexico Historical Review* and Powell's was published in limited edition in 1931 and 1984. Hunter's journal complements these two accounts in detail and in anecdote.[8]

Gradually, the gold rush excitement faded and the visions of easy wealth dimmed as disillusioned gold seekers sent discouraging reports back home. There was a large overland emigration to California in 1850, and then the number of people setting out diminished. The luster had worn off the California dream. In 1852, the *Fulton Telegraph* published this assessment of the gold rush: "It is calculated that out of every hundred persons who have gone to California, fifty have been ruined, forty [are] no better [off] than they would have been had they remained at home, five a little better, four something better still, and one has made a fortune."[9]

How Hunter fared in the gold rush is unknown as he fails to appear in California records. A terse note in a different hand on one of his hand-drawn map sheets reads: "Papers taken from chest sold at auction to pay charges. San Francisco. June 16, 1852." It is possible that Hunter obtained passage to San Francisco after his arrival at San Diego, placed some of his belongings in storage, and then set out for the gold fields. Why he failed to reclaim his property is unknown, as is his ultimate fate.

Little is known of Hunter before 1849, for although he wrote a detailed journal, he left himself out of it. There are no indications of his age, marital status, occupation, or any other background information in his journal. He mentions having lived in the West Indies and having traveled to Natchez and New Orleans. From his diction, vocabulary, and imagery, he appears to have been a well-educated man for his time. His comments and criticisms reveal a man of strong religious beliefs and of a conventional outlook. He was probably not a young man judging from the maturity of his thought, the respect he gained from his companions, and his ability to influence others. This may be inferred from the fact that the train members elected him to their judiciary committee, and that he was able to compose and have accepted a constitution for the train. These abilities are not usually found in a young man. But Hunter was also able to handle an ox team, which suggests that he was in his prime, probably his thirties.

Hunter recorded his experiences on sixteen unbound folios and two separate sheets. The folios measure 12 by 15 inches, which he folded in half to 12 by 7½ inches. Of the sixteen folios, one is marked "Memo," twelve constitute the narrative, and three make up the distance table. There are also four yellow sheets of various sizes upon which he drew a map of the route from the Rio Grande to San Diego. The map is drawn on both sides of the sheets, which when placed together measure 32 inches long. The folios are unruled, and Hunter used various shades of black-brown ink. The handwriting is the same throughout, but varies from a legible script to a minuscule hand that is difficult to read.

Hunter's work began, on about April 27, 1849, as a series of random observations and mileage calculations, which he labeled "Memo." Later, in the middle of June, he expanded the notations into a full journal with daily entries. At some later date he wrote a narrative account of his departure and the trip to Mann's Fort, for the period April 23 to June 12.

Hunter appears to have written most of his journal at different times along the trail. There are blank areas on some sheets which he intended to complete later. Just when the different parts of the journal were written is unknown, though the work was apparently out of his hands by 1852. One wonders why he went to such effort to record his

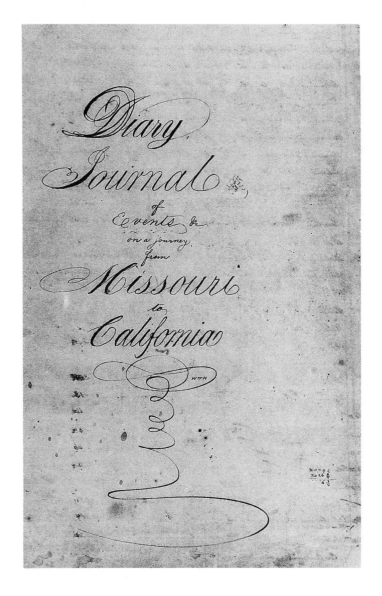

Title page from Hunter's manuscript. (Courtesy, Special Collections, University of Arizona Library)

First page of Hunter's "Memo." (Courtesy, Special Collections, University of Arizona Library)

First page of Hunter's "Journal." Hunter's minute hand, with its periods, dots, dashes, ink spots, and quotation marks, is not always easy to decipher. (Courtesy, Special Collections, University of Arizona Library)

First page of Hunter's "Distance Table." Appendix gives day's final campsite, distance traveled, and cumulative distance calculated by Hunter. (Courtesy, Special Collections, University of Arizona Library) experiences, draw a large map, and compile a detailed distance table which included columns for items such as road conditions and the location of water and grass along the route. He may have planned to publish the work as a travel book, for such books were popular in the nineteenth century, or to use it as the basis of a guidebook. Subsequent ownership is unknown; the University of Arizona Library purchased the journal from a book dealer in 1971.

Hunter paid little attention to punctuation or to paragraphing, and his entries usually appear as a block paragraph for each day. These block entries have been divided into paragraphs for publication and organized into nine chapters. Three of these chapters (One, Two, and Nine) result from breaks in Hunter's narrative. The other divisions were made at logical points in the journey. Hunter wrote comments in the margins of his distance table, and although these are usually limited to terse notes about the terrain and the weather, at times he made significant observations; these are given in footnotes. Hunter was an excellent speller and what few unusual or otherwise incorrect words that are to be found in the text have been allowed to remain, as they were in common usage at the time (eg. "Pimo" for Pima). He occasionally used parentheses and these have been retained. Editorial clarifications are indicated by brackets ([. . .]).

The overland roads of the nineteenth century often led travelers to places that are far from modern roads and highways. Consequently, there is disagreement in modern histories as to the exact location of important landmarks. Hunter wrote in precise terms and his journey can be followed on United States Geological Survey topographic maps, which have been consulted for locations in his journal and for modern spellings of geographic features. Illustrations are courtesy of Special Collections at the University of Arizona Library.

Introduction

Overall, Hunter's journal is a well-written firsthand account of overland travel in 1849. His work reflects a sense of immediacy, unmediated by revision for publication or by composition later in life. He wrote in the sentimental style then in literary fashion. Combined with his eye for detail and a wry sense of humor, these traits result in an entertaining narrative. In addition to a detailed physical description of the route (the mountains, the valleys, the streambeds, the plants, and the animals), Hunter includes graphic accounts of incidents, such as problems caused by a murder in his train, the shock and horror the emigrants felt as they witnessed the Papago Scalp Dance, and colorful descriptions of Mexican and Indian social life and customs. He also provides the human element in this great undertaking when he captures the psychological moods of the Forty-Niners, particularly the demoralizing and exhausting struggle across the deserts of Arizona and California.

Hunter's journal is useful as local history. He provides detailed descriptions of many localities and of their inhabitants in the Southwest at a time when the region was coming under United States domination. His style makes the journal interesting as a human document, for it records the impressions and thoughts of a well educated, mid-nineteenth century individual taking part in one of the major events in United States history. The "Diary-Journal" is a vivid, detailed account and a valuable contribution to the source material on the Forty-Niner overland trek in general and of the less well-known southern route in particular.

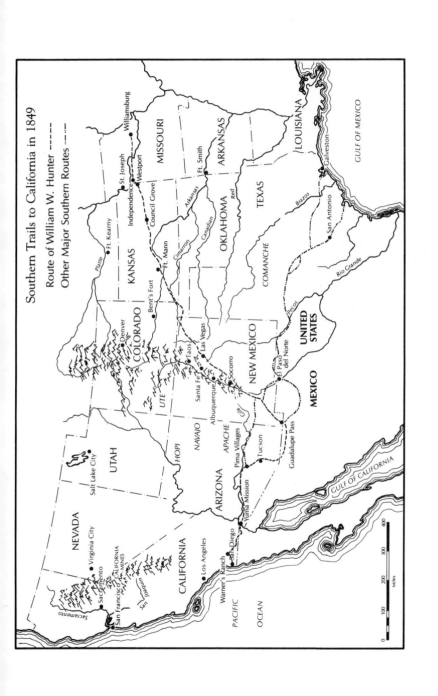

I

April 23–June 5

*"Nothing before was ever like this grand move, more like
the crusaders or Bonaparte's Grand Army for the
invasions of Russia . . . band[ed] together not for war
but for California's Golden Hills."*
—*J. W. Chatham,*
May 11, 1849

J. W. Chatham, an argonaut from South Carolina, was not
alone in recognizing that the overland journey to California
in 1849 was something extraordinary. However, it was not
an undertaking approached with courage and determination
in all cases. Plagued by doubts and hesitations, Hunter
and his partners experienced an emotional departure from
their homes in Montgomery County, Missouri, on April 23,
1849.

Hunter's party intended to follow the northern route to
California, which he referred to as the "South Pass Route."
However, as they neared the Kansas border, they met a
group from Williamsburg, Callaway County. The leader of
the Williamsburg group had read the 1848 edition of Kearny's and Cooke's reports and believed that the southern
route to California was practical. The argonauts voted to
follow the hitherto little-used route.

The cold and rain of late spring failed to dampen the
spirits of Hunter's party once they had joined with the

Williamsburg group and were under way across the Kansas plains. Although Hunter's company feared cholera and hostile Indians, only one member of their train suffered the dreaded disease, and he recovered. The Indians proved to be friendly and eager to trade.

As the Missourians became accustomed to the routine of overland travel, Hunter's journal, which began as a series of terse notes and mileage calculations, evolved into a detailed account of the route, of the Indians and mountain men, and of the plants and animals. At times he let his imagination wander and mused of lost love and of transcontinental railroads.

On May 21, Hunter's group reached Council Grove, the traditional point for travelers on the Santa Fe road to formally organize into trains. The Williamsburg group had grown to include 15 wagons, 51 men, 1 woman and 1 girl, 17 horses, and approximately 100 oxen. After some disagreement, they adopted a written constitution, elected officers, and christened themselves the "Callaway County, Missouri Pioneers."

Beyond Council Grove, the Missourians followed the well-traveled Santa Fe road along the north bank of the Arkansas River. They observed the standard overland routine of starting out early in the morning, traveling four to five hours, and then making a camp at noon. The oxen were unyoked and allowed to rest and graze. Late in the afternoon the stock were hitched up and the journey resumed until evening. This routine conserved the strength of the livestock and allowed the company to average sixteen to eighteen miles per day.

Of the forty-five days covered in this chapter, four were passed in camp, and Hunter traveled approximately 550 miles.

Journal

On Saturday at 1 p.m., of April 23, 1849, our wagon left the residence of Arthur T. Maupin, Esq., Montgomery Co., Mo., for a journey to California. The Company who started with it were: Almon Rollins, E. W. G. Wingfield, and Wm. W. Hunter. Wm. Newlee, Esq., would have also been with us but sickness in his family prevented it.[1] This was a trying evening to those who were leaving their families. A long, perilous, and doubtful journey was before us, rendered more terrible from the reports of Indian massacres, starvation, sickness, and death in every form, which now teemed through the County and were the everyday topics of conversation.

At an earlier period, when the first accounts of the "El Dorado" of California were received, nothing but the brilliant acquisitions of those who were then in that region were spoken of, and men, women and children of every age and complexion seemed half crazy to speed them to the "better land." "Oh! That I had the wings of a dove," exclaimed many a poor devil who had not courage enough to scarcely leave his chimney corner by any conveyance, "how soon would I land in the golden valley of the Sacramento."

But with the soliloquy ended their expectations, as their ardor became perfectly dampened by the horrible tales which subsequently became rife among us. To be sure, the letters which were ever and anon received from the "Gold Region" tended to keep up the spirits, and busy the hopes of many a fellow, who placed confidence rather in his wishes than in his resolution and for a time made him imagine that he was indeed hero enough to undertake the "hazardous enterprise." But alas! As the awful crisis of departure drew near the resolutions which had been only hoped, began to

3

wax sickly, and finally gave way to the huge prompting of prudence, and a pretty considerable "back out" ensued amongst those whose greatest anxiety was the safety and good case of their poor bodies.

To those who "dared be men" this was a trying moment indeed. Their lovely wives and beautiful children, fondly clinging to them, ere yet the terrible "goodbye" could be whispered, held them with grief too big for utterance. But as the wagons moved off the thought that it was to provide for the comfort and happiness of those "dearest of all treasures" filled them with energy sufficient to part the tender embrace that encircled them, and to rush from the presence of those they loved before affection should claim the mastery of their judgments and frustrate their long and best devised plans.

After giving vent to sorrow's first and keenest paroxysm, having other cares pressing their immediate attention, they mostly nursed their grief in silence, and soon became resigned and cheerful in prosecuting the enterprise, of which their best judgments approved.

We camped the first night and next day at "Hall Mill," in Callaway County, about six miles from the neighborhood whence the 100 had started, and were most scrumptiously and kindly entertained by the hospitable proprietor and his excellent lady.[2]

April 24, Sunday   This morning I took with me a negro boy and a couple of horses and rode bareback to Williamsburg, a distance of 9 miles, after my meat which had been left there by mistake, not having brought racks in which to put it.[3] I bought a cord and strung it (three hundred weight) through the corners. I then filled some old bagging with straw and laid it lengthwise along the horses' back, across which I swung my meat. I had about 7 miles to take it in this manner, during which it must have fallen off at least twenty times. In replacing it on the horses I got perfectly besmeared with grease and dirt from head to foot and was a certain target for the jests and witticisms from passers by who enjoyed many a hearty laugh at my presence. I cannot say much in favor of the agreeable state of my temper on the occasion, but I did know it should be the last time I would ever undertake to pack meat strung across a horse without being better prepared for it. However, this cross like all others soon came to an end, and it being night when I reached the wagon some 10 miles distant I rolled myself in my blanket and soon forgot the frustrations and fatigue of the day.

April 25th After breakfast this morning we recommenced our journey following the "Old St. Charles Road" through Callaway County.[4] The weather was dull and cloudy, and in a short time it commenced raining. Some little unpleasantries having transpired in our mess, the state of the atmosphere accorded well with the gloomy broodings of a mind altogether too susceptible at being hurt at discord or where good and friendly feeling was liable to be estranged.

Was the gloomy aspect of this, my first day's regular travel, emblematical of its final result? Did it indeed portray a dark and lowering destiny awaiting me? "No!" whispered a secret monitor within, "endeavor to do thy duty to Him who guides and protects thee, and to those by whom thou art surrounded, and all shall be well with thee. He can turn aside the weapon of the savage—smooth the ruggedness of thy way and cause the desert to bloom as the rose around thee. Be acting in conformity to His Holy Law, and placing all thy trust and confidence in Him Thou shalt find that like the glorious sun it shall soon dispel these mists. Behind a frowning Providence, He hides a smiling face."

With feelings chastened by the current of my thoughts, I could trace beauties and paint pictures which, though nearly wet to the skin, enabled me to trudge on my way rejoicing. This dreariness—these showers, were but the harbingers of the early spring, preparing the late frozen and barren earth for the reception of the germs which were to bestow countless blessings to sustaining life and to scatter peace, plenty, and happiness among the sons of men.

And then the idea of some beautiful writer whom I had read, "He who goes into his garden to hunt for them will certainly find them, but he who seeks a rose may return with one smiling in his bosom," occurred to me, and with a firm resolve to look at the sunny side of whatever might happen I soon enjoyed much serenity as I expected generally falls to our lot.

The roads were in places very heavy and we encamped for the night at William Alleins, on the Grand Prairie.[5]

Having made no minutes of dates, nor indeed but few of matter, owing to a protracted attack of sore eyes till we arrived at Council Grove, I must here generalize such items as my memory returns. We started for Columbia, Boone County, the next morning over a very good road till we struck the timber. Here it was muddy, hilly and rough, causing severe labor to the team. I was well pleased with the town of Columbia, its neatness, cleanliness, etc., but was disappointed in the view I'd formed of the magnificence of the University. I had not time to visit it, but from a distance it claims but a small share of admiration.[6] We continued moving on to Rocheport, stopping only at night to feed and put our cattle in a lot.[7]

The road from Columbia to this point, $13\frac{3}{4}$ miles, lay over one continued series of hills and hollows. The land is apparently rich and capable of producing the necessities and some of the luxuries of life in abundance. One feature in the surface of the country over which I passed particularly struck me. It seemed to offer a convincing proof that "agrarianism" must certainly be a humbug both in theory and fact. Its face was evidently formed for an exclusive adaptation to private right as each man on the plantations seemed to possess his "hill" and no more, and to glory in a residence on the summit thereof.

Rocheport is a thriving little business town on the river. Here we first came into the actual presence of the Cholera, some deaths having already occurred and four new cases being then under treatment.[8]

Our original intention of proceeding to St. Joseph by keeping altogether on the northern side of the Missouri River had been changed at or near Columbia, and we crossed the river at this point intending to recross it at Lexington, and so take a more direct route.[9]

We continued on to Boonville, Cooper Co., distant 10¾ miles, over a road, which along the river was deep sand. On leaving the stream, however, the road improved, and though somewhat hilly was yet good to travel. Boonville displays evident tokens of becoming at no distant day a very flourishing business town. All seemed life and animation. The storekeepers seemed to have their hands full waiting on well dressed customers. The steamboat at the landing was pouring out and receiving the treasures of commerce while the streets near the river were well lined with drays in rapid transit, and vocal with noise and bustle. Here also were many traders and trappers on the eve of departure for the Rocky Mountains. Most of these, together with some Californians, were armed to the teeth.[10]

On the road near Boonville I was delighted with the neat and sometimes handsome appearance of the dwellings instead of "log cabins," huts or houses with rail fences around a barren lot (a sight too common in some portions of the west). The buildings were either of brick or framed and neatly painted, with an eye to some little architectural taste on their construction. The yards around them, when not laid out in gardens (of which I noticed many), were surrounded with either paling or plank fences painted white, and around with a beautiful green sword of grass, through which towered rows of shade trees and clumps of evergreens.

I also noticed that the porticoes which adorned most of the dwellings were graced with a variety of creeping vines already gushing rapidly toward the roof. The ladies of this section seemed also to devote a large share of their attention to that most healthful, innocent and soul ennobling of all farming pursuits, the cultivation of flowers. Many of the windows were filled with flower pots containing geraniums and other beautiful plants, which they were early in trusting unsheltered to the caprice of a Missouri atmosphere.

At Boonville we heard of a highly respected company of Californians, raised in Cooper Co., who were then on the road ahead, and would rendezvous at Harrisonville in Cass Co., and thence start via the "South Pass" to California. This train my two partners concluded to join, and having procured a letter of introduction to two of its members we pushed on to overtake them.[11] Our route lay through Georgetown, Pettis Co., where we remained one day to have our wagon tire cut and to lay in little necessaries of which we needed.

Georgetown is a small place but pleasantly and healthfully situated. Four blacksmiths' shops in busy operation seemed full of work. Some 80 to 100 wagons were here under repairs to proceed to Santa Fe. This country mostly consists of rich and extensive prairies, well adapted to raising stock of all kinds, and is but thinly settled along the road.

We proceeded to Warrensburg, Johnson Co. This is a neat and delightfully seated little town in the midst of a fine fertile country. Our stay here was short. From the information here received we were led to believe that the Cooper Company would rendezvous at the "Lone Jack" in Jackson Co., and we therefore shaped our course accordingly.[12] It seemed, however, that either a maze of error overspread the country or that our informants placed a goodly distance between their assertions and the truth, for not one time in one hundred did we find [that] the results corresponded in the slightest degree to the statements we questioned.

The day after leaving Warrensburg we were joined by a gentleman of the name of West, belonging to Pettis Co., near Georgetown, who added much to the interest of our social circle. This gentleman, though having an ample fortune at his disposal, had either conceived the romantic idea of visiting far off lands or had become so fascinated with the dazzling tales of sudden wealth engulfing the inhabitants of the "gold region" that he determined to quit his home, and on a level with the poorest adventurer, to embark himself and his hopes on the tide of emigration now daring the dangerous transit to the shores of the Pacific. He overtook us driving his wagon and teams by himself, a party who were to have met him at Warrensburg having failed to do so.

In traveling the "Shawnee Trace" in this country we came to a hill or mound in the midst of a vast prairie called "Pilot Knob," which I ascended.[13] I should judge it to be elevated some 120 to 150 feet above the level of the plain. Its top was level and nearly square, rounded at the edges, and was some 50 to 60 paces long by about 20 at the broadest end, whence it gradually tapered to some 10 or 12 at the other.

The view from the top was not as beautiful as if the country around had been more diversified by hill and dale, or had been under cultivation. The prospect embraced a view of from 35 to 40 miles, and was delightful in contrast with the level prairie which we had traversed for some days. There were some mounds to the N.W. whose regular outlines and picturesque shrubbery added much beauty to the landscape in that direction. Nearly all the Western portion of Johnson Co. consists of a rich, gently undulating prairie, on which the grass had by this time spread a velvet carpet of deepest green, although yet too short to sustain our cattle.

There were no vast herds scattered over the surface devouring with eager appetite the first fruits of the welcome spring, or drowsily ruminating with well distended hides, in peace and superfluity, as my fancy had portrayed. On the contrary, the farms which we passed seemed destitute even of a sufficiency for use, and most of the habitations as well as their inmates showed plainly that they did not revel in a superabundance of worldly pelf.

On nearing the "Lone Jack," we were informed by several that there were some 500 wagons lying there and about to organize into companies for an instant start. We pushed on till we arrived there, and found *none*, nor had above 30 passed by enroute for California. Here we were much perplexed by doubts as to the best course to pursue. The cholera was raising violently at Independence, and there we dared not go. To be still was both expensive and useless, and about this time I believe the most serious notions of my companions to get clear of the dilemma was to wheel about and return home.

This, however, was utterly inconsistent with my views

and I was therefore obliged to use all my address to turn the current of their cogitations into an opposite channel. We finally concluded to start on the road and to fall in with some company about to cross the Kansas River tolerably high up, and by striking across the country obliquely to fall into the "South Pass" road amongst some of the foremost trains. We jogged accordingly, sometimes one way, then another, leaving Independence some 10 or 12 miles to the right, till we fell in company with Dr. N. E. Branham's wagons, together with two from our own neighborhood. This revived our spirits, and gave a new spur to our energy which had become most woefully lukewarm. [14]

The Doctor had started to California via Santa Fe, New Mexico, thence by Cooke's trail to the westward of the Rocky Mountains. A vote was accordingly taken as to which route should be taken, all hands except the Doctor agreeing to go with the majority. The vote of over three-fourths was given in favor of the Santa Fe route, and from this moment, in good earnest, we concluded to speed on our way.

We then proceeded to near the residence of Judge Yager, where we all encamped and remained two days. [15] We then crossed the "Big Blue," a large, well watered and finely timbered creek at or near the boundary line. [16] Here a fellow asked us 50 cts. per bushel for corn, so we concluded to graze from this moment entirely. Our road expenses from Montgomery Co. to this point, including fees, crossing the river, having wagon tires cut, etc., amounted to fifteen dollars seventy cents.

On crossing the creek at the upper crossing we entered a prairie bottom whose soil seemed incapable of being surpassed by any in the world. There is a tract of from 2 to 3,000 acres which nature seems to have intended as a site of a large and magnificent plantation. It is nearly surrounded on three sides by the creek, which contains an exhaustless supply of water. There is also timber directly on its margin more than sufficient to fence in fifty times as large a space.

About ½ mile north from the creek and near the center of the space, the gentle and beautiful ascent takes place till it strikes the level of the prairie country. This to the N.W. is covered with a magnificent growth of choice timber, while between it and the timber on the creek to the westward there is an open space of about ¾ of a mile, being a natural outlet to the vast scope of prairie which here commences. In the N.W. corner are beautiful mounds apparently specially formed for the site of a dwelling, offices, etc., as that a full and commanding view might be had of the whole planta-tion. Taken as a whole, I doubt much if nature ever did so much at any other spot towards *making* a farm. It is, I believe, in the Indian Territory, hence reason of its being unoccupied.

The road from Independence to this place was literally strewn with clothing, bedding, etc., of those who had fallen victims of the Cholera, and there were many cases in our immediate vicinity. We encamped at an excellent spring on the western side of the "Big Blue," and continued shifting our camp every day a mile or two to other springs; timber and grass being abundant our cattle and ourselves fared well. There was a vast detail of timber here injured or destroyed by fire, said by the Shawnee Indians, amongst who we were now sojourning, to have been caused by Santa Fe traders firing the prairie. The Chief, who paid us a visit with some of his councilors, requested us not to cut any of the green timber, but told us that we were welcome to use as much of that which was dead as we needed. He was a good natured, corpulent old fellow dressed in a French blouse and cap. [17]

This tribe seems to pay some little attention to agriculture, as I noticed several small fields enclosed with rail fences. Their houses are built of logs and covered with bark, cut to the requisite length; in breadth it is half the circumference of the trees. Stripped while green and flattened by pressure, it forms a neat looking and secure roof. While here we caught plenty of fish, but could see little or no game.

Four of our men about this time started out on a hunt, two agreeing to keep up one side of the creek and the others to range up the other. When they had attained a sufficient distance from camp, one of them who "had seen service" proposed to *scare* the opposite two, which was agreed to by his companion, who immediately secreted himself. The other then crossed the creek and commenced yelling, shouting and running towards them. Nearly petrified with terror, they stood with open mouths and eyes expanded to the utmost, awaiting his approach. As he dashed past them he told them that "there were some forty Indians, with guns, just above them and in full pursuit, that they had by this time got W's scalp and d——d if they would not get theirs in less than five minutes."

Waiting for nothing further they dashed through briar patches, over rock, stumps, and logs, and took the creek like a pair of frightened otters. On regaining the opposite bank, where were but few obstructions, every muscle bone and fiber was strained to the utmost, they cleared the ground in gallant style, and in a few minutes reached camp, breathless and all but exhausted. Their eyes betrayed the perturbation within and their bloodless and trembling lips showed plainly that they considered it anything but a joke. The others shortly afterwards came in breathless from laughter, and the way the jests and merriment flew about for some time "wasn't slow." The sufferers, however, bore it very stoically and in a few days other pleasantries succeeded in affecting its sting.

About this time we lost one of our partners. It appeared that his lady, after yielding a reluctant consent to his departure, had repented of the indulgence, and after using all other endeavors in vain had like a second Imogene undertaken the fatiguing and doubtful task of overtaking him herself. Foiled in her efforts, she was returning with feelings that may better be conceived than described, when fortune threw in her way a person who had spent the previous night with us. On becoming acquainted with this fact, she immediately offered him one hundred dollars to return to our encampment with a message to her husband. He had traveled off to another train at some distance when the messenger arrived and did not return until sundown.

On receiving the message for his recall, a deep shade over spread his fine and lively countenance, a severe struggle was passing within of hope, ambition, and the desire of novelty on the one hand and of conjugal affection on the other. Soon, however, the cloud passed; the strong desire to visit a foreign land whose streams seemed literally paved with gold, the prospect of almost unlimited wealth easily and in a manner instantaneously acquired, the destruction of bright hopes and brave resolutions to overcome difficulty and danger, so consonant with and animating to a warm and generous spirit, all, all of these with other cherished inducements must now be sacrificed on the altar of love.

I was highly interested in watching the workings of a noble soul at such a moment and as I marked the relaxation of the features, and a rising smile playing about the mouth, I felt confident that nothing but death could have the mastery, where love and all else were at stake. He immediately and cheerfully prepared for his departure, and ere morning dawned was no doubt far within the limits of the state. My partners here showed evident symptoms of a desire to return home, and they certainly would have done so could any plausible pretext have been seized.

We continued on by short stages via the "Lone Elm," distant 35¾ miles from Independence, and as the grass was excellent began to think of organizing a company for the trip across the plains.[18] Many wagons were traveling the same route but as yet seemed to prefer traveling separately or in small companies. Wood and water could always be obtained at or near the road, or by descending to some of the creeks.

Near "Willow Springs" we discovered a wolf den out of which we dug six whelps—five of which seemed perfectly sullen, refusing to move or note anything that passed. But one other manifested a most vicious disposition, snapping at everything that came in his way. We put them up as targets and shot them. The old ones kept themselves out of our reach, howling hideously and betaking themselves to flight at the least attempt to pursue them. The howling of these animals around our camp at night, though not so frightful as we had been led to expect from the stories that had been told us, was still sufficiently loud and near to frequently disturb our repose.[19]

At "110 Creek" we shot our first old one [ie., a coyote], and caught a gopher, an animal resembling a rat in size and color, with a short tail, immensely muscular and strong arms and claws to burrow in the earth, and a large pouch on each of its jaws to transport to the surface the earth it excavates to form its habitation. Their "hills" were very numerous all over this section of the country. We also caught several "prairie ground squirrels," a beautiful little animal, resembling a common squirrel of the states, but longer in the body with hair more glossy and soft, and beautifully full black eyes.[20]

At [blank] a gentleman, now of our company, received a wound which had well nigh proved fatal. One of his companions, a messmate desiring to see the pistol, had handed it to him, and while examining the action of the lock, the pistol by accident was discharged. Hamilton happened at the moment to have his hand on his face, the ball passing through two of his fingers, entered at the chin and passing round the lower jaw bone, forced its exit immediately beneath the ear. He lay for some time in a very precarious state.[21]

May 19   We this day arrived at "Big John," a fine creek 2½ miles east of "Council Grove."[22] The road hence to Independence cannot be surpassed in excellence by any in the world, and the country through which it passes from the boundary of Missouri is as magnificent grazing land as eye ever scanned. The soil is deep and rich within 30 miles of the grove, where it is somewhat rocky. The surface gently rolling, with streams meandering in sufficient abundance to furnish an ample supply of water and an abundance of wood, provided other than rail fences were used, to suffice for all necessary purposes.

The road to this point was literally strewn with the carcasses of cattle that had mostly perished on a trip from Santa Fe last fall and winter.[23] There were also many graves of persons who had died on this road and had here found in truly unconsecrated spots their long long resting place, with none but rough and lousy men to soothe their last moments, and naught save the wolf to chant their requiem. Here is a something at which nature recoils, to meet death under such circumstances, and in the dreary wild to breath out the spirit, with no sympathy to cheer, no gentle hand to minister comfort and no tongue to whisper peace or consolation to the departing Shade. A lonely and most desolate feeling occurs, even on the bare contemplation of such a death, how much more mournful than to meet it. Little, however, do the sleepers dream that in less than ten short years, if I opine rightly, their sepulchers will be obliterated. An iron road will embrace not only their narrow beds but the whole breath of the vast continent in whose bosom they slumber, while hundreds of their own living and energetic species will daily sweep over them, bearing the wealth and luxuries of the Indies, and the far off Isles of the sea, to scatter along the margin of the boisterous Atlantic, and amongst populous cities whose sites are yet unthought of.

To the right of the road, some 350 yards E. of the crossing of the creek, is a large spring of deliciously cool and pure water. In the evening we were visited by a large party of "Kaw" Indians, who came down the hill from the westward at a sweeping gallop, yelling and shrieking at the top of their voices and making a hideous uproar. They dashed up at the same speed to the wagons, where they halted so suddenly as almost to throw their ponies on their haunches. The first of these they endeavored to trade or sell to us, pointing out their good qualities and occasionally in parties of three or four scouring at full speed over the neighboring plains. The endurance of these generally shabby looking animals is prodigious. One half the hard treatment and ill usage they receive would inevitably kill our stoutest American horses.

One amongst them, their Chief, particularly struck me. He spoke English very fluently and bore himself with much dignity. His stature was almost gigantic, and his clean limbs and well developed muscles bespoke of an extraordinary degree of agility and strength. Some of our men, on his rebuking some little pleasantries that passed at his expense, asked him if "he was not afraid to express himself thus freely in such a crowd?" "Afraid?" said he, "I fear no man. I know what fear is!" and a haughty look of defiance beaming at that instant from his eyes seemed to vouch for the truth of his assertion.[24]

At night a committee of six were appointed to draft a constitution and bylaws for government during the journey to California.

May 20th   This morning the committee met according to appointment and proceeded patiently to the discharge of the duty imposed on them, and after much deliberation and discussion, finished the instrument and submitted it to the assemblage. Its reading produced an expression of opinions and sentiments, as diversified and irreconcilable as the languages that confronted "Babel's Workmen." After many of a "d——d if that will do" as the various clauses were negated and an explosion of each man's particular or general disgust, the ill-fated instrument, misconstrued, vilified and excoriated, was consigned contemptuously to the shades of Pluto's dominion. All now was anarchy and confusion. Every man wished to talk but none would hear, and the day, instead of being spent in devotion and reverence, echoed with nothing but liberties invaded, rights set at, all officers and no men. Citizens not soldiers, tyranny and humbug, &c., &c.

May 21st   All hands started for the grove, distant 2½ miles.[25] On rising the hill from the creek a fine view was obtained of a highly picturesque country. After about a mile we came to some Indian graves. One was shaded by an old tent cloth, set up on a pole above it. They were all covered with rocks to prevent the wolves despoiling them. Near them stood an old iron pot and some fragments of earthen-ware, old clothing, &c.; tokens of respect or articles of necessity to be used by the deceased on his journey to the "Land of the Spirits."

We now entered a bottom shaded by ancient and stately timber, of many varieties. On crossing the creek we ascended an abrupt bank and stood at once in the midst of the Indians' "Hall of Conference." Here was a store, blacksmith's shop, &c., and some fields were fenced in adjoining the houses. We stayed to purchase some few articles we needed and then drove some two miles to the bank of the creek and en-camped.

Here one or two "New Constitutions" soon went the rounds, each sharing the fate of the one that then slumbered. In the evening I concluded to try my hand solus at the business, and knowing that brevity was essential to the success of any measure that might now be proposed, I soon drew out a document to my notion and with much solicitude ventured to read it before the company. Not much was said contra to it, and on the whole a favorable impression had been made [though] still no action was taken on it.

After nightfall a committee of one [member] from each wagon was selected, whose action was to be binding on their respective messes. My "banting" have been first submitted, and a vote taken on each clause separately, was unanimously adopted "verbatim et liberatim" and our company was christened the "Callaway Co., Missouri Pioneers." And now a spirit of unity usurping that of discord and contrariness, each retired to his bed to refresh himself for the morrow.[26]

May 22 Started for the "Diamond Spring," distant 16 m. from Council Grove.[27] The country was a rich prairie destitute of timber as far as the eye could roam. We arrived here early in the evening and encamped some 150 yards from a cold spring of delicious water. Near it grew profusely a weed called in the West "Lamb's Quarter," making a very good and palatable vegetable. I had gathered and used several messes of it along the road. There was also another plant weed called "Crows Foot," which we dressed. This, however, I did not relish as well as the other.

At sundown we assembled to elect officers when Samuel H. Berry, of Callaway, was elected Captain. Freeman S. McKinney, Esq., of Fulton, Orderly Sergeant, and Adam Dickerson, John Reddick and William W. Hunter, Judicial Committee.[28]

24th We yesterday encamped at the "Lost Spring," and this evening arrived at "Cottonwood Fork" of the Arkansas River.[29] This has been reputed as a very dangerous spot from the thefts and attacks of Indians. The night sat in rain and [was] very dark, broken by vivid lightning. The guard have been cautioned to be wary, but it is a time on them.

25th We this day remained encamped. About daybreak an alarm was excited by our horses taking fright, tearing up their picquets and rushing furiously past us on the road back. A stampede—A stampede! loudly vociferated brought all hands instantly from their dormitories to a caucus, each face indicative of anxiety to ascertain the cause of so unceremonious a summons. Six horses having passed out of sight, a pursuing party was soon on their trail. Three of the runaways were stopped by a train some 15 miles in our rear, and a fresh party pushing after the others ran them about 10 miles further, when their speed seeming unabated, the chase was abandoned.

[Remainder of sheet blank]

[At this point there is a break in Hunter's narrative. The remainder of the sheet, front and back, is blank, and Hunter probably intended to fill them in at a later time. The gap in the narrative covers the period from May 25 to June 6, when the train traveled from Cottonwood Creek to Mann's Fort.

N.K. Grove, a member of Hunter's train, wrote to his wife a lengthy account of this portion of the trip, and it was published in the Fulton Telegraph *on July 13, 1849, and is as follows:*

May 23 We moved this morning, and drove some five or six miles to breakfast and to graze our stock. While we were doing so there came up a heavy rain and [it] gave us all a smart drenching. We again hitched up and put out, and after driving fifteen miles camped at the "Lost Spring," which is a small spring of brackish water that boils up in the bed of a little creek entirely destitute of timber. We hauled wood to cook with, and to make us a little fire to warm by.

I have to stand guard tonight, and in [the] drawing I am thrown on the last relief, which is from two o'clock till day light. It rained very hard this evening, and turned so cold that I have to put on my blanket coat and mackinaw over that. It has rained on us nearly every evening since we left the "line." We always have had wind and rain, and sometimes a good deal of hail.

May 24 We have traveled seventeen miles today, and are encamped at Cottonwood creek, a consider-

able stream, timbered entirely with cottonwood. . . .
This is considered a dangerous place, and those who
have to stand guard tonight are joking each other
who will run first, in case the Indians attack us
tonight.

May 25   Owing to the continued rains which have
fallen, we concluded to lay by today, to sun and dry
out our goods and chattels. About noon our horses
took a stampede, and turning into the road towards
home, away they went, horses, picket-ropes, picket-
pins and all. We, however, caught some of them
pretty soon; but three of them got entirely off, not-
withstanding Frank Berry [who] ran them near forty
miles. It has been a delightful day, and we took out
our bacon, flour, fruit, &c., and sunned it nicely.

May 27   We moved on to the Little Arkansas today,
a distance of 27 miles. . . .[30] We have killed seven
buffalo, and caught one antelope, which I think is a
very good Sunday's work . . . as soon as we got to
camp every man went to cooking and eating as hard
as he could. The [buffalo] meat tastes a good deal
like beef.

May 28   About 4 o'clock this evening a herd of buffalo came heaving across the head of our train, and
in a moment there were more than 20 guns fired into
them.

May 31   Our line of travel lies up the Arkansas
River, sometimes bringing us within a hundred yards

of the stream, and at others taking us some three or four miles from the Arkansas. The river here is about 200 yards wide. It is lined on the south side by a succession of sand hills, which appear in the distance like pyramids of fire, as they reflect the rays of a burning sun. They are composed of pure yellow sand.[31]

June 2   We were awaken this morning by the firing of the guard, and the cry of "Parade, men, in the car'al! The Indians are upon us!" It was just at daylight, and three of us sprang up at the same instant, and seizing our guns, we rushed out in front of the wagons and looked eagerly for the enemy, but could see none. The men were rushing out of their tents in all directions, with guns and pistols, but we soon ascertained that it was [a] false alarm. We came six miles today, and are now camped on Pawnee Fork, on an old battle ground of the Pawnees and Camances [Comanches].[32]

June 3   We were on the road this morning before sun-up—came 19½ miles today, and are now encamped on the left bank of the Grand Arkansas. This river runs through a most delightful country, so far as prairie is concerned, as there is scarcely a stick of timber on its banks. It is broad and shallow.

Our road today has taken us close by the edge of this river, and along a bottom as level and dry as a floor. We haul some wood to kindle our fire, and then we throw on some "buffalo chips" which make a very good fire.[33]

Missouri '49er

[The gap in Hunter's journal is also partly filled in by his early notes in the "Memo," which are as follows:]

Nothing of much interest occurred for some time after organizing the train at Council Grove. The same dull outline of Prairie surface marked the rising and setting sun. The grass was excellent and our cattle fare sumptuously. About "Turkey Fork" we first discovered the Sand Hills on the south side of the Arkansas River, and in a few hours saw a herd of Buffaloes quietly grazing some 5 miles to our left.[34]

This was a long looked for moment. Every pulse quickened, and fellows who but a moment before would not have moved a dozen steps from the wagons now seized the "deadly rifle," and prepared to sally forth in quest of the "Prairie Monster," though the whole Comanche Nation should interpose to thwart them. We succeeded in killing three—2 calves and a young bull. The meat was delicate and juicy and as deliciously flavored as epicure or gourmet could desire. We now continued daily to slay Buffaloes frequently, indeed in mere wantonness, each being desirous to say he has killed one.

While engaged in the chase—especially of a morning when the balmy breeze come sweeping from the west (which is the most prevalent) across an endless scope of prairie, I have thought that I could sensibly distinguish health and vigor imparted to the frame, as I inhaled its life-imparting soul-cheering breath, and have said to myself "Could but our poor dyspeptics, hypochondriacs, &c., &c., leave their beds or closely smothered non-ventilated chambers, or those who in street or alley drink in the stagnant and poisonous vapors of our towns and cities, be instantaneously transported here, they would certainly imagine that they were on a visit to some other planet, or that here at least was the Elysium of their own."

I do not believe, with moderate experience, that disease or sickness can exist here. Already those who at the start had been complaining or who evidently labored under indisposition began to dread the voracity of their appetites, while their cheeks tingled (through bragging) with nature's own demonstration beyond all doubt that the trip which we are now engaged, and that mode of living necessarily followed, is a sure and certain "Panacea" for all the physical infirmities to which we poor mortals under other circumstances are liable and subject.

Oh, that tight lacing were out of fashion amongst our fair country women and that they could as damsels in days of yore mount their gallant palfreys, and with hawk in hand sally forth in pursuit of the antelopes who in troops are continually bounding before us. Then indeed would new life inspire their frames, new tints be added to the rosette hues which would mantle their lovely cheeks, as roses, the odor of a thousand species of wild flowers, with eyes beaming health and pleasure [next few lines illegible, partly due to cross-outs and minute size of writing]

June 3   We encamped for the first time on the banks of the Arkansas, a shallow but rapid stream, and at this place about ¾ of a mile wide. At night the breeze ceased and a quiet calm pervaded except for the low murmuring of the river as it sped on in its course towards the blue ocean. The beautiful moon shed its silvery luster on the stream, and as I stood guard on its margin, musing after the vicissitudes of my past life, Moore's beautiful song "Flow On Thou Shining River" thrilled through my brain. Like a spirit from the stream it portrayed the image of her whose memory was too indelibly engraved on my heart to be obliterated. She too had lived in a far-off isle. Might not the current now flowing past touch the shore where we had rambled ere it becomes lost in the briny depths to which it runs. Foolish though like your bright drops new glistening in the moonbeams, now dashed into a thousand particles on the sand beneath.

I tried to sing, but a choking sensation in my throat caused me to take the current of my thoughts to a party of Cheyenne Indians who had come to our camp through the day and who now lay buried in sleep about 100 yards from my post. And these are savages, thought I, and in such close proximity I found myself involuntarily playing with the trigger of my rifle, while a pistol and an enormous Bowie knife graced my belt. I must keep a sharp look out or they will get my scalp. I peered with all the power of vision amongst the group of sleeping beings, partly surrounded by their horses and mules, which though unfastened manifest not the slightest disposition to leave. But there they lay, quiet, motionless, wrapped in the arms of refreshing slumber, and unconscious of the presence of the White Man who is fast sweeping their race from the face of creation and hurrying all save their *name* into the vortex of oblivion. Savages! Call them rather the victims of an inexorable fate whose name is "extinction."

We had traded considerably with them through the day, horses, mules, blankets, Buffalo robes, &c., &c., and in their dealings it was very surprising to observe the shrewdness and tact with which they dealt. Of the two parties I believe we made the worst bargains. Their neatness and cleanliness of person and apparel would not be surpassed, while their ingenuity in the preparation and ornamenting of their Buffalo robes, moccasins, shot pouches, purses, belts, leggings, &c., all beaded with surprising taste.[35]

2

June 6–July 5

"I believe we are the only company that has not become
discouraged . . . it does seem that we have been
especially favored by Providence."
—J. P. Grey

Grey, a member of Hunter's train, made this comment in a
letter reprinted in the *Fulton Telegraph* on August 17, 1849.
He wrote the letter while the train crossed northwestern
New Mexico, and it reflected the argonauts' growing opti-
mism and confidence.

The Missourians traveled west from Mann's Fort and
forded the Middle Crossing of the Arkansas River. South of
the river the train followed the Cimarron Cut-Off, blazed by
William Becknell in 1822 and used thereafter by the Santa
Fe caravans. This route offered a level grade for wagons,
although it led across the first of the jornadas Hunter encountered on the southern route, an arid expanse of prairie
known as the Cimarron Desert. Though mild compared to
the later jornadas in Arizona and California, it presented
the first major challenge on the southern route.

The Cimarron Desert involved at least fifty miles of
waterless travel, and Hunter's company followed the standard procedure for crossing arid regions. Before setting out,
they rested and watered their livestock and filled water
barrels. Movement began at dusk and the train traveled all

night, stopping every two hours for a short rest. At sunrise, the emigrants made camp and turned the stock out to graze for two hours. They resumed the journey until noon, when camp was made again. In the late afternoon, they hitched up the oxen and the process began again until the desert was crossed. This system took advantage of the cooler night-time temperatures and allowed the train to cross a barren area with the least injury to their stock.

Santa Fe caravans often encountered hostile Indians along this section of the road, but due to their large numbers the Forty Niners experienced little trouble. The jornada ended when Hunter's train reached the Cimarron Valley, which they followed to the southwest for eighty more miles. The Cimarron was an intermittent stream, and the only reliable source of water came from three springs along the riverbed. Beyond the Cimarron, the Missouri train ascended the tablelands of northeastern New Mexico and came in sight of the Rocky Mountains.

Las Vegas was the first town on the road since Westport and the first Mexican community the Forty-Niners encountered. Hunter devoted a considerable portion of his journal to descriptions of the local inhabitants, their customs, and the appearance of the buildings. He included an amusing account of an event experienced by many Forty-Niners on the southern route, local dances known as a *fandango*. The travelers also sampled locally distilled spirits, the famous *aguardiente*.

During this portion of the journey, Hunter's train spent twenty-one days in travel and eight in camp, traveling over 380 miles for an average of 18 miles per day.

June 6 Reached Mann's Fort, a Cat-e-cornered structure (as might "all angles" and no shape as can well be conceived) built of turf cut about the size of bricks. The roofs of the rooms were composed of logs placed slantingly and covered over with turf. It is situated near the bank of the river, and from its position on the plain must have been impregnable to attack by Savages armed only with bows, arrows and spears. It is now disused.[1]

In and about the fort were from 70 to 100 wagons, some perfect and others mutilated for fire wood, with great quantities of log chains and other useful irons scattered in every direction. In the river opposite the fort is an island which must have been thickly covered with timber. It is now all cut down and used for the erection and consumption of the fort.[2]

While here a party of traders, who had been in the mountains all winter, arrived with wagons heavily laden with buffalo skins and pelts. One of the wagons had on a load weighting 7500 lbs., and had been hauled by four yoke of oxen from Fort Laramie to the crossing of the Arkansas at Fort Mann. They worked five yoke. The party consisted of seventeen men and a Delaware Indian and his child, which he was bringing down from amongst the "Indians" to which tribe its mother belonged, to see and pass the summer amongst his own tribe. The traders paid him $50 per month to hunt for them.[3]

On the arrival of the train he was absent after game, but a few minutes afterwards he came riding into camp with all the choicest parts of a buffalo strung across his pony behind him. The child, about four years old, immediately extended her arms to him, commenced crying and seemed in much distress. He requested one of the men to hand her to him, and on receiving her into his arms pressed her to his bosom, kissed and fondled over her, and setting her on his lap rode up to one of the wagons to dismount, on accomplishing which he led her to the camp fire, gave her some water and then retired from my sight bearing her in his arms. Can such manifest affection warm the bosom of the savage? thought I.

While conversing with some of the traders I was forcibly struck with a reply made by one who was cooking and whose appearance indicated "good health personified," to a question asked by one of our men. They had obtained some flour from a train just ahead of us, the first they had seen for months, and the cook was frying some cakes in a pan full of the melted tallow of the buffalo brought us by the Indian, when one of our men asked if he, the cook, thought bread fried in as much grease was healthy. "Healthy? Anything is healthy that you can get to eat out here!" was the reply, and truly from experience I can all but entirely coincide in this opinion.

We remained at Ft. Mann three days recruiting our cattle and waiting the recovery of Mr. Freeman S. McKinney, who had been attacked with every symptom of Cholera. He had let the disease proceed unheeded till seized with most distressing cramp, vomiting and purging, which was followed by an apparent absence of all vitality in the extremities, especially the legs which were cold and insensible up to the body.

He now consented that Dr. N. E. Branham, who accompanies us, should be sent for, altho he had previously declined his attendance on account of the Dr. practicing entirely on the Botanic system and rejecting all mineral aid *in toto*. The change wrought after a dose or two of medicine had been administered and some friction &c. used, was as if by magic, and he who but two short hours previously had been looked upon by all as tottering on the brink of eternity was now, from the effects of the medicine taken, lying free from pain and apparently enjoying a refreshing slumber.

June 10 Left Mann's Fort and arrived at the crossing of the Arkansas River. This we first forded about ½ a mile across to ascertain the best route for the wagons. We found the water from 2 to 3½ feet deep, and after doubling teams and quadrupling drivers, we drove in and before nightfall succeeded without accident in reaching the opposite bank.[4]

From a train that passed towards Bent's fort we this evening got possession of a fine mare, one of the runaways at Cotton Wood. Here a party of our men wounded and gave chase to an old Buffalo Bull and altho he must have received at least a dozen wounds he succeeded in reaching and crossing the river with several on horseback at his heels. On gaining the opposite bank he succeeded in making his escape—and here I would remark that clumsy and every way ill-qualified as this animal appears to be for running, it takes a fleet horse to keep pace with him after he once gets fairly started.

We now had a journey of 60 miles before us without wood, water or grass, and remained encamped till 2 p.m. on the 11th, when we started in order to take advantage of the cool of the evening and night to travel in. About 11 o'clock we reached "Battle Creek" where there were some holes with a little water in them.[5]

The cattle were so anxious to eat that they did not heed them, and after rambling about in search of grass and finding some, and manifesting a disposition for a "Stampede" we deemed it prudent to corral them. This is done by forming the wagons into about seven-eighths of a circle and running chains across the spaces. The vacant eighth is left as a means of ingress and egress.

At 1 o'clock a.m. on the 12th we resumed our journey and drove till 9 or 10 o'clock, when we halted to get breakfast and let the cattle rest awhile. At about 11 o'clock we again proceeded forward and about 3 p.m. reached "Sand Creek," where luckily we found plenty of water and some little grass, and concluded to stay for the night.[6] Our route from the Ark[ansas] had been over sand hills nearly destitute of vegetation, called by the Mexicans a "jornada" (signifying Desert), and truly a journey of desolation it was, the occasional sight of an elk, antelope or buffalo alone breaking the dreary monotony.

It chanced to be my day to drive, and having been on guard from midnight to the time of starting, I of course did not feel greatly refreshed from the quantities of sleep that fell to my share. I walked by the side of my team, sometimes trying to sing, at others to whistle in order to beguile time, but an irresistible drowsiness would steal over me, and I have no doubt but that I slept several times while jogging forward. A while after sunrise, some seeds and dust having got into my moccasins, the wagon descending a hill, I thought I would get in to rest a little and to cool and ease my feet. I had not been there more than five minutes when, in spite of the jolting of the wagon, I was unconscious of everything and came well nigh to upsetting it. The steers at the foot of the hill striking across the gully, the jostling nearly threw me under their feet, which served as a very good admonition for me to keep my "eyes skinned." My partners being nearly as badly off as myself, I of course had to plod on and make the best of it.

At this place we met a party of some 100 Mexicans from Taos or thereabouts who were out Buffalo hunting in order to dry the meat to take back with them (this is done by cutting the flesh into strips or slices and suspending it in the air and sun. It soon dries and may then be packed up and used in any way the most agreeable to the palate. It is excellent). They were a set of dirty, ill-looking fellows, mostly armed with bows and arrows, and I have no doubt but that a party of 20 Comanches would have terrified the whole posse back to the settlements. They were full of politeness and vermin, both equally disgusting. The one cloaked in a garb of grease and filth, the others obtruding themselves into notice "sans ceremonie."[7]

June 13th Reached the "Cimarone" at the "Lower Spring."[8] Here the pictures formed by my imagination of the appearance of this stream proved all at fault. It is represented by our geographers in the atlas as a river of considerable size, with tributaries, &c., &c., cutting as big a figure on paper as though it was worthy to rank in the 3rd or 4th class. Instead, it is a mean, baggerly, pitiful stream (where it runs at all) hiding its face amid the roots of rushes and dank grass, as if ashamed of the notoriety of its name. In others it becomes so bashful as to disappear altogether in the sand. In fact, the best way to find the "Cimarone" is to walk through high weeds, rushes, &c., across where you think from appearances its course should be, and when you get about half-leg deep in mud and water you may conclude you are about [in] the middle of the "Cimarone."

The roads up to this point had been excellent, the best natural or unimproved ones I ever saw, and really, for the major portion of the journey, preferable to the McAdamized roads of Europe or of our own country.

We continued traveling on this stream till we reached the Upper Crossing on the 17th, over desperately bad roads. It was in reality nothing but one continued bed of sand into which the wagons cut deeply, causing severe labor to the teams.[9] We were, however, favored with frequent showers accompanied with tolerably severe thunder and lightning which purified the air and kept it cool and pleasant. The grass was excellent and abundant, and we had plenty of water.

June 18th   Crossed the Cimarone at the Upper Spring and commenced ascending the "table lands of Mexico." In the evening we reached a gorge amongst the hills, the first we had seen for some time. Their ruggedness added variety to the prospect, and tended for a time to furnish new topics of conversation. At night encamped at "Cold Spring," a fount of water as delicious as I ever drank. It was cool, pure, and transparent as crystal.[10]

The next morning after breakfast I proceeded up a beautiful vale in search of wood. On a point near its head about 1–1½ miles distant I perceived some cedar trees and made my way thither. On reaching the spot I regretted that I was not a landscape painter. Not that the vista was extensive, nor that there was anything of the sublime or grand to captivate the admirer of the extraordinary and wonderful. But it was a romantic spot, a "multus in parvo," a miniature whose outlines, had they been expanded, would have vied proudly with the choicest specimens of Alpine scenery. But above it all was a home scene, nestled there to itself with nothing remarkable around to distract the attention. All its charms were its own, nothing was borrowed. It was just such a picturesque spot as would be chosen by modest unassuming youth when first love's flame he feels. There to retire and meditate on her who now seems the mainspring of life and action, whose semblance pervades every thought and where unmolested revel in daydreams of bliss too exquisite to be ever realized but in anticipation.

Such were my ruminations as I ascended a rugged cone of rock some 40 feet in height, forming part of the side of a beautiful grotto nearly surrounded by similar pinnacles. On the top lay a slab as though it had been capped by art, in the center of which was a font of pure and crystal-like water. His must indeed be a flinty heart who at such a moment and in such a place would not overflow with gratitude ever to Him who was the Architect. I would have offered my orisons aloud had not others come up at the moment to destroy the silent but deeply impressed rapture which at that moment pervaded my whole frame. All that seemed lacking was a holy man in sacred vestments to sprinkle me from that font and to bestow his benediction.[11]

The spell which had bound me was now broken by intrusion, yet it seemed to me like desecration to touch the cedars that flourished in the clefts of such a spot. The same evening another large train for California came up and encamped in the vale below us. On the next night at about midnight, the rain pouring down in torrents, it seemed as though a perfect wall of water came sweeping down through the vale, which in a few minutes was deep enough in some places to swim the mules, which were picqueted out, and to float off many articles from the wagons. The men, by prompt attention, prevented any serious accident. Had the rain continued it is highly probable that great damage and possible loss of life might have ensued.

June 24th Crossed "Whetstone Creek" just below an excellent spring, round and about which were stones of as fine grit as I ever saw. We procured some and pushed on. At a distance of some 6 or 7 miles to the N. W. were some isolated peaks from 5 or 600 feet high.[12]

Dark clouds were fast driving through the sky, until at length it seemed as though a dense mass had gathered directly over the summit of the tallest peak, when bending as if from a superabundance of moisture, or from the attraction of the peak, they gracefully curved down to a point resembling a water spout, and seemed to pour their contents within a circle formed by the summit and upper portion of the hill. The spectacle continued for several minutes and was truly beautiful.

June 26th Crossed the N. Canadian fork of the Arks. [Arkansas River], the first running water we had seen since the 11th. The current, about 10 to 12 yards in width, is deep and rapid, and the bottom and sides very rocky. It abounds with fish. [13]

At night encamped at the "Wagon Mound," a hill some 120 feet high, so called, I presume, from its resemblance to a covered wagon. Here we found springs of deliciously cool and pure water flowing from the summit of a hill, and a super abundance of excellent grass for our cattle, the first chance they had had of a feast since leaving the Cimarone. [14]

The next morning, while rambling near camp, some of our men discovered the clothes and a part of the skeleton of a man apparently not long since dead. They brought in with them the upper jaw bone. I proceeded to the spot. It was a lonely place in the bed of a drain grown over with long rushes and matted grass, and at the foot of a knoll of rugged rocks. On one lay the unfortunate man's socks, one of them slit from the top to the toe as if with a knife, the other perfect except the under part of the foot, which looked as though it had been torn by a wolf. I could discover none of the skeleton save the upper part of the cranium, too small to show if violence had been used. There lay the clothes and clothes-bag scattered around, and I determined to examine them if perchance I might discover some clue to the name of the deceased or to the manner of his death, his pockets containing no papers nor were his clothes marked.

He had belonged to the U.S. service from his uniform. The cap was new and apparently as good as when last worn. The shirt and pantaloons were much mangled by beasts of prey, but a blue blanket coat, somewhat torn, was stiff at the back with blood. Murder had evidently been committed, but by whom? Had the Indians slain him they would undoubtedly have taken his clothing. Money or revenge might possibly have been temptation enough to the "White man" to commit the deed. Perhaps in company with his very comrade he had trusted himself to that fatal spot, and there from hands, in whose care he would have confided as in those of a brother, received his bloody death.

Alas, Alas! Could that skull but have spoken it would have told of a fearful scene, a death horrible to reflect on, unsoothed by sympathy, and closed in frightful shrieks and struggles of self defense. Oh could the mother who once dandled thee at her breast and whose throbbing bosom had often pillowed that now tenantless skull, have foreseen thy tragic fate, she never had lived to rear thee through the bright and joyous days of youth nor see thee reach the spring of manhood. But thy race is run. Thou hast "past that bourne whence no traveler returns." Thy name and nation are both unknown, and thy fate though open and palpable to the eye of a just and retributive God, for a season lies hid in the bosom of thy fiend-like murderer.[15]

On returning to camp a party who had ascended the "Wagon Mound" had described two tigers [pumas], but having gone without their guns, they were enabled to effect their escape. We also, while antelope hunting, saw several black-tailed deer. On the summit of the mound (composed of a mass of rock) is the crater of an exhausted volcano, filled with masses of lava and other matter bearing evident marks of volcanic action.

June 30   Drove to "Owl Creek" where [there] was plenty of grass and water.[16] Here the skeleton of another man was discovered. After grazing a while, we proceeded on [to] the "Rio Mora," a small but rapid and clear stream.[17]

Here the first marks of American industry and ingenuity were plainly visible [for] a fort to our right had been raised, called after its builder Fort Bartley. A large bottom on the margin of which the river ran had been ditched, through which the water flowed freely for purposes of irrigation, and two other large dwellings to our left were in process of construction.[18]

But what tended most to excite our admiration was a mill just ahead of us. On coming up "all hands" (some of whom had passed here last fall, when some of these improvements existed) went to it, to wonder and speculate on the proximate fate of this land of apathy and idleness. It was a cheering sight to see the water leaping over the dam, and rippling as it were in very ecstasy as it bounded below, at having fallen into new hands, to become a ministering agent of plenty and comfort to those whose energy would soon cause the "desert to blossom as the rose." Soon this section of country, now the haunt of the "wild deer and wolf" and their still wilder and more savage pursuer, will be filled with an intelligent, enterprising population of the land, parched in appearance, is good in quality, needing humidity only to render it highly productive.[19]

On crossing a branch of the Mora we encamped, near a party of soldiers and volunteers from Santa Fe, who were there to protect some herders and cattle. A few minutes previous to our arrival an express had arrived from Rayo stating that the herders and inhabitants were entirely surrounded by a body of Apache Indians and would in all probability be cut off unless immediately relieved. A party instantly started and would probably reach them (70 m) the next evening.[20]

While conversing with one of the men, he informed me that the murdered man was a young man with light hair and had been shot near the "Wagon Mound" [and] had been discovered some two months since by a person (a Wm. Woods), now in Santa Fe. He had found two muskets near the corpse, one loaded, the other discharged and broken off at the breech—both of which he brought in with him. This tended to prove that the foul deed had not been the work of Indians.

Here we saw the first wheat and corn growing since we had left the States. Both were about hand high, and looking green and flourishing, altho the one was miserably sown and the other worse tended. They, however, improve on entering. Here an express had arrived the evening previous from Rayo for more help, and all the soldiers in the town but 8 had left.

On our way we passed through the "Plaza" (public square), a space some 30 to 40 yards square, ornamented on one side by a "hotel" (par excellence) and a range of rooms, on another by mud barracks. Here at every corner and almost at every house stood from one to 3 Mexicans with large flowing pantaloons open at the sides to display a pair of white cotton drawers. Sockless, and many shoeless, with an enormous "sombrero" or broad brimmed coarse straw hat on their heads resembling in shape the hats generally worn by witches at our theatres, smoking their "cigaritos" or paper covered cigars, and wasting their precious time in listless apathy. How surprisingly different to that activity and bustle to which we had all been accustomed.

We soon left town and proceeded to seek an encampment about 4 to 5 miles from town. We passed through the first Cañon or Mountain Glen we had seen. It consisted of a narrow pass between two abrupt hills, which at the entrance scarcely afforded room for a wagon to pass. Through this our gallant Volunteers in 1846 made their way when, if properly resisted, ten times their number could have been cut off to a man, and that too with but little or no exposure to those occupying the Pass. Nothing surely but imbecility on the part of the Mexican government or a total recklessness of the lives of their subjects can be offered in extenuation for their neglecting to fortify and hold all such points if for no other reason than to repel Indian attacks and massacres. [21]

About a mile and a half from the Cañon we encamped at the foot of one of the most beautiful hills I ever saw. From our position it seemed a perfect cone whose top had been stricken off as evenly as though it had been sighted by a water level. Its sides curving regularly and gracefully inwards from its base, which consisted of a huge mound regularly and beautifully formed, as if it had been specially formed and placed there to be the pedestal of so magnificent a superstructure. The sides and tops were adorned with clumps of trees while its base was encircled by a grove of fine timber, reminding me strongly of some of the grounds gorgeously attached to the country seats of the English nobility.

July 2nd Passed through Vegas (or San Vegas), the first Mexican town on the road from Independence to Santa Fe. On descending the hill to the eastward of the valley in which the town lies, we obtained a full view of the place, a clear and very correct idea of which may be formed by anyone who has ever seen a large brick-yard, which is an exact resemblance of it. The houses are all one story high, with flat roofs covered with earth, built of adobes or unburnt brick, and from the outside present a very mean and dirty appearance. I walked up to several, but from the filthy appearance of their occupants, who out of every door obtruded their heads, I was fearful of entering, as ocular demonstration corroborated the statements I had often heard of their abounding with vermin.[22]

At length I reached one more respectable in its external appearance, and by an aged Senora was invited to enter. I availed myself of her politeness, and doffing my "Buena Vista," was introduced to a middle aged man, indisposed, and sitting in an arm chair. His wife was leaning on his shoulder while two other females sat on a buffalo rug spread on the floor.

I was escorted to a seat on another rug on the opposite side of the room, and after an interchange of civilities began to look about me. The room was about 40 ft. long by 15 ft. broad. The floor, of nature's own formation, was nicely swept and sprinkled with water to lay the dust and to cool the atmosphere. The walls were plastered and whitewashed and ornamented with crosses and miniatures of the apostles and of half the saints in the Romish Calendar.

At the upper end were a couple of beds where the snowy whiteness of whose furniture spoke volumes in praise of their fair mistresses. At the lower extremity was the fireplace and chimney in one corner, with sundry vessels of household use. The ceiling was composed of cedar joists with planks laid on them, on which was a thick layer of earth forming the roof. Over one-half the length of the floor on one side were spread rugs and mats on which were beds rolled up tidily against the wall, which showed that its

inmates at night were numerous. The window was composed of isinglass which admitted light almost as freely as
glass.

Almost all the females that I had seen, with the exception of this family, had their countenances besmeared with
paint (after the Indian mode) to prevent sunburning, which
tends to disfigure them very much. I had not yet seen one
female who would have been entitled to the compliment of
"good looking."

The man's wife, however, above alluded to, was an
exception. She was of fine stature and when in motion
moved with the dignity of a queen. She was about 25 years of
age, with long raven hair, and her features, though not
regular, were yet pleasing. Her nose, though slightly con-
cave towards the point, did not terminate in a retrograde
curve towards the forehead, as though the upper lip and
itself held their proximity in peculiar disgust (the certain
index to your real spitfire), but curved again to the face in
about the same angle which characterizes this peculiar member amongst our own fair daughers of Judah. Her teeth were
of ivory whiteness, and as she stood with lips asunder and
partially bent reclining on her husband's shoulder and the
back of his chair, listening to the account of "far off lands,"
she reminded me more of a graceful statue than of a human
being.

Her eyes were large, full and black as jet, their dark and
ample fringes now raised in wonder, and anon modestly
shading the beautiful orbs it was their office to defend,
seemed as though they needed not the noisy assistance of
the tongue to give utterance to the sentiments which like a
mirror they reflected from within. From such a pair might
have beamed the love and admiration of a Cornelia when
viewing the Gracchi or the heart rendering anguish of Vo-

lumnia pleading with Coriolanus for the safety of Rome. The withering ire or contempt of an Elizabeth while spurning a Senate or the deathless devotion of a Petrea as handing the fatal blade to her husband she bade him imitate her example.[23]

Such were my thoughts and such an ill delineated picture of the pair of eyes that encountered my gaze as I rose from my mat to return thanks for a handful of roasted piñon, which their possessor politely offered me. She was dressed in the loose habiliments peculiar to their countrywomen, which precluded all chance of tracing the outlines of her figure. I remarked, however, that she possessed a very, very pretty foot and ankle.

On being refreshed I took my leave and on passing through the yard I noticed a hog tethered to a stone, which I was informed was almost the only one in the country. Chickens, altho they might be raised in prodigious numbers, seem to be exceedingly scarce as I saw very few and heard but one or two crow while I remained in town.

Two Americans resided here and had more land under cultivation than probably 20 Mexican would have done. The town is situated on a creek affording an abundant supply of excellent water.

On the road today we met several Mexican ladies riding on mules and asses. They ride on the off or right hand side of the animal, and where they ride double the gentleman mounts behind and holds on by his fair partner's waist or over her shoulder discharges the animal (a most enviable method, certainly).

In the evening we reached "Vernale," a small village distant 17½ miles from Vegas, where we found a large and very excellent spring. The children ran out in crowds to beg tobacco and pipes, and after emptying my pockets and bestowing all I had they would still raise their tiny hands for more. Little "muchachos" who could scarce lisp the word "tobacco" were yet vociferous and constant in their petitions and would scarcely fall back even after we had passed the village, about ½ mile from which we encamped.[24]

At supper time we were visited by several men who partook with us, and after nightfall proposed that if we would walk with them to the village they would have a "fandango" for our entertainment.

This was just what several of us had wanted to see so we were not long before we stood at the door of the adobe-built ball room. Its inmates, mostly female, had scarcely time to leave their pallets (to which they had retired) ere we entered the room. It was about 30 ft. long by 12 broad, rather too narrow for comfort—and it was not over 8 ft. high. Had I not felt secure of an exit when necessary, I should most certainly have fancied myself in a "Calaboose."

Seats were arranged along each wall, the men using one side and the females, as they arrived, seating themselves on mats laid on the floor in front of the seats on the opposite sides. Our fiddler (one who belonged to the Company) now played several airs accompanied by an old Mexican on an instrument, which in the Western States we call a "banjo" (a kind of miserable guitar). The music, tho' not such as to have enraptured a Paganini, was from the evident willingness of the girls to be "up and doing," relished very well as what it lacked in melody it accomplished in speed, while the gesture or attitude of the performers was altogether lost sight of in their smiling self-complacent countenances. If old "Orpheus" did move "Old Nick" our musicians beat him hollow, for in fifteen minutes they had some twenty pair of feet in motion, which not all the "stocks" in the country could have kept still while that music lasted.

The Mexican youths soon led out their partners for a waltz, which was the only kind of dance they seemed acquainted with, and it was pleasing to see the grace and ease with which they moved through its mazes. We soon had them dancing cotillions in which, however, they did not seem to take much pleasure. Some of our "awkward squad," by this time excited by the amusement [and] aided by the stimulus of a little "aguardiente," now seized their partners for a waltz, and of all of the ridiculous actions that I ever saw it was the Cap-a-pie.[25]

Here might be seen a stalwart backwoodsman, his face flushed from the heat of the room, his Dulcinea suspended in his brawny arms and struggling to obtain a footing on terra firma, while he, jumping with distracted feet straight up and down, would not think of relaxing his exertions till warned by the scream from some female whose foot had been almost crushed beneath his massive shoe.

Here again, thinking that the beauty of the dance consisted in the multitude of revolutions, might be seen a pair widely separating as the poles are heretofore, until they pitched against opposite walls owing to some unlucky trip-up or from the rapidity of their whirl acquiring such centripetal force that she, poor soul, discomforted, sought a momentary retirement, and her half-stunned and unwitting swain would be deprived of his trophy by someone on the alert for mishaps. Another, a six footer who had jumped round till he became dizzy and lost his partner, might be seen with the good natured girl pulling at the skirts of his coat (if he had one on) while he, with awful and bad Spanish, endeavored to discover her whereabouts, still jumping round to seek her there, stood an unfortunate as though in agonies of toothache, holding her head, and doubting whether it still pertained to the body, from the paralyzing stroke of that "gentleman's" elbow who, with his shirt sleeves rolled up, manfully clears his way of all opposition. Such a scene would have disturbed the gravity of [blank] self.

About midnight we broke up, each one fully content with what he had enjoyed and full of mirthful incidents for a laugh on the morrow. On contrasting the evenings entertainment with some that I have witnessed amongst those said to be "well bread," I could not help according my admiration to our "fandango." The females on entering the room, instead of entering into a tete-a-tete on the demerits of a sister, commenced a general and lively chat amongst themselves, and throughout the whole evening seemed to enjoy a pleasure in rectifying instead of criticizing on the blunders and mistakes which happened. On leaving the village we fired a volley of pistols in honor of the 4th July eve, and so ended the day.

July 3rd Passed through "Tecalote," another "brick yard" looking village, which as I had a little more leisure I determined to spend an hour or two in. The houses generally were as mean looking and dirty on the outside as those of Vegas.[26]

The Warm Springs near Vegas are situated about five miles north of that place, in the opening of a gorge of the granite mountains, about 20 feet above the level of a fine creek that comes soaring and foaming down the gorge. There are some 120 or 150 of these springs, of every variety of temperature, from the tepid to the scalding hot. Some of them are slightly impregnated with sulphur, others with sulphur and antimony, while others again seem to possess no mineral qualities whatever. They extrude from between the cracks of the granite rock which is at that place in a vertical position, forming a sort of low bench of some 30 yards in width, and extending about 200 yards up and down the creek, sloping from the escarpment of the mountain down to the creek.

A somewhat broken valley commences at this place and extends southward about ¾ of a mile to a fine prairie country, well adapted to agricultural purposes, especially when it shall be irrigated by the aforementioned creek, which is of fine size for that as well as for manufacturing purposes. Altogether this is a place of no inconsiderable promise, and should Uncle Sam in his munificence make his National Railroad through this region it will become one of the greatest places of rest for the invalid in the U.S.[27]

July 4th Remained encamped. Everyone talked of celebrating the day but no one would begin. We endeavored to purchase a fine heifer for a barbecue, but the owner would not sell, sheep, chickens, any and everything, but we were equally unsuccessful. At length we turned it into a washing day, and so exchanged frolic for utility. There were no ardent spirits in our camp, and after work we determined at all events to have a sweetened dram—each one threw in his mite and the messenger was dispatched for it. But lo, he returned empty as he went. The vendors asked one dollar and a half per pint for whiskey, which we knew to be abominable. So we divided out our money and again pocketed it. Awhile before sundown the rain poured down in torrents, driving all hands to their tents or wagons and so ended the 4th.

July 5th Passed San Miguel, a large Mexican village, where I remarked that more attention seemed paid to fencing, titling the ground, &c., and the crops of wheat and corn looked much more forward than any we had seen [in New Mexico].[28]

We now followed the base of a range of mountains which extended hence to Pecos. They are singularly regular and uniform in appearance. Their surfaces from their base to the summit, which is nearly flat, are formed in semicircles obtruding outward in some places as uniform as if they had been chiseled by art. Their base for about two-thirds of their height is composed of loose rock and gravel on which lie horizontal strata of rock, the uppermost as level as line could strike it, and presenting the appearance of once having formed the barrier of some vast water course.

At night encamped within ½ mile of the Ruins of the Pecos, and the next day proceeded to pay them a visit. I had heard many tales respecting these ruins previous to our arrival.[29]

3

July 6–July 28

*"[The Callaway County Pioneers] are in fine spirits,
while those who have taken the Northern route are
nearly everywhere lamenting their folly in having started
at all."*
—Editor of the Fulton Telegraph,
August 3, 1849

Hunter's party traveled leisurely through north-central New
Mexico; of the twenty-three days covered in this chapter,
only seven were spent in travel, and they moved approximately a hundred miles. The Missourians took their time in
order to rest their livestock and to wait while the grass
ripened farther down the road.

Hunter visited several Mexican villages and noted the
distrust between the emigrants and the local population. Rumors of thievery and murder by Mexican outlaws abounded,
and he witnessed instances of both. There were a few Anglo
settlers in the area. Most of them carried unsavory reputa-
tions and were not trusted by the Forty-Niners.

Hunter's train left the Santa Fe road west of Glorieta
Pass and traveled to Galisteo, a popular campground because of the good pasturage found in the area. Hunter made
a side trip to Santa Fe, where he saw the first signs of
disillusionment among the Forty-Niners. There were many
in the town who were out of money, unable to procure

needed equipment or otherwise unable either to proceed to California or to return home.

Approximately forty miles south of Santa Fe, Hunter stopped at the placers, a center of gold mining activity. Some of the Forty-Niners examined the gold deposits in New Mexico with an eye to working them rather than proceeding to California. Hunter's party, like most Forty-Niners on the southern route, decided that the placers' ore was too poor to be worthwhile. Nonetheless, a few Anglos worked the deposits, hoping to earn enough money to continue on to California.

July 9th Went 5 miles to Cotton Wood Spring. The water of this spring, which is in the bed of a branch to the right of the road, is as cold as iced water and truly refreshing and delicious. Here we discovered tracks of bear, which from their size must have been of the grisly monster which I was told were numerous in the adjacent mountains. We obtained good grass by driving up a valley to the right of the spring.[1]

July 10th Passed through the great Cañon, a deep gorge about 4 miles in length between hills from 3 to 400 ft. high. Through this the road runs and it is possible that without immense labor it is the only practicable wagon road to approach Santa Fe from the east. It is truly surprising on surveying this ravine to think of the ease with which New Mexico fell before the arms of our gallant volunteers. One thousand resolute men could undoubtedly hold this pass against any odds. Had the Parisians, who thoroughly understand the art of defense, but had time to barricade it, not all the troops in the world could have dislodged them.[2]

We encamped for the night at the west end of the

Cañon where to the left was a rather poor spring. Wood plenty, but little or no grass for the stock.

July 11th Arrived at the forks of the road leading to Santa Fe and Galisteo, distant 6 miles. Here was a grocery established in a tent, the first we had seen since leaving a villainous looking hovel of the kind on the Shawnee Trace in Johnson County. There is a tolerable good spring in the bed of the branch near the descent of the old road.

We turned to the left and after passing over about 5 miles of heavy sand commenced a gentle and pleasant descent to Galisteo, distant 11½ miles. The town is not visible until you arrive directly below it. It is built on a hill commanding a pleasant view of an extensive vale in which we found an abundance of excellent grass and water, but no wood within four miles; what we used we purchased from the men of the town who brought it to us packed on asses, and for which they charged us from 25 to 37½ cts. per load.[3]

This, like all other New Mexican towns, is built of adobes resembling a huge brick-yard in appearance, and contains from 250 to 300 inhabitants, among whom are some very wealthy individuals. Here were large herds of cattle, goats, and sheep, some few hogs and pigs, and a beginning for a stock of barnyard fowls, altho here as in all the other settlements I have visited, I have seen neither goose, duck, turkey nor indeed any other kind of poultry. There are two houses at which refreshments may be had and where a stranger might be accommodated.

We were treated with much courtesy by the inhabitants, who every night of our stay favored us with a fandango (in somewhat better style than at Vernale). One old gentleman of the town started a Monte Bank but a "knowing one" belonging to another train of Californians encamped near us, broke the bank, which so disheartened the proprietor that he quit the business. Some gaming on a smaller scale was carried on, which I believe resulted generally in favour of the visitors.[4]

There were some excellent stone fencing round the farms, one of which, better than a mile in length and about 4 feet high, would have done credit to any of our Eastern States. The crops of corn and wheat, though young, looked green and flourishing, and their cornfields were kept as clean and free from pernicious growth as well tilled gardens. I noticed some cabbages growing which were probably the first raised here, as on inquiry of several Mexicans I could learn no name for them more than that they were a something "Americano" with which they were not acquainted.

On the 13th I went with 2 or 3 companions to pay a visit to the "far famed" city of Santa Fe. My expectations of something more than ordinary had been raised very high, and I pushed on eagerly to gratify my curiosity. The weather was cool and beautiful, and the road moderately good. About 7 miles east of town we came upon and shot a tremendous wolf, who stood with great indifference watching our advance till we arrived within some 30 paces, when his temerity cost him his life.

On nearing Santa Fe the first object that attracted attention was Fort [blank] which seemed seated on the projection of a mountain frowning in sullen dignity upon a surrounding waste. But on a little nearer approach, that beautiful emblem of liberty, the "Star Spangled Banner," shot as it were from the earth, dancing and fluttering in the breeze like a thing of life. Its wavy folds streaming from the top of its graceful staff in the grand "Plaza" seemed to rejoice triumphantly in their glorious pre-eminence, and to proclaim that freedom had made another gigantic stride and now reigned omnipotent from the bleak and rugged coasts of New England to the sunny shores of the beautiful Pacific. "Hail Columbia" dwelt in fancy and played upon the tongue, with all those patriotic and glowing associations connected with its soul stirring words as I entered the first fruits of my country's conquests.[5]

But oh! What a shock to sight and scent. What a revulsion of feeling instantly occurred as I descended the hill and entered a narrow filthy lane, barely wide enough for the passage of a wagon. The mud walls on either side banished what little air was stirring, and the fetor arising from the decomposition of every kind of offal, of which the streets appeared to be the receptacles, seemed enough to suffocate one, or to taint the olfactories with an effluvium which not all the roses of Persia could ever dispel. I pushed on through similar abominations till I found myself standing on the "Plaza" (public square). Here was a respite from the disgusting traverse of the preceding ten minutes. The germ of drunkenness was visible, altho it had yet barely struck its roots.

The "Plaza" is a moderately sized square, say 100 yards across. The barracks in which the U.S. troops are quartered form one of its sides. The other three consist of stores, hotels and taverns, all of one story, with a piazza 10 feet wide in front of them, except where two streets intersect the angles of the square. Under this terrace a lounge is delightful. The center of the Plaza is paled in, and young trees planted equidistant around it. On the side next to the barracks are ranged in neat order the U.S. pieces of artillery with their ammunition wagons. Midway of the train is a neatly executed sun dial, whose gnomon indicated that it was exactly noon at the moment of my visit. One mistake on its face, however, seemed to whisper that perfection did not dwell in

Santa Fe. The artist, in engraving his name and profession, had inverted the letter "S" in "Sculptor," which to a true eye gave the whole an awkward appearance.

I next visited Fort [blank], which stands on a hill on the side of the city, commanding entirely all its most densely inhabited portion. It is built of adobes, as also its barracks, a two story building near its entrance, and its magazine near its centre. From its position and substance I should think it capable of resisting any attack the Mexicans or Indians might ever feel inclined to make.[6]

Within the fort was an open grave with the case off a coffin, from which one with its mortal tenant had probably been exhumed. There were many graves outside of, and near the fort. From the ramparts I had a fine view of the valley in which Santa Fe is situated. The buildings and cultivated spots were scattered for about 3 miles up and down the vale, which appeared not to exceed a mile in width.

After strolling through the suburbs I again visited the Plaza. Here at the Bar rooms might be heard yells, imprecations and drunken clamor. At the stores might be seen, instead of purchasing customers, parties of card players, regardless of everything but of fleecing each other, and on the side of the barracks, a calaboose filled with the victims of intemperance and vice.

In one store I noticed a woman who appeared to be its proprietor, seated on her counter display, engaged at cards with a male opponent, while another sat at her feet humming a Spanish song. Her features were sharp and somewhat haggard, and such was a malicious, money-loving glance as occasionally stole from her eye towards her opponent [that] had it been directed at and perceived by me, would assuredly have deprived Santa Fe of the honor of my presence. Fortune, however, seemed to smile on her propitiously while I remained a spectator. [7]

On the Bar room doors were placards thus: "Gentlemen wishing to play will please not do so at the bar, but retire to the gambling room." And on the pillars of the Piazza: "A Fandango will be held this night at &c., &c. The best liquors will be kept at the bar, &c."

At nightfall, as to satisfy curiosity was the object of my visit, I visited the gambling rooms. The business of the day being over, the rooms were crowded. A large number of Americans who now filled the place seemed to vie with the natives in their passion for this accursed amusement.

One American present, in less than an hour, lost seven hundred dollars at Monte, and then sought the Bar room, there to drown in inebriation the stings of conscience and remorse. Several thousands of dollars changed hands while I remained. Other games at cards, which I did not understand, Billiards, &c., were all in full operation, each having a full quota of votaries. Fifteen pistol shots were exchanged in less than ten minutes after I retired to my lodgings, five of which were at one individual. None, however unfortunately, took effect.

On Sunday morning the same scenes were again enacted. As I was about to leave the place I saw a fellow make a stab at another with a large butcher knife, which he parried with his hand, receiving a severe gash on it. Friends of both then interfering, the affray was checked till an officer arrested the fellow with the knife and hurried him to the calaboose.

I had visited, I thought, about the worst places on this habitable globe, amongst the rest, New Orleans, Natches, &c., but never did I in so short a time see so much licentiousness and villainy as graced the Capital of New Mexico. The atmosphere of the place, though tainted with disgusting and noxious effluvia, is yet pure compared with the moral pollution which seems to disgrace each sex and condition of its inhabitants. When the church bell rang for service, there were many who quitted the card tables, ran hurriedly to the church, and then returned straightway to the hell whence they had emerged.

There were in the place a great number of California Emigrants who had arrived there with wagons and teams intending to dispose of them and purchase mules to pack them through. But owing to the low prices of wagons and oxen, the best of the former selling at from 20 to 25 dollars and the latter at from 12 to 15 dollars per yoke, and mules at the same time ranging from 40 to 75 dollars, they were unable to do so. After selling out and staying awhile at enormous expenses, they could neither get one way nor the other, and were in deplorable condition indeed. Their situation in a strange land without money or friends rendered them desperate and reckless, and many among them appeared ripe for anything. I was glad when I ascended the hill to the Eastward and once more breathed freely the pure mountain air. Nor did I stop till I encamped for the night some 12 or 13 miles distant.

The next day I returned to camp at Galisteo, where I found all hands busily engaged in something useful or recreating themselves at some innocent pastime. After enjoying the luxury of a bath in a pond hardby, I took my supper and soon lost in sweet forgetfulness the fatigue of body and pain of mind from my visit to Santa Fe.

We remained encamped in Galisteo till the 17th, at which time we moved on to a spring on the Placea Road, distant 8 miles.[8] The road to this place was rough and broken. We found good water about 100 yards to the left of the road. Grass was scarce and only to be obtained in the hollows some ½ mile to the right.

Here we discovered the body of a murdered man, about 35 to 40 years of age judging from his hair, which was a deep auburn lightly sprinkled with grey. He appeared from his dress to have been a California Emigrant, and to have been murdered only three or four days. He had apparently been shot some 100 yards from where we found the body, dragged to a ravine and covered up, but the wolves had torn him from his bloody sepulchre and mangled the remains considerably.

The face, hands, one arm and one foot with the toes of the other, were gone, together with the flesh from the breast and the upper part of the abdomen and its contents. His clothes and an oil cloth cap lying near were also much torn. We examined the clothes and pockets as well as we could to see if any traces of the unfortunate's name or residence could be discovered, but could find none. The body, from exposure and violence, emitted a dreadful factor. We at once paid it the last sad rites of humanity by shrouding it first with a layer of cedar boughs and then covering it well with earth.

Peace to thy manes brother! Thou hast started no doubt fearlessly on thy perilous journey, with hopes as bright and visions of the golden country to which thou went speeding as glorious as could warm a human heart, but here thou art, wrapped indeed in a bloody mantle, thy name unknown and thy journey with all its fair prospects brought to a close. Ere thou hast entered the portal of the promised land thou art verily laid low in a most desolate spot, whence none can call thee, till thou hearest the blast of that trumpet which shall call alike thee and thy murderers into His Holy presence whose omniscient eye witnessed thy bloody downfall.

After musing a while on the sad scene, we took the trail made by the body as it was dragged along and followed it to where he had probably been sitting under the shade of a cedar tree. At the time he met his death he had apparently been trimming a limb of the tree for a walking cane, as the place whence he had cut it still looked fresh and its top, bark, &c., were scattered around. There was a place in the sandy surface as though it had been beaten bare by the victim in his last agonizing struggle. Here we found several lumps of clotted blood mixed with sand which the sun had hardened, and here too was a part of the lower jaw bone, so that subsequent violence might have been done to his remains.

July 18th A few minutes previous to our departure this morning Captain Bostick of [blank], Mr. Williams of Cooper Co., Wisconsin, and the Alcalde of Placea arrived in our camp, having in charge two villainous looking Mexicans, the supposed murderers of the man whose remains we discovered yesterday, who they were conducting to Santa Fe for trial and safe keeping.[9]

The two former gentlemen, in company with three others of their train, had discovered the same body almost unmutilated two days previously and took the trail of a pair of shoes and a pair of moccasins leading from the victim down a deep ravine. This they followed till they pounced upon the two villains now in their custody, whom they made come back with them, and whose feet they measured in the tracks they had followed, which exactly corresponded. The moccasins were deeply stained with blood. A pair of pistols and a horse were found in their possession, which they claimed, and which it since appears some Americans now encamped at Galisteo are ready to swear belonged to the murdered man, whose name was Wilburn and who came from Tennessee.

The eldest villain was a dark, scowling looking wretch whose physiognomy would have suited him for anything else than a safe or agreeable companion. His junior, who sat behind him on the same horse, nature seemed to have stamped for deeds of darkness. He was sparse, gaunt and lean-favored, his eyes downcast, were ever averted, except when they leered for an instant in a thievish glance to see if he were noticed. His frontal region, from the brow, seemed evidently disposed to repel all advances from the intellectual and moral faculties and sentiments, and to strike the nearest possible line for a closer acquaintance with self esteem, a large share of which would certainly be requisite if the opinions of others were required. I was afterwards sorry that I did not request permission of the Alcalde to Phrenologically examine their "bumps" that I might have made a minute of their more prominent traits for future reference or comparison.

We shortly started for Placea, distant 14 miles over some few miles of very rough road, the remainder being level, firm and excellent. [10] At midday we saw the mines on the side of a hill to the left of the road. At 2 p.m. we corralled in town and watered our stock from a branch running through it.

Here we found many Americans who had stopped at this place to work the mines. On conversing with several they informed me that they had found their labor very unproductive, and that in the fall they would either leave for home or proceed to California. They mostly seemed exhausted of funds, and from many sitting about on the fences or lounging in the shade, while others half intoxicated, with many a bitter imprecation on their "luck," were gambling in a neighboring house. I was constrained to believe that their time and energies, instead of being directed to laudable objects, were here prostituted to the worst of purposes and that instead of cursing the unprofitable yield of the mines which they were unwilling to work, they had better saddle the blame on their own misdeeds and lack of industry.

While in town (which contains some 200 inhabitants) we noticed several holes which had been dug in different places in search of gold, with the washing machines, &c., near them. Most of these had been disused. We saw some men, however, at work lower down the branch, in the banks of which they were digging, one of whom had just found a piece of gold worth about $5.00 besides some dust which he kept in a quill. They washed the earth in gourds, sheep-horns, broken earthen vessels, &c.

At 4 p.m. we started again for San Pedro, distant 8 miles, which we reached in a perfect torrent of rain about an hour after nightfall. We were then compelled to tie our jaded and hungry oxen to the wheels all night, for fear of having them stolen, which is sure to be done whenever a chance presents itself, and we ourselves retired supperless to bed. [11]

July 19th   The 8 miles traverse of yesterday evening was over the worst road we have yet seen. It was mostly over rocky spurs of the Placea Mountains, and was one continued ascent on one side and steep descent on the other. The best judgments amongst us computed the distance at 12 or 13 miles, but on reference to the roadometer, it told of only eight. [12]

Here was the largest as well as the best Rancho or farm I had yet seen. It was well irrigated, and the wheat especially looked splendidly. It was of the kind known in our Western

States as "golden chaff," or smooth headed. The heads were long, plump and full, and from a superficial view I should say it would yield from 30 to 35 bushels per acre.

A large crop of corn in beautiful order was also planted and altho it was not leg high, it was tasseling. Beans, peas, melons, onions, some few potatoes &c., were all in rapid growth. The village contained some 80 to 100 residents, the men and some few of the women of which labored on the Rancho. The grass here was scarce, but in the course of two or three weeks will no doubt be plenty.

About 10 a.m. we moved on to Santa Antonietta, a Rancho 3½ miles distant.[13] The road to this [place] was as good as the previous 8 had been miserable. At this Rancho we found some U.S. troops in charge of the rations of a detachment which had been sent here by Col. Washington (Gov. of N. Mexico) for the arrest and punishment of some Indians said to have murdered two Americans (gold hunters) near this spot about three weeks ago.[14] They are now out in pursuit, but from what I have seen I should with perhaps more justice lay the blame to the door of some infamous Mexicans nearer the scene of the tragedy. Here was a considerable quantity of Pine plank that had been sawed by a circular saw belonging to some Americans now in Santa Fe, which tended to remind me forcibly of scenes I had often witnessed at home.

This Rancho is owned by an American, as is also another about ½ mile W. Here we found an abundance of excellent water and about 1½ miles N. very good grass in the valleys. Wood in abundance all around us, and a most excellent spot for encampment. We concluded to remain here several days, and to have a thorough and perfect refit of wagons, as well as to rest and recruit our stock before we cross the "Rio Grande del Norte."

July 20th   We had purchased at Santa Fe some blacksmith's tools (for which they charged us $125) and having a blacksmith and an excellent assistant along, we at once set to work to burn a coal pit for their use. We also put up a tar kiln, and what with some washing of clothes, and dispatching a party of hunters to the neighboring mountains for game, this day passed busily improved and pleasantly away.

July 21st   This morning Captain Bostick's train came up and joined us. This gentleman and Mr. Williams informed us that on their leaving us on the morning of the 17th, in charge of the murderers of Wilburn, they had proceeded but a few miles when they halted for breakfast. After dispatching their meal they were making preparations to start, when the gear on the mule held by Mr. Williams becoming deranged in some way, he stopped down to arrange it. In doing so his pistol dropped from his breast and fired, mortally wounding the animal and consequently disabling them from proceeding any further.

They accordingly returned to their camp within some 200 yards of Placea, where the Alcalde said he would take charge of the prisoners till they were otherwise disposed of. Between this and the town, however, short as the distance was, the wretches managed to escape, without any signal or effort on the part of the Alcalde to arrest their progress.

This Alcalde, from their apprehension, had seemed utterly averse to all interference in the matter, and the first night they were taken the Americans there had to procure a house, secure and guard it themselves, or this praiseworthy functionary would have at once washed his hands of the business. Mr. Williams states that the older villain repeatedly offered him a large reward to let him go, and from appearances one would judge that the Alcalde, not being quite so scrupulous, profited of the liberality of his friend and winked (as great men sometimes will do) at his escape.

Indeed, a partner in business of the Justice did not scruple to tell a poor spiritless, dastardly soul who had been purchasing some eggs of a woman, that was then caviling at the price, that he would pay the difference, that it was to his interest to be friendly with the Mexicans, and that he often had to do so for d——d Americans, another of whom he never wanted to see. Would to goodness the fellow had used these expressions in the presence of some of the "boys" there would not have been enough of the rascals left to have ever contained another curse.

I am sorry to say from what I have seen that the Americans, or rather a majority of them, now settling among the Mexicans seem with their superior knowledge to outdo the natives in their own abominable vices, besides adding their own imported stock to the list. Were I to draw a scale as a measure of confidence, I would divide it somehow thus: "I would not trust 'Old Nick' on any terms." "I would as soon trust him as an Indian." "I would rather trust an Indian than a Mexican." "And I would doubly rather rely on a Mexican than on most of the Americans I have found settling amongst them."

Charity and the honor of my Country constrain me to believe that most of them certainly must be refugees from justice, who having violated the laws of their own land are fain to find an asylum amongst the rocks and mountains of New Mexico, where they may safely indulge in those excesses which were the cause of their exile from their home and kindred. I should, however, have expected much better things from those now in progress through the country, who yet have a reputation to sustain, most of whom have left comfortable homes, graced with amiable wives and smiling babes, whose only earthly anxiety is for their absent parent's safe return. Such men as these, one would suppose, would be the proper stock to set examples of piety, order, decency, and obedience to the laws of civil society for which their country is eminently distinguished.

But alas! Unchecked by the restraints of propriety— unmasked by the eye of, and uncontrolled by the influence of his almost guardian angel—Woman—with evil examples continually before him, the man whose virtue is not deeply rooted, or whose philosophic eye is unable to scan the gulf before him, falls by degrees into the pit laid for his soul, and by little and little becomes dissipated, reckless, irreclaimable. Such will be the picture of numbers, I am persuaded, now on the route, or who may hereafter start for these regions—unless their course differs materially from most of those now on the road, whose Sabbaths especially, if not spent in traveling, are devoted to card playings, pitching dollars, games of ball, singing profane songs, running, jumping, wrestling, &c., &c. All of which being practiced, as a salve to conscience are politely designated "innocent amusements." Truly do I believe that physical dangers, though great, are the least to be apprehended during the prevalence of the California "gold manias."

July 22nd (Sabbath)   This morning we heard of the recapture of Wilburn's murderers in or near Santa Fe and that an express had arrived at Placea with a summons for Capt. Bostick and Mr. Williams to attend there on next Thursday. The Alcalde, however, having started for that city, the summons were not served.

While out herding the cattle in a "vale of the mountains" at an early hour, I was particularly struck with the silence which reigned around. The spot was graced with some lofty and majestic pines, with here and there a beautiful cluster of small oaks, and cedars with their deep green foliage from the summits of the surrounding mountains, giving the whole the appearance of more of a park than of a wilderness. Yet scarce a feathered songster warbled his matin hymn. True, there were a few "Corn Birds" resembling jays, with a piping note like the Western "sap sucker."

During my guard I heard but one solitary approach to melody, and that was from a songster I did not see. Its notes resembled those of our Red Thrush. This dearth of the feathered tribe and consequent silence in the woods I have noticed ever since our arrival in New Mexico.

One fact possibly worthy of notice occurs amongst us all here, and that is a shortness of wind or breath. Many of us who could have run a quarter of a mile at home without experiencing inconvenientousness now puff and blow on the slightest exertion. The cause may arise from a greater rarefication of the atmosphere or it may possibly be the effect of our eating too much, of which we are all guilty. There are some amongst us, however, who live abstemiously and yet suffer a like inconvenience. The natives (probably from use) do not appear troubled with it.

July 23rd   Today has been all hurry and bustle. The black-smiths have commenced work at their forge (which was built on Saturday). Those skilled in the art of handling tools have been mending wagons, &c., &c., while others have tended the coal kiln and tar pit, and been employed in odd jobs, such only as a camp can give birth to.

Our hunters brought in a fine blacktailed Buck, which makes two since Saturday, and all our cooks have been engaged in the preparation of soup. This evening the troops sent in pursuit of Indians returned after an unsuccessful chase of several days.

July 24th Last night one of our sentinels fired at a fellow skulking around our cattle. The shot grazed the back of his neck and the rascal took to his heels. This morning a fellow belonging to San Antonio, a small town about 4 miles distant, was taken by the soldiers, and not being able to give a satisfactory account of himself was severely whipped. He was the same fellow our guard shot at. [15]

News reached us today that there were two men (Mexicans) lying dangerously wounded at San Miguel. These fellows had stolen a splendid cow and some mules from Mr. William's train (now merged with ours) during the night they lay near that town. [16] The next morning several men went in pursuit and after much fatigue found the mules some 5 or 6 miles off, quietly grazing among the mountains. Their piquet ropes had been taken off and they were well hobbled. They could discover no traces of the robbers.

The party who struck and followed the trail of the cow were equally successful. They came suddenly upon two Mexicans who had killed and were then engaged in skinning her. These they secured and were deliberating whether it would be best to hand them over to the proper authorities or to let "Judge Lynch" at once pronounce and execute summary vengeance on the offenders when they [the Mexicans] offered in payment for the cow, one mule worth $60, one pony worth $25 or $30, and $12 in cash. The transfer being agreed to and duly received both parties separated.

That night, however, an attempt was made to recover by theft what they had been compelled to pay over in the morning, with probably a large interest. Some 15 men came creeping cautiously towards where the horses and mules were picqueted. They were observed by the keen-eyed sentinel who held back till they arrived within a few feet of him, when he discharged the contents of a double-barreled shot gun at two of them with effect. Their companions aided them in a precipitate retreat, since which time till the present nothing has been heard of them.

One of our hunters yesterday got a shot at an ocelot or tiger, but missed his aim. We daily see "signs" of Grizzly bear but have not yet had the luck to encounter one. The mountains abound in deer, and there are many rabbits in the valleys. We had shot but one squirrel (grey) in New Mexico.

July 25th   We still continue encamped. The mechanics are busily employed, but those who are more idle are beginning to manifest symptoms of uneasiness at lying still so long, and here I would remark that I think this trip well calculated to disqualify most men, especially youngsters, from ever again resuming cheerfully or contentedly the labors of the farm. A spirit of adventure and of a roving life I noticed to be daily engrafting itself more deeply in their minds, and they already emphatically declare that they would rather lead their present life on half rations than exchange it for the dull routine of any settled business avocation. Should they be disappointed in their expectations in California, their whole after life will feel the ill effects of this adventure.

July 26th   The same dull routine of camp duty &c., still continues. This evening a rather suspicious looking old fellow (an American) who has a small and ill-tended Rancho here invited some of the boys to take a hunt with him in the mountains, promising to show them plenty of game. Several accordingly got their blankets, packed up provisions and started. At night fall they returned and stated that the old fellow had wanted them to tie their horses some three miles from the place designated as a camp, and from certain movements on his part they concluded it was neither safe nor advisable to trust him any further, so they wheeled about and came in.

He had raised some suspicions among us by stating that since his residence here he had had some difficulties on account of the authorities accusing him of being connected with or leading a band of robbers who prowl about these mountains, which accusation I should believe more true than otherwise. Had the party not returned it is highly probable they would have lost their horses and henceforward have found the proprietor of the Ranch amongst the "missing."

July 27th This evening we had a tremendous storm of hail and rain. Many of the hail stones were as large as partridge eggs, and they fell so thick that their noise on the tents and wagon covers sounded like incessant peal of musketry. The rain which ensued completely deluged the earth to the depth of 5 or 6 inches. Happily the wind was not very violent or we might have sustained some loss or damage.

The wolves last night seemed to have congregated between us and the mountains on purpose to greet us with a frightful serenade. Old and young, big and little, brought their notes into requisition, and it was almost impossible to say whether the noise or the discord of tone was most insufferable. They continued their wild concert till near midnight, when one more daring than the rest made his way amongst the cattle in order to seize a young calf which was quietly sleeping at the side of its dam, thinking no doubt that his services in the orchestra were fully entitled to at least a supper of veal. In this, however, he was disappointed as a watchful cur belonging to us soon told of his whereabouts and on a couple of rifle balls whizzing close to him he quickly sought some other conservatory.

July 28th   This morning our washer women brought in the clothes and were busy in settling up their accounts. They charged 5 cents per piece, the employer furnishing the soap. They do not iron the garments. Here as at other places through which we have passed they wash admirably well and do it quicker than I ever remember to have seen it done.

One of our "boys" paid a visit to San Antonio, and there started a Monte bank in company with another American. They won all the money the Mexicans could raise, together with some of their clothes. One fellow they completely stripped, leaving him nothing but "night vestment." So addicted to this vice are they that they seldom think of quitting a game while either themselves or their opponent have anything to lose.

4

July 29–August 11

"The best camping ground we have had for many a long day. . . . This is the only place since we have entered the territory of New Mexico fit for a settlement of whites."

—H. M. T. Powell,
July 17, 1849

Powell wrote this comment in reference to a campground near the mission of Quarai, in central New Mexico. Hunter's company planned to travel around the Manzano Mountains and proceed directly to the Rio Grande but took a wrong turn and arrived at a site where they found two other trains camped. Hunter's group joined them and this marked the beginning of a unique episode in the Forty-Niner overland journey, the two-week encampment of several trains near Quarai. A long stop such as this was a luxury not available to travelers on the northern route, who had to keep moving in order to cross the Sierra Nevada before the onset of winter storms.

While Hunter's party rested their livestock and waited for the rainy season to improve the grazing along the route farther south, several other trains arrived, and the campsite formed a temporary community of over 300 emigrants. They entertained thoughts of remaining in the area and working local gold and silver deposits, but after a futile expedition to investigate gold mines said to exist at Sierra Blanca, the Forty-Niners packed up and resumed their journey.

Quarai marked the halfway point on Hunter's distance table; by his calculations, the mission was located 1,090 miles from Williamsburg, Missouri, with an equal distance yet to San Diego. During this period, his company traveled only about fifty miles and spent eleven days in camp.

July 29th   Broke up our convenient and pleasant encampment and started for the Cibolo (Buffalo) Springs, distant 22 miles.[1] In consequence of forsaking the route via Albuquerque, distant [blank] miles, we had to travel nearly due east some 5 miles, where we took a right hand road which gradually turned south and entered a magnificent valley some 25 to 30 miles in width, leading from the foot of the Galisteo Mountains.[2] The road was mostly level and excellent, composed of fine gravel and sand.

We passed through some splendid grazing land interspersed with clumps of trees and occasionally large bodies of timber during the early part of the journey, but on entering the vale we found it destitute of any large growth. Several species of cacti and wild currants, with a few dwarf shrubs were all that met the eye as it scanned the wide expanse. I noticed some of the largest prairie dog villages I had yet met with and they seemed more populous. During the morning they were sunning and yelping in every direction around us.

Some 3 or 4 miles north of the [Buffalo] spring we again struck the timber which to the south became thinner and more dwarfish in appearance till it again ceased within 1½ miles of the spring, on nearing which we thought we could discover traces of a Rancho once having existed here. The road for the last five miles was literally beaten with wolf tracks amongst which I could discover one huge track of a bear.

The spring furnishes excellent water in abundance and flows from the base of a hill towards the north. It is some 30 to 40 paces to the right of the road. The grass was good throughout the journey.

This day was the Sabbath, and unfortunately like most we have spent since we started, it has been devoted to the accomplishment of one of our longest journeys. Several of our company would wish to lie by, on this sacred day of rest, not only with the view of meditating on and returning their thanks and gratitude to Him who is the author of all good for the mercies and blessings which daily crown us, but also for the less laudable but to us important object of letting our cattle rest and recruit. We are, however, in a minority, and so for well or ill we have to succumb.

July 30th   This morning at starting we missed the Captain's horse, nor could he be found in any direction. One of the guards had observed a Mexican shortly after daybreak clambering over the hill south of us, but concluded that he lived possibly not far off and was hunting sheep or something. From his movements and other circumstances there can be no doubt of his having stolen our missing horse.

Between 9 and 10 o'clock we halted at the "Ojo Veundo," distant 8 miles, a beautifully transparent and cool spring flowing from a limestone basin directly in the road. Its stream supplies abundantly a large pond near it, and the grass around being excellent our stock fared well.[3] During our stay to breakfast a Mexican came charging up to us in a sweeping galley and offered his horse for sale. He was an American pony of deep chestnut sorrel color and appeared latterly to have endured much hard treatment. Our Doctor became his purchaser for $10. The Mexican had no doubt stolen him from some train ahead of us.

About noon we again resumed our journey south. I rode on in advance of the wagons till I arrived at the Ojo La Estancia, distant 6 miles.[4] Here were many springs, or rather holes dug, into which the water flowed, and escaped into a large pond below, on the banks of which I found a party of four Mexicans with their "Carratas" or carts. On conversing with them they told me that this place was a favorite resort of the Apaches and Navajos, and that only last week they killed three Mexicans here. They appeared, while talking on the subject, to be then in dread and anxious to pursue their journey to their homes. The fellows were very well armed and needed not to have feared 20 Indians if they had not been base cowards.

They asked if we intended to proceed down the Del Norte and through the Indians to reach California? I answered yes, on which they rolled up their eyes, shrugged up their shoulders, and uttering a smothered hem! hem! started to drive up their oxen. These they tie by the horns with strips of rawhide to a round stick of timber notched near the ends and centre, to serve as yoke.

The "Carrata" consists of two clumsily constructed cottonwood wheels, about 4 feet in diameter. The wheel consists of three pieces, the longest in the middle, the other outer two fastened to it by means of long wooden pins and then rounded at the edge so as to form a circle. The centre of the wheel is about a foot thick, which it gradually tapers to 4 or 5 inches to the ring as to leave a kind of hub, through which a huge pine axle presents itself, making a most hideous noise when in motion. On the top of this axle tree the tongue is secured, which is again surmounted by the body, resembling in appearance the skeleton of a crockery-ware crate. Over this the Mexican throws his blanket for an awning and in its shade smokes his cigaritas, or luxuriously reclines amid thumping and jolting apparently sufficient to dislocate the limbs of a Hercules. The axle is seldom in the centre, the rim never round, and I have seen what appeared originally to have been a square wheel some 3 feet in diameter, while its mate on the opposite side was anything but circular and from 4 to 5 feet between its longest angles. A deaf man will leap for joy at his infirmity when he passed one of these vehicles.

Here we encamped for the night, the guard receiving strict orders to keep a sharp look-out or that the fellow who had sold us the horse today would be back and steal him again after dark. This is a fete often practiced on travelers by these wily and expert gentry, whose only excellence seems to consist of a preeminence of villainy.

July 31st   We left with the intention of taking the road via Chico, but missed it somewhere and took the one leading to Pueblo Quarra. This was plain and good, being mostly a plain destitute of timber till within 2 or 3 miles of Quarra. Here we found plenty of water and very good grass by driving the stock off the road a short distance.[5]

From the extent of the ruins at this place, still visible, it must at one time have been of considerable size. The walls of a Cathedral or church are still standing, but the roof has fallen in. The walls are some 2 feet in thickness, built of thin flat sandstone not more than 2 inches thick, and laid with mud mortar; they are perfectly smooth on the outside and from 35 to 40 feet high. The ground plan of the building is that of a cross. It has a venerable and time worn aspect.

I asked one of the villagers, whose countenance bespoke more than ordinary intelligence, the probable age of these ruins. He replied that they were about 300 years old, and had been built by or under the direction of the Spaniards shortly after their conquest of the country. From their appearance and the implements that must have been used in their construction, evidently such as only could have been used at that period by civilized people, I judge to be about the date and truth of their origin.

Attached to the church were other ruins, partly demolished, which some of the villagers had metamorphosed into modern habitation on their own rude and uncouth plan. There were several acres of land in cultivation at this place, the crops on which looked well.

On my arrival I noticed a Mexican woman who had three or four infants from 1 to 3 years old in a pond close by. These she would now and then immerse and then wash and dash the water over them as tho' she considered this pond a "Fountain of health." The little things, although they would cower and sometimes gasp for breath, seemed to be used to it, and to relish the sport amazingly. I was informed that there were three or four other such Pueblos within the circuit of a few miles.

Aug. 1st We left Quarra and took the road south for "La Joya," at which place it is probable we shall cross the river. After traveling about 3 miles we came to a trail leading west. This we took and kept for about 5 miles, till we arrived near the foot of a chain of mountains running nearly at right angles. Here we found three other trains for California encamped, resting and recruiting their animals as they think we are nearly a month too early to proceed much further south. We accordingly halted till we shall form some plans for our future movements.[6]

The place at which we are encamped is a plain stretching from near the southern end of a chain of mountains to the eastward. It is thickly overspread with a luxuriant growth of gigantic pine timbers, interspersed here and there with a few oaks and small dense patches of live oak. The grass everywhere around is about a foot high, springs and rivulets from the mountains abound, while the hillsides and valleys are thronged with game.

Aug. 2nd   Two of the trains who have been here some days have been making arrangements with two Mexicans to guide a party of men to the "White Mountains," at which place these fellows state that there is an abundance of gold.

One of them belongs to "Manzano," about 3 miles off, and the other to Quarra, distant 4 to 5 miles, where is the veritable "Jose Lucero" mentioned by Abert in his Report, Ex. Doc. N. 41, pp. 487–488, as having discovered the greatest gold and silver mine in the whole country.[7]

Their first proposition was that they would go and in five days return with three pounds of gold as evidence of the success of their mission. This, however, would not satisfy as our men by this time are more or less acquainted with their thorough proficiency on the art of deception. They next proposed that we should pay them Seven Hundred Dollars, provided the exploring party became satisfied after visiting the mines of the truth of what they stated, and we to protect them and allow them to work the same as ourselves after we should commence operations. This we agreed to and after a little shuffling on their part they came into our camp this evening and reported themselves ready to move forward.[8]

A company of thirty-seven horsemen was immediately organized, all well armed and mounted (on an average each man could fire six shots without reloading) and about 4 o'clock they started in high spirits, the good wishes of all who remained attending them. They intended traveling all night so as to reach the edge of a "jornada" some thirty miles across which they would have to traverse the next night without water.[9]

Aug. 3rd Last night three of the "exploring expedition" returned and this morning three more came in. The first stated that after traveling a few miles the guides wished to proceed to "Manzano"[10] to procure some large gourds in order to transport a sufficiency of water across a "jornada" which they now stated to be 90 miles across without a drop of water, and unless they took some with them they and their animals must inevitably perish. On seeing the wrathful countenances which this piece of information begat, and the unanimous disapprobation of the trip to "Manzano," the younger remarked that "as there had been abundance of rain lately there was a possibility of finding water on the route."

They were then asked how long it had been since they were at the "White Mountains." One of them replied that he "had not been there for twenty years," and the other "that he had been taken prisoner by the Indians when a child, that at the mine he and the younger Indians had often played with lumps of gold, unconscious of its value and which existed in profusion, but at the age of ten years he was rescued and returned to the place of his nativity, since which period he had never visited these mines for fear of the Indians." He further stated that "they would now run great risks of being cut off by Indians, and that it would no doubt be more prudent to return."

Persuasion and encouragement were then used to calm his fears and to quiet his scruples, but on his still manifesting an unwillingness to proceed, threats became plentiful as "apples in Autumn," and such threats too as no one wishing to preserve a whole skin would have dared put to the test.

So, considering danger in perspective [the threat of Indians was] too remote to be compared with what surrounded them, they sullenly agreed to prosecute their journey in all speed. Should they fail in the object of their mission, "I'd rather be a dog and bay at the moon than such a Mexican." We, of course, now have to await the return of the "gold hunters," which will probably be some two weeks hence. So, today we have been busy in putting up our blacksmith's forge, stripping wagons, &c.

A party of hunters have just returned from the mountains with two common and one black tailed deer. These latter are much larger than the common deer, with eyes more prominent and beautiful, ears longer and more velvet-like, and tail smooth and long, with a tuft of long black hair at the extremity. They, however, do not run so swiftly nor are their bounds so graceful as those of the common kind. We have also had a party out in search of two of our men who started out too [sentence not completed]

Aug. 4th Our mechanics have been crowded with work from the other trains and several hunting parties have returned from the mountains loaded with game. One party, while traversing a cañon (mountain gorge) saw a bear and fired at it. The shot took effect and the animal sprang at the hunter who turned and fled. At this moment the growls of some 5 or 6 more close to, and nearly surrounding them, were heard, which put all hands to flight. The hindmost, who was the one that shot, lost his knife, a pistol, &c., in the race, but having no relish for a real "bear hug," he did not halt till he arrived in camp. Vengeance for such unceremonious behavior on the part of the bears is the order of the day for tomorrow, when hill and dale, rock and brake are to be scoured by a formidable force—so that Bruin may yet have to regret publishing his whereabouts.

There is a man by the name of Roberts who is in company with the train of Captain McSwain of Audrain Co., Mo. Himself and a younger brother had started with an ox cart and had got as far as Galisteo. On leaving this place they started on ahead of the rest of the train. As they were driving along the road some 40 miles from town, they were approached by two Mexicans who came up to them from the woods and after shaking hands with them and manifesting the most friendly feelings towards them, asked for a drink of water, obtaining which they took leave but shortly returned for more, this also without exciting suspicion.

Scarcely were their backs turned when the two muskets carried by the treacherous villains, the Mexicans, were fired almost simultaneously, killing the younger brother dead on the spot, and passing through the flesh, glancing from the ribs of the other. He did not fall, and springing towards his cart for his gun, the two cowardly and fiendish murderers fled precipitately.

The wounded man then lifted the body of his murdered brother into his cart and brought it some six miles back, where meeting with a couple of gentlemen, they interred the corpse. The rest of the train at this time came up, and after paying proper attention to the wounded man, they proceeded on.[11]

Our absentees returned today about noon, and right glad were we all to see them alive and well. They had been lost and in endeavoring to make their way round the foot of the mountains, instead of clambering over them, they had got much farther off than they suspected. Their appetites were pretty keen from exercise and the purity of the mountain air, and they had been appeasing them since yesterday on the last remains of a fox, who like a self-devoted victim to minister to them in their necessity, walked straight up to one of them and was shot down. They had also the remains of a hawk in their shot pouches when they came in, on which they had been regaling their palates this morning. Verily hunger is a great sauce.

At nightfall those who had been searching for them returned, hungry, weary and dispirited, but on learning of their safety, all gloom soon gave way to pleasure, and jokes on their diet were freely circulated.

Aug. 5th Another blessing sabbath has nearly passed. In the morning it broke upon us calm and beautiful. The sun, as he mounted the heavens, beamed in cloudless majesty upon us, and the morning breezes murmured in music amongst the lofty pines which overshadowed our encampment.

All else was noiseless. A profound serenity seemed settled around, inviting the soul to wing its meditations to Him whose throne is in the blue and spotless firmament above. There is an inexplicable rapture, and exquisite sensibility of feeling, nameless and utterly above the reach of language, which seizes as it were by force the soul of him who on such a morning delights to revel in contemplation on the stupendous, the glorious handiwork of the Great and ever blessed God who sustains him. Blessed with perfect health and safety, and surrounded by innumerable comforts of which he is totally unworthy. That man must have indeed a flinty heart who at such time does not feel a sense of his dependent state, or where such is not arrived, to pour forth praise and thanksgiving, and in humble gratitude to acknowledge the goodness, the love and mercy of his Creator.

An appointment had been made by a gentleman in Captain Turner's train (Mr. Rickets of Henry Co. [Missouri]) to preach at 10 a.m., which, however, was recalled and the time changed to 2 p.m.[12] As I proceeded to the spot appointed, I was delighted with the beautiful prospect that broke upon the view on nearing their camping ground. I entered a pretty glade about ¼ of a mile in length by about 100 yards broad, gradually but gently ascending to the camp.

Before me was a range of conical shaped mountains whose summits were now embosomed in clouds, their bases seemingly all but near enough to touch with my hand, altho they were at least 1½ miles distant. Behind one was an extensive and magnificent view. At the foot of the glade and on each side were undulations of hill and dale, here densely covered with forest trees, there stretching out into beautiful meadows dotted with clusters of deepest green shrubbery, while still further east lay an extensive vale tinged with every variety of color, correspondent to the vegetation or sterility of its surface. An extensive range of lofty mountains occupied the background, sketching their blue peaks far up into the regions of others. Truly did "distance lend enchantment to the view" and "robe the mountains in its azure hue."

The preacher, on my arrival, stood under the shade of a huge and lofty pine. He was a man who had passed the prime of age and his looks were fast silvering over with age. His appearance, though not strictly venerable, was interesting, and it was the first opportunity any of us had since leaving home of hearing the word of God expounded by one of His Servants.

I sat me down on the green sward in front of the minister that I might lose neither word nor gesture. He had just given out his text: "Who is the Almighty, that we should serve him? And what profit should we have, if we pray unto Him?" (Job Cap. 21:v15). I tried while he repeated it to get ahead of him in the application of the subject to our circumstances and the occasion, but any foresight was completely babbled. I could not see its applicability in any light. I thought he would have chosen a text from the New Testament, so favorable in its reference to our present position that the most obtuse intellect would have at once realized its bearing.

After some very appropriate introductory remarks he warmed as he proceeded, and in a plain but forcible manner answered the question contained in the first interrogation, showing our dependence and the necessity there was for us more than ever to place our whole trust and reliance on Him who is mighty to save. On the second glance he was touching and eloquent, and his eulogy on prayer me thought sufficient to convince any one that it is one of the most blessed privileges enjoyed by man to have the power and indeed to be invited to pour forth his sorrows and supplications before a throne of grace.

Dense clouds were gathered around the mountains near us, and formed as it were a canopy of solemn grandeur above us, highly appropriate and imposing, while distant but subdued peals of thunder echoed along the mountain's sides and cavities, as if fearful of disturbing this first scene of Christian worship which this spot or almost this whole land ever yet witnessed, for:

> "The sound of the church-going bell,
> These valleys nor rocks never heard;
> Never sighed at a sound of a knell,
> Nor smiled when a Sabbath appeared."

After singing part of a hymn and receiving a benediction we returned to our own camp, more thoughtful and, it is hoped, more thankful beings. [13]

Aug. 6th   There is a silver mine about 12 miles S.W. of us, which from specimens that have been brought in by some of our hunting parties, must be very rich indeed. One of our company, who is an old and experienced miner, declares that if the ore at the mine is abundant (which is reported by those who have visited it to be the case) and of as good quality as the specimens exhibited, he with ten hands and proper apparatus could smelt 300 pounds weight per week. We have tried some experiments with the specimens, but have failed on eliciting any satisfactory result from our want of proper materials to thoroughly test it. We have not even a crucible amongst us. There is some talk of trying other modes while we wait for the return of our "White Mountain" party. [14]

Today the men have been busy in getting out saw stocks and have commenced sawing them into plank. This we shall haul in our wagons to the river, provided we proceed to California, and there construct a boat should the stream continue as high as it now is to ferry us over. We are also burning coals and tar kilns, so that when we again move forward we may prosecute our journey to an end without further stoppages.

Col. Jackson's train from Howard Co., Mo., came up to within three or four miles of us on the 3rd, and it is possible we may all push on together. We can then muster 300 men. [15]

Aug. 7th   Our hunting parties continue to bring in game in abundance, tho' as yet we have only succeeded in killing one bear. Last night a party of Mexicans succeeded in carrying off six or seven head of cattle from a train encamped about 3 miles north of us. This morning on discovering the loss, their trail was immediately taken and followed for some distance up the mountains where the party in pursuit came upon them just as they had slaughtered one of the oxen. On discovering their pursuers the Mexicans fled, but were fired on and one of them, it is thought, dangerously wounded as others had to assist him on a horse. They then effected their escape, leaving behind them a horse saddled and bridled, which was taken possession of by the Americans, and brought into their camp, together with the stolen oxen.

Aug. 8th Mr. Williams had a fine young mare stolen yesterday. She must have been taken from within one hundred yards of our camp.

This morning a Mexican entered the camp in great haste to inform us that the Apaches and Navajos were committing frightful ravages between us and the river (Rio Grande), and intended to cross the mountains at whose bases we are encamped to attack us. He states that they had had a desperate fight yesterday morning with an American train for California which was passing between the mountains and the river, and some Mexicans, killing two of the latter and two of the Americans, while their loss amounted to one killed and several wounded. The fellow was almost naked, without arms, and showed us several wounds about his person, which he said he had received from the arrows of the Apaches in former combat.

From his apparent composure during his stay amongst us and our skepticism on anything a Mexican can say, we were led to suspect some sinister design on the part of his "compadres," and his startling information elicited no more sensation than the most trifling "ipse dixit" he could have invented. The fellow was suffered to sneak off without further notice.

Aug. 9th Last night was a desperate night indeed. The wind blew in fierce blasts from the mountains, howling and screeching as though the "spirit of the storm" had left his hall to riot in midnight tumult and wild disorder. The lightning danced and glared incessantly through the sky, while sharp crashes of thunder seemed to shake the hills to their very foundations. The rain poured down in torrents, and the ravines near us added their roaring to the awful sublimity of the scene, as the rushing waters from the mountains bounded and whirled over their rocky beds.

About an hour before daybreak the war of elements subsided and awhile afterwards a fellow was seen stealing towards our corral. On being hailed by the guard, he instantly wheeled his horse and made off at a gallop. The guard fired at but did not bring him down. He halted some 3 or 400 yards off and raised a shout which was immediately answered by several others to our right and left. On searching the spot he had occupied when shot at a piece of shirt was found, looking as tho' it might have been torn by the bullet. If the fellow escaped a wound, it was a "hair breath 'scape" which will teach him to be more cautious in the future.

After breakfast we endeavored to trail them, but the cattle and horsemen from the different camps had obliterated or defaced their tracks. The rascal who told us yesterday of the Indians being in our vicinity was no doubt among this gang.

Aug. 10th During the storm on the night of the 8th, three oxen were killed by lightning in the corral of Capt. Turner's train, who have today moved off some four miles south. This evening we finished sawing enough plank to build us a boat. We shall get the gunwales on the banks of the R. del Norte some four miles S. of La Joya, at which point we shall no doubt cross the river.

Aug. 11th This morning our "White Mountain" party returned safe and well, and what I scarcely looked for, brought the two Mexican guides back unharmed along with them. Below is a sketch of their trip, politely furnished by N. Grove, Esq.:

"We left the encampment at 4 P.M. on the 2nd August., in company with our Manzano guide, and proceeded to Pueblo del Quarra, which we reached about dark. Here we were joined by Jose Lucero (the fellow mentioned by Abert in his report Ex. Doc. No. 41, pp. 487–488), who was to act in concert with our friend from Manzano in guiding us to the gold mines said to exist in the White Mountains.

Here some of our men, becoming alarmed at the privations which these Spaniards said were inevitable upon this expedition, turned their backs upon us and made for the camp. This desertion left us only thirty-one Americans. After as little delay as possible we set forward, intending to travel most of the night, which our guides reported would enable us to accomplish our journey across the jornada in our front by 12 o'clock the next day. After riding ten or twelve miles we discovered that one of our horses was very lame. We induced his rider to return, and two others volunteered to accompany him. This second falling off left us but 28 men. We pushed on till two o'clock when we became so sleepy and tired that we concluded to stop until daylight.

The first blush of the morning found us in the saddle, with our Capt. and guides in front. We again took up the line of march for a mountain then distinctly visible, and which our guides observed was on the opposite side of the jornada we were traversing, and at which they expected to find water. After we had traveled some three or four hours we struck a range of low sand-hills some two miles in width and which greatly fatigued our animals in our passage over them. They ranged N.E. and S.W. After considerable labor and fatigue we reached the mountain about 3 in the afternoon, and were greatly delighted to find a plentitude of excellent water and grass. We remained at this place until 12 o'clock.

The next day, when we again set forward and crossing two lofty spurs of the Sierra, we encamped by the side of a beautiful little rill which had its source on the mountain side and flowed N. and into the plain below. Here we remained until 12 o'clock the next day, when we again mounted and pushed on. Our course, which had been nearly east to this time, now lay within a few points of due S., thru a valley of considerable width, and which was covered with the best and most beautiful grass I have ever seen in New Mexico, and were it not that this valley is extremely destitute of water, it would be one of the best and most delightful grazing grounds in the world. This valley abounds with deer and antelope, which must of course resort to the mountains to slake their thirst as there is no spring or pool on the plain known to the white man or Mexican.

About twelve o'clock today two of our men who had been hunting came in and reported three Indians a short distance on our left. Supposing them to be spies Capt. Gulley immediately gave orders to charge and take them prisoner.[16] As soon as the word "Charge" was uttered a portion of our little band wheeled to the left and swept down the plain in noble style.

But instead of three hostile Savages we found nothing

but two bare horses quietly grazing under the large cedars, and which, not relishing our hostile appearance, proudly arched their necks and uttering two or three snorts, loud and shrill as if to challenge our speed, rolled their tails over their backs, bounded a few paces forward to stretch their limbs, and then like a tornado swept over the plain and were soon lost in the distance.

After we had adjusted our packs, which had been disarrayed in our formidable charge, we again pushed on and discovered another horse, but not feeling quite so full of fight as before, we sent out one of our guides, who with great address lassoed him and brought him in. We then moved on rapidly until dark and encamped without water.

We mounted at daylight next morning and traveled over a broken country until 1 P.M., when we reached a spring strongly impregnated with sulphur, but which afforded great relief to our suffering animals, as they had not tasted one drop for twenty-five hours. We remained here about two hours and then set out for the White Mountains, which rose in lofty grandeur at a distance of fourteen miles to our right and which we reached before sundown.

There in a large cañon we found another spring, also impregnated with sulphur. This was the mountain in which our guides said the gold was to be found. As soon as we had breakfasted, our guides, with 5 or 6 men to protect them, set out in search of the place where the precious metal was to be found in such abundance. Night again returned and with it came our hunters and guides without having discovered the least evidence of the rich deposits we had so hoped to appropriate to our own little necessities. Our guides seemed much dejected but expressed their determination to renew their search in the morning and with apparent confidence in their ability to find the much desired spot.

Our Capt. thought it most expedient that the whole party should aid the Mexicans in their endeavor the next day. We did so, riding where we could and leading where we could not ride, until sundown, when our guides declared their inability to accomplish the object of our expedition and begged to be allowed to return home. A few long visaged boys would not have been difficult to find at this minute. Concluding that the White Mountain was not the only spot where gold was said to be found, we turned our reins for the encampment, which we reached on the tenth day after our departure."[17]

5

August 12–August 31

" 'Goodbye,' we say, from the bottom of our hearts to this muddy stream and the horrible roads we have had since we crossed this river."
—David Brainard,
September 10, 1849

Brainard expressed a commonly held opinion among the Forty-Niners on the southern route, formed after several days of traveling down the rugged west bank of the Rio Grande. This segment of Hunter's journey fell into two distinct portions as his party left the tablelands of central New Mexico and entered the Rio Grande Valley. The first portion, from Quarai to Socorro, was generally easy travel. Hunter's company crossed the river at Sabino and then traveled for thirty miles through a narrow ribbon of irrigated fields and orchards.

The second portion of the journey began when Hunter passed San Antonio, the last town the Missourians would see until the village of Santa Cruz, Sonora, 400 miles and a month's travel away. South of San Antonio the main road crossed the river and followed the desolate Jornada del Muerto, a ninety-mile stretch with little water, though the ground was level and offered few impediments to travel. Hunter's company kept to the west side of the river and followed the road blazed by Cooke and Kearny in 1846. Numerous ravines cut the road and made travel difficult at times, although water and grass could always be found. It took Hunter's train nine tiring days to cover the ninety miles to the turnoff for Cooke's road. The rugged valley road constituted difficult travel for Hunter, though it would appear less so when contrasted with the deserts he would encounter later.

Of the twenty days covered in this chapter, two were spent in camp. The train covered 180 miles for an average of only 9 miles per day, reflecting the slow pace down the Rio Grande Valley.

Aug. 12th   Sunday. Today has been spent in travel. This morning we left our pleasant camping ground with the intention of reaching the "dripping spring," but our cattle having been gorging themselves for some time on grass, we deemed it more prudent to halt at the first watering place we came to, since leaving the bottom which stretches from the foot of the mountains lying westward. [We traveled] A distance of some 10 miles.

We have been traversing a "jornada." These "jornadas" vary considerably in their appearance, some being perfectly sterile while others, like that over which we have passed today, put forth grass, shrubs and a dwarf growth of scrubby Cedar &c.

An immense vale running nearly north and south, and distant some 25 to 30 miles from the "Rio del Norte," while others lie in the summits of the elevated table land, or undulate gently with surfaces always sandy and sometimes interspersed with rock, while yet others are broken, cut up with hollows, ravines and fissures, and present nothing but a naked face of rock and gravel. The grass here is excellent, over a foot high, and for the most part looks like a luxuriant meadow about ¾ of a mile.[1]

To the northwest lie some ruins called "Pueblo de Abo."[2] On visiting them this evening I was particularly struck with the loneliness and desolation which attached to them. Only one feature seemed to remind me that it was a spot where civilization had once smiled. This was a narrow skirt of cotton wood trees, which looked as tho' they had been planted on the banks of a small water course (supplied by a few springs) which lay between me and the ruins as I descended from the hill from the Eastward. Their bright green foliage contrasted strongly with the deep color of the Cedars which grew plentifully near them, and beautifully relieved the sombre aspect of the time worn and dilapidated buildings but a few paces behind them.

The Cathedral, or Church, is the most entire building now standing, altho it is fast going to decay. The outer wall, built of sandstone from 1 to 4 inches thick and cemented with mud, is about 5 to 6 feet thick, by about 4 feet in height at the highest points which are now left standing. It is impossible to trace its original height, but from the stones and rubbish fallen on each side, it must once have been considerably higher. It encloses an area of about four acres.

The walls of the Church itself, the construction of which would do credit to any of our masons considering the materials used, are some 50 feet high by 2½ broad. It is built perfectly square like all the rest I have seen lately, in the form of a cross, from the entrance (S) to the extremity of the cavity for the altar. It is 40 paces long through the arm of the cross 15 paces, and its mean breath almost 9 paces (the same measurement at the church at Pecos). The top of the walls are castellated, and the windows, two in number, are built in gothic style but have arms near the top resembling a cross.

The entrance has fallen in, as also the roof, gallery, orchestra &c. The ends of some of the rafters, joists, beams &c. still remaining embedded in the masonry have been burnt off, which might possibly have been the fate of these edifices altho the walls show no evidence of fire. There is no woodwork left about the ruins except a platform over a cell some 3 feet square like a huge square column standing N. against the western wall on the outside, and resembling very much those living sepulchers in which incontinent nuns and probably others have been oftimes incarcerated to meet the most horrible of all deaths. My blood chilled as I contemplated the use of that dismal looking niche.

The ruins resemble those at Pecos, but it is impossible now to form a correct idea of their ground plan, as they have fallen down and scattered their materials in every direction.

Outside the enclosure the ruins would indicate a once populous village. An "Acequia" [irrigation ditch], long since dry, passes through the enclosure S. of the ruins and runs for some distance under a wall, probably supplying or at one time having been supplied from or through a large cistern, the cavity of which is still visible in a small court or yard amongst that portion of the ruins which formed the cells or habitations of its founders or occupants. Pieces of earthen vessels (some neatly painted) lay thickly strewn about the enclosure.

We passed this morning some singular looking hills. They were covered with vegetation from their tops to about half way down their sides. Here a cornice seemed to protrude and thence downward was a perpendicular face of red sand-stone, excavated here and there into cells, and occasionally obtruding into massive columns supporting the cornice. One to the eastward somewhat resembled a Chinese pagoda as it rose in lessening tiers towards the summit.

This morning Capt. McSwain's train, who were incorporated with ours yesterday, took up their line of march with us. We now number 25 wagons and [blank] men.[3]

Aug. 13*th*   About 1 o'clock this morning we were all thrown for a moment into considerable alarm by a noise somewhat resembling distant thunder, rapidly approaching us. It evidently proceeded from the earth, which seemed to tremble as tho' some fearful visitation was about to overwhelm us, and for an instant of anxious suspense, was enough to paralyze all action on the part of most of us.

The night was pitch dark, so that no object was visible at a distance of five paces. The dreadful sound grew more distinct and nearer each instant—when "a stampede—a stampede" was yelled by 50 voices from an encampment (Capt. Turner's) near ½ mile below us. "Parade, Parade. All hands corral the cattle" was vociferated by our Captain, and echoed by every one as he sprang or tumbled helter skelter from his wagon, and it is but due to our energy or our fears to say "that our cattle were never before corralled in double the time."

A herd of some 180 to 200 cattle had taken fright, and started at the top of their speed, directly towards our camp. The noise caused by the trampling of so many huge beasts was now heightened by their affrighted bellowings. On they came, like the inch of the sweeping torando, threatening destruction to whatever might oppose them, when suddenly, thank God, at a distance of only a few rods from us, the advancing column separated into two divisions, one passing on each side of us, at which I at least, was devotedly thankful.

These same cattle had several times before shown their agility in this kind of dangerous frolic, once breaking 5 wheels from 3 wagons and damaging others. I am informed by those who should know that when thoroughly alarmed they will dash through a body of wagons or over any similar impediment to their advance, destroying whatever impedes them, and entirely regardless of the presence of man. Fire-arms discharged at their front are said to be the only way to turn them.[4]

Our route this morning lay through a long and pictur-esque cañon for about 4 miles. We shortly after left the road and encamped to breakfast near a deep hole of water, about ¼ of a mile in a ravine to the right called "Salado." The water was very salt, and unfit for any culinary purpose. Our stock, however, drank it with avidity. The grass around was excellent.[5]

Near the southern end of the cañon by the road side to the right were several huge rocks covered with hiero-graphics, which from appearance and designs, I should be led to ascribe to the aborigines of New Mexico.

From this place we proceeded 2 miles to the "Dripping Spring," a name which would convey an idea of a somewhat romantic spot, but its location, appearance and flavor, once seen and tasted, destroys all illusion. It "drips" indeed, but so slow that it takes some time to fill a bucket, and altho somewhat better than the water at "Salado," it is brackish and by no means palatable. It is, however, the last water to be had till you reach "La Joya," distant 25 miles.[6]

In the road today I caught a Centipede, a disgusting looking kind of worm, said to have 100 feet, whose sting or bite is very venomous. It was, however, unlike those of tropical climes, being round and black, about 8 inches in length and coiling itself into several folds when molested, while those I had seen in South America and the West Indies were of a brown color, flat and of a light yellow underneath, and but slightly round across the back. The horned lizard is also different from that we had previously noticed. Its head, instead of being armed with sharp boney spikes, is only furnished with two projecting ears, giving the reptile a very singular appearance.

Aug. 14th We last night had another stampede amongst the cattle belonging to Capt. Gulley's train. They flew past our camp like the wind, but owing to prompt attention and good management on our part we again escaped difficulty. [7]

Our route this morning for some 7 miles was over a tolerably good road through the mountains, but one bad place had to be passed, and when we descended the last hill we entered upon a beautiful area of plain, stretching some 12 to 15 miles to the celebrated and much talked about Rio del Norte. From this to the summit of the hill overlooking "La Joya de Ciboletta" the road is most excellent. Near the base of the last hill we descended. [8]

Mr. Williams informed me that he examined a vertical stratum of quartz running nearly east to west, directly across the road in the interstices of which he could discern particles of gold in abundance, and it is his opinion that at or near this spot there must be rich deposits of this mineral. His reason for not mentioning the discovery at the moment was a desire to proceed on our way to California as speedily as possible, much time having already been spent in useless explorations or idle research.

We did not arrive near La Joya till after dark, in a heavy

shower of rain. Some of us had ridden on early in the evening to town in order to swim the river, so that we might have something to boast of when the others arrived. We were, however, ashamed of the adventure. When the rains came on we were kindly and politely welcomed by the inhabitants. They also courteously provided us shelter and refreshments for the night.

The town is situated near the river (the river is not over 200 to 250 yards wide here and very shallow, instead of being at least ¾ to 1 mile [wide] as we were led to expect) on a bottom about 3 miles long by about 1 to 1½ miles broad to the foot of an elevated range of sand hills, a large part of which was under cultivation, the crops evincing industry in their abundance, and a bountiful harvest at maturity, the remainder apparently being reserved as pasture ground. The town itself is another brick-yard looking place, containing some 250 inhabitants. Its vicinity and itself not being especially remarkable for anything but swarms of gigantic mosquitoes with extra-pointed proboscis.

Aug. 15th We have been traveling since early breakfast (except an hour or two at noon when we stopped to graze) through deep and heavy sand, very fatiguing to the teams, our road lying over sand hills and hollows near the river. By the road side were many monuments or piles of rocks commemorative of the spot at which some murder had been committed by the Indians.

Here were the first thrifty looking Mezquite bushes we had seen and this probably forms the Northern boundary of their plentitude. The climate evidently changes its character here. The weather is much warmer, and the flowers, shrubs, &c. begin to assume an appearance more resembling those incidental to the tropics.

This evening we encamped at the village of "Joyeta," [Joyita] distant [blank] miles from "La Joya."⁹ This village contains a population of about 100 adults. It is built on a sandy bottom and contains houses which, though they are built in the same style as the other towns, are more commodious, many of them having windows which tho' square are arched with plank above so as to bear a resemblance to the Gothic. The inhabitants are better looking here than those we have seen [previously], and their dress and general appearance evince an improvement over those we have left behind. They treated our boys to a fandango, which indeed has been the case wherever we have stayed amongst them. The soil here seems to be highly productive, altho their crops are some what backward. They have no grapes as yet, and their onions, which throughout this country surpass in size and flavor any I have ever seen, are yet too small for them to use.

Aug. 16th   On leaving "Joyeta" we had a laborious ascent of nearly a mile up a steep range of sand hills. The view from the top repaid us for our toil for directly before us lay the vale through which the river, like a sheet of silver, wound its tortuous course, skirted at intervals by a scattered growth of cotton wood trees.

The pleasant little village of "Pulvidera" [Polvadera], situated on its western margin and embosomed amongst the cotton wood and fruit trees, and surrounded with corn fields, contrasted beautifully its reddish brown aspect with deep green foliage. About 4 miles below lay the village of "Limitar" [Lemitar] characterized by the same features, while in the back ground towered a lofty pile of rugged mountains, with bright misty clouds flashing around them about midway of their height.¹⁰

Our road still continued through deep beds of sand, but about noon we reached the town of "Sabino," on the eastern bank. Two of us had gone ahead and on our arrival we entered a hall or entry into a square pile of buildings. The front of each side [was] occupied as a store, the other three sides facing inwards on a square courtyard comprised the dwellings &c. of its inmates. In the hall sat a remarkably fleshy old lady and her daughter, both seated on the ground enjoying the fumes of their "Cigaritos." They politely invited us to enter and take chairs, and immediately ordered some cool water to be handed to us. This was a treat, as we had not tasted any liquid since breakfast.[11]

The elder lady must have had at least ¼ of a pound of gold on her fingers, while from the ears and neck of the younger it swung in superfluous profusion. Her fingers also were scarcely less encumbered than her mamma's. Both excelled in politeness, and in our conversation were very social and communicative.

A pair of large and strong folding doors defended the entrance to this and most of the other houses in this town, while at "La Joya," "Joyeta," &c., they [the doors] frequently consisted of a single narrow plank, and were so low that the body had to be bent nearly to right angles before an ingress could be effected. Several of them [the doors] also had ladders sat up by their sides, communicating with the roof through an aperture in which in times of danger the inhabitants always pass, the doors being barricaded.

On descending to the river I encountered a woman with a bottle of "aguardiente" (spirits) which she was urging on all she met. This was the first time I had seen anything of this sort since my arrival in the country. Here too those of our company who chose were favored with another fandango.

As the river is too steep to ford we this evening made an arrangement for two canoes to ferry us over tomorrow. We have to pay eight dollars per day for them and to do the work ourselves.

Aug. 17th   Last night a platform was laid over the canoes with the plank we had sawed at "Santa Antonietta," the Mexicans charging us 12½ cents each for 3 small poles to bind the canoes together, and this morning by day break all hands were in motion. To those unaccustomed to aquatic labor, the crossing of the wagons promised nothing but frolic, and some 15 or 20 might be seen floundering about in the water, laughing and hailing at the top of their voices and in perfect ecstasy at the change of employment. After ferrying over two or three wagons, however, and becoming chilled, their ardor abated considerably, and they began to perceive that they were engaged in one of the most laborious of undertakings.

The river for about 60 yards near the eastern bank was from 4 to 5 feet deep, and the current so rapid that it was utterly impossible for a man to keep his feet. The water was so thick with sand and mud that it swept everything with almost the force of a solid body. From this to the western bank, some 450 to 500 yards, it was shallower and we could get along very well.

About the sixth or seventh wagon we were crossing over, the canoes, owing to a lack of force sufficient to manage them, drifted on a snag and immediately filled and sunk, upsetting the wagon into the river, the contents of which were soon drifting in every direction. By prompt assistance we succeeded in saving most of the property. This accident was the more to be regretted as the wagon, belonging to Capt. Bostick, contained the wearing apparel, trunks, bedding, household furniture, &c., &c. of his family, whom he was removing to California. His loss was probably something over a hundred dollars.

Aug. 18th   This morning we finished getting over our wagons, &c., and are now encamped below the town of "Limitar" on a plantation belonging to Gov. Armijo. One or two of our friends were entertained and treated by him with the greatest urbanity. [12]

A Mexican came down to one of our wagons which had been landed apart from the rest, and before the eyes and under the very nose of its owner, picked up his axe and dashed with it into the river. Some of our men happening to be on the opposite bank, the alarm was given, and the fellow dropped his prize in the river. He was taken, but after receiving a hearty kick or two and a few sound cuffs, he again escaped and this time made good his retreat.

"Limitar" is the largest town we have yet seen S. of Santa Fe, and contains 150 to 160 male adults. The crops and vineyards in its vicinity look thrifty and beautiful. Here we obtained as many grapes as we wanted. They were of large size and most delicious in flavor, and some of the branches would measure half the length of a man's arm. The natives, however, charge very high for them. We caught several fine catfish and soft shell turtles from the river, and have here fared sumptiously on turtle soup &c., for some days.

Aug. 19th (Sunday)   This morning we passed through the town and commenced descending the western bank of the "Rio Grande del Norte." About 3 miles from town the road forks. The left, leading down the river bottom, is almost impassable, the wagons in many places cutting into the axles. That to the right, leading apparently to the mountains, is an excellent road. From the hills here we had a fine view of the village of "Parida" on the eastern bank of the river, [blank] miles below Sabino.

Early in the morning we reached "Socorro," a large village on the western side of the river. Here is a very good looking church, built of adobes, with towers of three stories above the roof. In front, each story contains a hall, and the summits of the towers and centre of the fronts are ornamented with crosses. Here was also proudly floating the "Star Spangled banner." This place at present being occupied as a military station, and having a squad of dragoons in readiness to operate in any direction.

A party of them are now out in search of a gang of ruffians who a few days since committed an atrocious murder. A man had been sent out into the mountains to herd some mules, and while thus employed he was murdered and his body burnt. They have one fellow now in irons on suspicion, and anticipate further discoveries in a few days.[13]

Here were the first melons we have seen. They were small, however. There were also some thrifty looking peach trees in some of the gardens, the fruit not yet ripe. Plenty of grapes could also be obtained. A short distance south of town are the ruins of an ancient town, nearly level with the ground. We encamped for the night some 2½ miles south of it amid most excellent grass and plenty of water, altho it was the Sabbath, still several of our company were promised a splendid fandango at night. A heavy rain, however, opportunely prevented their attendance. In the morning we had met crowds returning to "Limitar" who had been down here to attend mass or divine service. Many of these (females) were expected back to join the dance. Such is the mode of spending the Sabbath where Catholicism reigns predominant.

Aug. 20th   Today we have driven [blank] miles over a good road, in ordinary times, but as it rained heavily all last night, two thirds of our journey along the flat bottom that here skirts the river had been through water from 1 to 3 feet in depth. We are encamped about a mile N. of the village of "San Antonio," on the bank of the river, and have excellent grazing for our cattle. For some 5 miles south of "Socorro" it is nearly one continuous plantation. Here is situated the village of "Los Lopez" [Luis Lopez], a small, mean looking collection of hovels, altho their fields have better fences than any we have lately passed.

This evening we have caught some fine catfish and soft shelled turtles from the river. The town folks here, as well as at all other places in this country, flock in crowds to the camp immediately after we stop, bringing horses, mules, fruit, vegetables, &c. for sale and somewhat annoy hungry men by hanging around the fires, smoking their cigaritos. We are constrained to believe also that their main object is to spy out some opportunity for theft and to take immediate advantage of any neglect on our part.

Last night some time after dark, one of our sentinels brought in a fellow whom he caught creeping towards the camp, whose ready excuse was that "he had come to request us not to let our cattle get into a corn field above us." This was at least 2½ miles off, and the rascal certainly knew that had we let our stock ramble at night we should long since have lost every head.

Aug. 21st   From "San Antonio" to where we are encamped it is 11 miles.[14] For nearly the whole of this distance there is a magnificent bottom from 1 to 3 miles wide, skirting the river, and covered with a dense growth of the most luxuriant grass, the blade of which resembles "timothy," while the stalk, bearing a heavy head of seed, resembles that known as "blue grass" in the western states.

The houses in "San Antonio" are all built of poles placed perpendicularly in the ground and plastered only on the inside, giving the exterior a very mean appearance. Here I met a Mexican just returned from the "Rio Colorado" of California. He states that the "Camino Real" by which he came is an excellent road, but that "Cook's Trail" is very bad, that the Rio Colorado is from 2 to 3 miles across, and that there is an abundance of grass and water throughout the whole route.[15] He says, however, that the Apache Indians are very numerous and daring in their attacks along the whole route, and that the Indians on the Colorado are very hostile, having attacked some American troops whom he had piloted out and killed 5 of their number—they losing 18 men in return of their action. He offers to guide us to the Colorado for twenty-five dollars, but as no faith or confidence can be reposed in any of them we deem it better and safer to trust to our efforts.

Here I tasted the wine of "El Paso." It is delicious and resembles choice old Madeira in flavor. It is, however, of a deeper color and somewhat too sweet.[16]

Aug. 22nd   This morning we traveled a continuation of the same magnificent bottom we did yesterday. The same [illegible] of grass still continues. The river still affords us an ample supply of fish, and we have had some excellent duck shooting at several ponds near which we have passed. The rifle is, however, unsuited to this sport as it tears the birds too badly. We have shot guns, but unfortunately no shot. I have noticed today several fish hawks hovering over these ponds.

We nooned at the foot of the "Table Mountain," a singular mountain some 250 feet high, rising from the river bottom on the eastern side. Its top is perfectly level and projects over its sides so as to resemble a cornice. Its sides ascent from its base at an angle of about 45 degrees and are fluted with much regularity. Its river face is about a mile in length and it occupies an area of some 557 square miles.[17]

The weather for the last two days has been delightful. We yesterday passed two wagons encamped whose company wished to join us. From appearances, however, we concluded not to augment our forces. This evening we left the bottom and ascended a body of "table land" lying before us. The road still continues excellent and the Plain around us was covered with luxuriant grama grass. At night we encamped near the river on the summit of a sand hill, after having traveled 18 miles.

Aug. 23rd About a mile from where we had encamped the road abruptly left the river and took a due west course up a cañon to the right. The road was excellent and ascended gently for some 4 miles when we reached the level of the hill tops to our left. We now traversed some high land running from the foot of the mountains to the river, forming entire ridges throughout their length.[18]

The weather was warm and our cattle would have been the better of a good drink, but there was no water to be had. On leaving this elevated region we descended by another cañon which made nearly due east to the river. For more than ½ of a mile the descent was very bad, the gorge at the bottom being scarce wide enough for a wagon to pass, and so steep, rocky and uneven that the wagons in some places seemed to bound from one rock to another. We, however, passed down without accident, and after continuing some 5 miles through this pass, we turned off to the river and encamped.

I noticed today several coveys of quails. They are somewhat dissimilar from those of the States in color, and have a
crest of fine long feathers on their heads. I also saw two new
varieties of cacti. This makes 7 different varieties I have
noticed.

Aug. 24th   This morning our route lay over a dreadfully bad
road. We have been crossing the points of numerous sand
hills, stretching to the river, and through sand from 6 to 15
inches deep. Altogether it is the worst piece of road we have
traversed since leaving the boundary of Missouri.

We are resting near a singular looking mound or wall of
earth, distant 49½ miles south from "San Antonio."[19] From
a distance we all thought it to be the remains of some old
temple, but on visiting the spot I found it to consist of
almost a perfect wall some 8 feet thick, its length about 60
feet and its height about 30 to 35 feet. It is formed of a kind
of cement or mortar composed apparently of gypsum and
sand, well intermixed, and stands on an elevated knoll near
the river. Its appearance from the north is highly picturesque. Its resemblance to some ruined fortress is very striking, and it seems still to frown proudly on the neighboring
scene less lofty than itself. The base of the knoll on which it
sits is surrounded next to the river with a grove of cotton
wood, while its western side, dreary, ragged and steep, seems
to forbid approach. The river winds in brilliancy around its
southern and eastern base, while the lofty range of the Fra
Cristobal mountains rises in gentle slope for 8 miles beyond
it, suddenly spring [sic] from their velvet looking base, and
raise their black looking and rugged peaks into the regions of
the clouds.[20]

The road near and beyond this spot is very bad, a
continuous succession of sand hills lie directly south and we

have had to encamp at least 3 miles from the river, with no water nearer. The grass, however, is excellent.

Aug. 25th   Today we traveled but 4½ miles, the same bad road continuing. We encamped here, on the river, as we think there is a stretch of 18 miles from this place before we again reach water. The river here is not 100 yards wide. The bottom, in which we are now, is about 1½ miles long by some 300 to 400 yards wide, enclosed in a semicircle of sand hills. The grass is excellent. The water from the river being very sandy and bad has given several of our Company severe diarrheas, and they complain of the pain attendant on it as excruciating.[21]

Aug. 26th (Sunday)   Today we have been traveling over a good road, and are encamped till evening near the river. We have made but 6 miles. The weather is very warm, and even this distance caused our cattle to show symptoms of fatigue, so that our future traveling will be prosecuted early in the morning and in the cool of the evening, whenever circumstances will permit it. I have noticed today several large coveys of quail.

Our evening journey has been 6 miles, nearly the whole of which has been over a tolerably good road, forming a gentle ascent for over two-thirds of the distance. We are evidently fast increasing our elevation and as we see a mountain in the southeast which all look upon as Cook's point for turning west, everyone is anxious to hear the opinions of his neighbor, as it is from this point our "leap in the dark" commences, no one among us ever having been this far. A variety of opinions having been expressed as to the practicality of this route by those who assume to be acquainted with the country. Some anxiety is very naturally entertained.

Aug. 27th   This morning for some 2 miles the same ascent continued, at this point the summit of the hill was reached, when a very gradual and easy descent occurred to the south, over a sandy but good road. A little beyond the foot of the hills we turned W. up a cañon which wound around till we again turned about S.E. till we struck the river bottom.[22] The road is good except in 2 or 3 short stretches. One steep and difficult hill was climbed with severe labor to the teams. We have traveled 10½ miles, and this evening would have proceeded further had not Dr. Branham complained of being too ill to move.

While the wagons were progressing I took a ramble through the hills near the river. They were greatly diversified in aspect and character, some being of a deep orange or brown color, apparently containing or being composed of ochre. Others were white or streaked with red and composed of fine clay and gravel. One mountain was a vast mound of ashes, with here and there a black or brown pocket jutting a few feet above the surface, composed of what to me appears iron, it exactly resembles the cinders or conglomerate substance thrown away by blacksmiths from their fires, but it is not so hard. Others again were covered with masses of rock and large pebbles of every hue and form, all more or less indicative of having undergone volcanic action, or betraying the existence of mines in the earth beneath. The river gradually grows less in width and depth, from absorption in the sandy country through which it runs, and from evaporation, which must here be very great. It has no tributaries to replenish the loss.

At the spot where we are encamped we found a piece of plank with the names of several companies and many individuals who passed here en route for California during the month of July. It is rather a singular spot, being composed in nearly a semicircle by hills whose fronts have nearly all been washed away, so that we seem to be encompassed by walls of red clay, furrowed and washed into a variety of fantastic shapes, some of them of sufficient architectural accuracy to appear beautiful.

East of us is a high ridge of mountains, while further south some 10 or 12 miles is a mountain which we all look upon as "San Diego," Cook's southernmost traverse on the "Rio Grande del Norte."[23]

Aug. 28th   This morning at a distance of 4½ miles from last night's encampment we came to a creek some 12 feet wide and from a foot to 18 inches deep.[24] Its current was clear and rapid, flowing east and entering the Rio Grande a mile from where the road crosses it. This was an unexpected treat, not only because its waters were clear and good, but because none of us had any idea of meeting with water, other than the river, till after we should leave it entirely, and thus to stumble upon a fine stream, roaring and dancing over its pebbly bed was indeed delightful. The river water with its ¼ sediment of mud was immediately emptied from our water kegs, and its place supplied from the creek, which tho' not very cool was pure and wholesome.

Near the mouth of the creek we caught some fine cat fish and killed several rattle-snakes. One of these was over five feet long and had upwards of twenty rattlers altho the extreme point of the tail had been broken off. I noticed also many large and beautiful horned lizards. This creek, from appearances, is supplied from the plains and short ridges of mountains to the westward, and I should judge is dry except in the rainy season.

Evening—Good fortune still seems to attend us. At a distance of 6¼ miles from the last creek we have encamped on the bank of another, narrower but deeper, with water cleaner and cooler, and this seems to be a lasting stream. Its course and sources of supply seem to be the same as those of the last.[25]

We have today traversed three cañons to the west to cut off bends and elbows in the river. At the head of these were steep, rocky and severe hills to surmount. The balance of the road was firm but gravely, and hard on the oxen's feet.

The wood we have used for fuel for the last few days has been the dry branches and roots of the mezquite and willow, which though scarce and small, make a lively and good fire. The roots of the mezquite, altho putting forth boughs seldom as thick as one's wrist, are themselves frequently as large around as a man's body, and farther south, I am informed, are dug up with much care and labor, by the wood cutters. A growth of cotton wood, dissimilar from ours, occasionally skirts the river banks, but for the last few days' travel there has been swampy ground between us and the river covered thickly with willows or rushes, in many places impassable.

Aug. 29th   Today we remained encamped on account of the protracted illness of Dr. Branham. The morning was warm and sultry. This evening it has been cooler, with flying showers and thunder and lightning. From the river we have taken some fine fish and one of our hunting parties killed and brought in a fine deer (common). The grass in the bottom where we are now halting is of the best quality, and the water of the creek being clear, affords us the first opportunity of washing clothes we have had since reaching the Del Norte. Most of the men have consequently profited of the occasion and shown their ability to beat many a laundress in the U.S.

Aug. 30th   We this day moved one mile and encamped on the south bank of "Berry Creek" (so named in compliment to our worthy Captain, no other sobriquet being known). This is a bold and rapid stream flowing east, its source and supply being probably the same as the two last. It flows through a vale running east to west. The view up, which is here perfectly open till it strikes a lofty chain of mountains to the west, running apparently about N.W. and S.E. The only growth near it, at least for some miles towards its source, is mezquite, willow and shrubs of small size. At its mouth, however, is a goodly skirt of large cotton wood trees.[26]

We have noticed for the last two days several flocks of Sandhill Cranes flying south. These in the Western States are generally the harbingers of cold weather. The wind is and has been for some time from the N. and N.W., and the air is cool and we still continue to catch plentifully of the best catfish I ever saw. They are somewhat dissimilar from those caught in our western waters, and are so full of fat that they need no other grease to cook them. Dr. Branham still continues very ill, hence we are remaining stationary.

Aug. 31st   We still remain encamped. Three trains have passed us today, and two more are in sight.[27] Some of our hunters who have ascended the creek have seen several deer, antelope and turkeys, but were unable to obtain any. They also noticed the impressions of moccasins, pony tracks &c., indicative of the presence of Indians.

A serious affair had like to have occurred the day before yesterday to a member of a train just behind us. He was hunting amid the tall cane grass that here in many places extends from the river far up into the bottom, forming dense and almost impervious jungles, when he saw a large grizzly bear, which he fired at and wounded.

The infuriated beast immediately sprang at him, [and] his mule wheeled and threw him. By this time the bear was on him, and trampling on the man in the scuffle, pursued the mule, which when at liberty, struck for the river and dashing in, has not since been heard of. The bear stood gazing awhile on the bank and [then] retreated. The man, on seeing Bruin's departure, thought it high time to attend to his safety and accordingly made for the wagons with the speed of a roe buck.

6

September 1–September 13

*"While we are confident that we can have nothing worse
ahead of us, we will hope for something better."*
—Joseph R. Simmons,
September 3, 1849

Simmons's comment reflected the argonauts's anxiety on
leaving the Rio Grande Valley. Although the valley presented difficult terrain, the road to the west was little
known. Hunter reflected this feeling also when he wrote,
quoting Cooke, that "our 'leap in the dark' commences."
Previously, Hunter's train traveled over established roads;
some of the train members had seen the country during service in the Mexican War. After they left the Rio Grande and
entered Cooke's road, they would be following a route little
used prior to 1849, with only Cooke's vague description to
guide them. Hunter's initial misgivings were quickly dispelled as the eastern portion of Cooke's road crossed generally level terrain which presented few difficulties for wagons.

The major problem experienced by Hunter's party
proved to be a murder within their train. Beyond any legal
jurisdiction, the emigrants were hesitant to impose capital
punishment. This quandary occupied several days, and the
final disposition of the case illustrated the problems of justice on the frontier where citizens were on their own.

When they turned south at Ben Moore Peak (east of present day Lordsburg, New Mexico), the Forty-Niners entered Mexico. The Treaty of Guadalupe Hidalgo, which ended the Mexican War in 1848, established the Gila River as the boundary between Mexico and the United States. At the point near where the Gila intersected the modern day boundary of Arizona and New Mexico, the boundary line dipped south and then followed an east-west line to the town of Mesilla, on the Rio Grande. The precise line was in dispute in 1849, a disagreement settled by the Gadsden Purchase in 1853, which moved the boundary south to its present location. Hence, Hunter's party traveled through Mexico from a point south of Ben Moore to Yuma Crossing on the Colorado River.

During the thirteen days covered in this chapter, five were spent in camp, and Hunter's train averaged twenty miles of travel per day, their best average on the entire journey.

Sept. 1st   This morning we traveled over an excellent road for 8 miles when we entered a beautiful little dell, with a fine grove of cotton wood trees standing at its extremity nearest the river, under the cool and grateful shade of which we watered our stock in buckets from the river.

On ascending the hill to the south my attention was attracted to a group of our company some 200 yards in advance, whose movements indicated something uncommon. On pushing to the spot I found Mr. W. Wigginton of Boone Co., Mo., stretched on the ground and bleeding profusely. He had been stabbed from behind with a large dagger knife by Wm. Gadson. The knife entered between the shoulders a trifle to the left of the back bone and ranged horizontally towards the right breast dividing the motor and [blank] nerves, passed through the mediastinum and severely wounding the lungs, entered the inner surface of the chest.

Our own physician, Dr. Branham, being too unwell to attend the case, a messenger was dispatched to a train in our rear, who promptly returned with Dr. Porter of [blank] Co., Illinois. This gentleman at once pronounced it a highly critical and dangerous wound, but with much skill and ability soon succeeded in stanching the exterior bleeding. The hemorrhage from the lungs, however, still continues, and the patient lies apparently helpless and sinking fast.[1]

This evening I received a present of a little animal about 4 inches long, of a light brown color, striped horizontally with white. Its tail is twice the length of its body, bare to the point where it is tufted with long scattering hair. Its head and body resemble those of the guinea pig. Its fore legs [are] very short, while the hind ones appear disproportionally long and shaped exactly like those of the Kangaroo. One of its legs was broken when it was presented to me [and] I had therefore no opportunity of watching its movements. It burrows in the earth, forming a conical hill above, around which are several apertures for ingress and exit. Its teeth are like those of a mouse.

Sept. 2nd (Sunday) We remained encamped today watching with anxiety the fate of Wm. Wigginton, who still lies very low. This evening we are gratified with an excellent sermon from 1st Epis. John Chap. 2 or 3, by the Rev. [blank] of [blank], Illinois. The spot selected for preaching was the beautiful little grove on the river bank, at the foot of the dell before mentioned, which lay about midway between his camp and ours. His prayer was appropriate and touching, and the music of several excellent voices harmonizing in the sacred songs, seemed to impart tremulous motion to the leafy shade above us, as it ascended through the pure, still atmosphere to the throne of Almighty God, whose praises were our theme.

It was truly a delightful sight to see the hardy adventurer, the spirit that would have dared anything and which would have disdained submission to a thousand mortal foes thus fraternizing with his brethren and bowing in humble reverence at the footstool of his Maker. It is no doubt the first time this spot was ever consecrated to Divine worship as we are some 90 miles below the settlements and the savage who roams over these wilds, if he has any conceptions of an Over-ruling Providence still "sees God in clouds, or hears Him in the wind."

Sept. 3rd This morning we renewed our journey. As our patient was in too dangerous a state to move for at least two weeks, even should he finally recover, the wagons that joined us at Quarra and to which he belonged, remained with him, as also some of his relations from another train. We also left the perpetrator of the deed with them. We had him in custody ever since this murderous attempt at assassination, and had Mr. W. died before we left it was the opinion of our company that it was our duty to have delt summarily with him. [2]

Our Judiciary Committee, however, had serious scruples as to the legality of such a course, and as I happened to be one of their number I was not sorry to leave the fellow with those who seemed to have the best right to take charge of him.

Last night, on delivering him to the guard, our Orderly Sergeant happily searched him, when he discovered in the fellow's pockets a quantity of bacon, a large pocket knife,

&c., and on examining the chain by which he was confined it was found that the link through which the one attached to the padlock had been opened so that he could have freed himself of his shackles in an instant, and had fortune favored, effected his escape. A horse belonging to one of [blank] having been found saddled and bridled, tied on the grove above us. This discovery, opportunely made, caused his more secure confinement, but through the night one of our camp guard overheard two of his friends plotting his escape. It will, however, be a most dangerous experiment, try it when he will.

The hemorrhage from Mr. W's lungs ceased last night, and this morning he appeared much easier. It would, however, seem a miracle should he recover.[3]

After traversing 6 miles of good road we stopped to noon near the river, opposite the mouth of a large cañon. At 2 P.M. we entered it, this being the point where the river is left and the journey to the westward commences.

This point cannot easily be mistaken. Just before reaching it a large bottom is entered, having scattered here and there a few trees over its surface, at the southern extremity of which is a cañon of some 50 to 60 yards wide running about S.W. opposite the hollow between the second and third hills. To the right as you ascend the cañon a drain crosses the cañon, and from the base of the third hill protrude horizontal strata of rock. This is the only one throughout the whole extent of the pass, which is about a mile long, where the rocks are visible, and as the table land at its upper end is reached, the road turns abruptly to the east, and following this direction some distance again curves quickly to the westward, forming almost a complete letter S.

As this is a spot of interest to those on the route and the place where all the water vessels had better be filled I have been somewhat minute in this description.[4] The "San Diego" of Cook is, I presume, a mountain ridge 12 or 15 miles S.E. It may be easily known by its tapering down to a point towards the river, while all the other ridges to the E. increase in abruptness as they approach it.[5] We made 6¼ miles over a good road and encamped on a dry creek, although water might have been obtained by digging in its bed.

Sept. 4th   We made an early start and arrived at "Foster's Hole," distant 5¼ miles by breakfast time. This is a large pond ¾ of a mile to the left of where the road enters the bottom in which it lies. I did not visit it, as we had plenty of water in a creek which here crossed the road. In the evening we reached a sulphur spring at the angle of the "Proposed Road," and the route traveled by "Lt. Col. Cook" in 1846.[6]

Eye, I think, has seldom rested on a more gorgeous scene than that which this morning burst upon our view at sunrise. Just as the sun, in peerless majesty, had climbed above the eastern mountain and robed each object in a flood of rosy tinted light, we had gained an eminence which overlooked a large scope of surrounding country. It was a sort of dividing ridge, leading from the river to the upland westward. On each side were extensive clusters of minor conical shaped hills, their western sides being buried in shade which revealed their regular and sun lit outlines, and presented a sublime aspect as the surface of the troubled ocean immediately after a tempest.

To the eastward lay the low ground, ornamented with clusters of trees and shrubbery through which the river with its silvery flood might be seen peering at intervals from amongst the dark foliage which fringed its banks. Beyond this a lofty ridge of mountains reared themselves abruptly into the air, their crests representing a variety of grand or fantastic objects, as their dark outlines were boldly penciled on the clear bright sky. Many had spots on their sides, especially where shade yet held dominion, and where rugged and bare rocks were no doubt piled in wild disorder might be traced cities with temples and towers, boldly standing forth by their own grey color against the dark ascent surrounding them. And then the rapture which thrilled through the frame at such a glorious moment, each nerve, each atom seemed big with ecstasy. The cool mountain breeze, as it swept across the ridge, whose crest we were traversing, seemed freighted with health, inspiring the whole system with a vigor that bid defiance to fatigue or suffering.

Sept. 5th   This morning, about an hour and a half before day, we started for the "Mud Springs," distant 13 miles.[7] The moon, nearly full, shone clearly and brightly, and the air being cool our teams traveled rapidly. Our course was nearly south till we reached the springs. Here we halted and breakfasted, and in about two hours entered a long and beautiful cañon running west some 2 miles.

After leaving it and bearing south-west, we turned the point of a hill and faced to the N.W. This course we followed in momentary hope of finding water. The drains which we crossed, however, were all dry, and the surface of the country, presenting no flattering prospect to dig for it, we concluded to push on till we reached some.

Our route lay round a semicircular ridge of barren mountains. On coming opposite their western extremity a gradual descent commenced and we pushed on briskly. This descent continued for about 8 miles till we struck the Rio Mimbres, which we reached about 11 P.M. and encamped, after traveling 31½ miles, and accomplishing in one [day] what it took Col. Cook three days to perform.

Sept. 6th   During last night a party of men brought to our camp Wm. Gadson, the murderer of Mr. Wigginton, who died of his wounds on the evening of the 3rd Inst. The prisoner seems in no way daunted.[8]

The country around us, as far as eye can see, is one vast plain with here and there an isolated peak or short ridge of volcanic mountains rising from its surface. This plain is sandy or covered in spots by patches of gravel or rock of volcanic origin. Its growth consists in most places of a luxuriant coat of grama grass, wild sage, cacti of several varieties, a species of what in the West Indies we use to call Spanish Daggers, called by the New Mexicans and the emigrants generally "Soap Weed," mezquite of small size, the creosote plant, besides a great variety of shrubs and plants whose names I know not, and a hundred different varieties of wild flower, many of them the most beautiful tints, but nearly all void of fragrance.

Sept. 7th   Today we lay in camp till evening when we crossed the river Mimbres as there was a great deal of rain above us and we feared least it should become swollen and prevent a passage. This is a singular stream. At and near this spot it forms two channels some 60 to 100 yards apart, the space between being thickly overgrown with Cotton Wood, ash and a dense mass of willows, amongst the roots of which the water courses in shallow channels, or in places overspreads its whole breath. The main channel of the stream is about three feet deep by 25 to 50 broad, clear and rapid. Here we obtained the first really excellent drink of water we have enjoyed since leaving our encampment below Manzano. It looks like an elegant "trout" stream if there were less brush about it. I did not try it.[9]

Tonight we have tried Wm. Gadson for the murder of

Mr. Wigginton. An impartial jury having been summoned and sworn, from amongst those to whom the prisoner had no objections. Our Judicial Committee sat as judges. Milton Williams, Esq., of Boonville, Cooper Co., Mo., appeared as attorney on the part of the Plaintiff, and Freeman S. McKinney, Esq., of Fulton, Callaway Co., for the defendant, who entered his plea "guilty." All the testimony elicited went to prove the prisoner's guilt, and after hearing the arguments of Counsel, the case was submitted to the jury, who after but a short consultation ordered the following verdict: [space for the remainder of sentence left blank]. It being some time after midnight the Court adjourned *sine die.* [10]

Sept. 8th   This morning at sunrise Wm. Gadson received his punishment and was then dismissed. [11] We then journeyed on to "Rock Creek," distant 14 miles, which here rises at the road and runs S.E. In it was found some deep holes of good water and we remained there till evening. [12]

From the road about a mile East a view is obtained of two singular looking white rocks to the left, which look like two wagons in the act of corralling, while below them are scattered some bushes resembling the teams.

Two miles west of this we passed the "Ojo de Verra" (Cow Springs), and near it crossed the Janos road to the copper mines north of this. About 8 P.M. we encamped amid excellent grass (Cow Spring). [13]

Sept. 9th   We started at daybreak and drove to "Ben Moore," a mountain at whose base we expected to find water. The party sent in search, however, returned unsuccessful.

A party of five of us determined to try the ascent and started accordingly. We found it very steep and rugged, abrupt rocks springing from its sides in all directions, from amongst which a few stunted Cedars here and there peep forth, while the large leafed prickly pear flourished luxuriantly, bearing its pleasant fruit in great abundance, and of a large size.[14]

I met with one some 12 or 15 inches in diameter and about 20 high in the form of a cone from the top of which sprang a cluster of magnificent blossoms, whose leaves partly enveloped each other, like those of the rose, but narrower and expanding at the extremity into a bell-shaped flower. Their color near the top was bright red, changing imperceptibly to a deep orange near their base, while the centre was filled with hair-like petals surmounted with yellow seed. The exterior surface of the plant was lined perpendicularly about an inch apart at the centre and verging towards a point at its summit and base. These lines or ridges were armed with large thorns projecting in every direction. It would have made a beautiful present to some of our fair American florists, to whom I much regretted I had no means of presenting it "in propria persona."

We startled two deer during our ascent, one of which we shot at but missed. Another singular but beautiful plant also flourished here. It consists of a number of round stems frequently 10 feet high, springing from one root. Some straight, others serpentine or curved in various ways. These stems are thickly armed with thorns which obtrude from amongst the leaves, which grow in clusters and lie nearly flat with the stem. When green the stems are exceedingly tough.[15]

On reaching the summit a most extensive prospect burst upon the view. Its height I judge to be from 8[0] to 100 feet above the plain. All around might be seen elevations

from the size of a prairie dog's mansion to that of a respectable mountain ridge, all, however, having a very broken
appearance. To the S.W. lay a plain bounded in the distance
by mountains of some magnitude.

Through this plain could be traced the road pursued by
Cook, which here forms an angle and takes a course about
S.W. by S. To the west and where Mr. Leroux on Cook's
map proposes a due west course cross what he believes to be
an open Prairie, we could discover from our superior elevation innumerable ridges and hills from south to north,
which from this point would seem to forbid any route other
than the one pursued by Cook. [16]

On scrutinizing near us to the north, we thought we
could distinguish signs of water near the base of the mountain. One of our party accordingly descended in that direction and found plenty in a rocky ravine about a mile from
our encampment. It lay in holes among the rocks and had to
be closely approached before it could be discovered. We also
noticed a well-broken trail north of the mountain running
about N.W., probably used by the Apaches as a marauding
trail to the northern Mexican settlements.

Could old "Ben Moore" have found a tongue he could
have told us many a wondrous tale. He could have told us of
once having overlooked a densely populated district, whose
tenants like their habitations had long, long since passed
into oblivion. The surface of the valley at its base was strewn
with fragments of broken pottery, similar in substance to
that found about the Ruins of the Pecos, Abo, &c., but
seemingly more ancient in its style and design. Not a vestige
remains of any other monument or memorial.

The gentleman who discovered the water, not having
arrived till we were in motion, we pushed on into the

prairie.[17] In about five miles we came to a grave, having a head board surmounted by a cross on which was inscribed "H.E.L. Hanleying, Augt. 5, 1849."

We caught two large tarantulas, the first I had seen, altho one of my messmates informs me that he caught one among our bedclothing some few days since and merely threw it from the wagons, not knowing its dangerous character.

These were hideous looking creatures. Their form was that of our large spiders, about 2 inches long in the body and larger round than a man's thumb. Their color on the back was a dirty whitish brown, the lower extremity covered with brown hair, with eight long and powerful legs (4 on each side) covered with dark brown hair and two obtuse antenna ½ inch in length. Their under surface was coated with a kind of feathers, variegated with black and white shades. Its mouth, nearly the whole diameter of its body, was at the distance of about ⅓ its length from the point of its head, of a blood red color. From each angle projected a strong claw armed at the point with a fang resembling that of the rattle snake. These were worked so as to draw whatever they touched into the centre of its frightful mouth.

On annoying it with a stick it manifested every symptom of the most violent rage, striking its fangs into the stick, with a noise that we could plainly distinguish, and with such force that its body could be suspended for several seconds from the tenacity of its hold. Its mouth also seemed to dilate and compress with great muscular energy, but whether armed or not I could not distinguish, having no glasses of magnifying properties with me.

The plain we were now traversing abounds in rattle snakes. The grass was excellent, and our road being level and firm as a turnpike, we moved on rapidly not knowing where we should strike water, and our animals having had none since they left Rock Creek. Fortunately about 10 P.M. we came to a "sink in the Prairie," covered with water from 3 to 4 inches deep from recent rains. Here we encamped.[18]

Sept. 10th   Eight miles from our encampment we entered a rugged cañon about 2 miles in length. Near its centre were holes 3 to 4 feet deep which had been dug and were now full of water. From their appearance I should say there were springs in this vicinity, and that water might be obtained by digging at any ordinary time.[19]

Here a specimen of lizard genus was brought to me, differing from any I had ever seen. Its length from the nose to the extremity of the tail was about 9 inches. The breath of its body about 1½ inches, its fore feet were pointed with claws placed like the fingers on the human hand, having a thumb also similarly situated. Its back was striped alternately with regular black and white bands which extended in rings from the insertion of the point of its tail.

Its ears were short and projecting, and it was covered thickly with short, formidable spikes, excepting the underside, which was smooth and of a light straw color. Its form, except in being rather roo flat, was exactly that of an alligator.

Nine miles from the southern extremity of the cañon we reached Las Playas or the "Dry Lake." This is a shallow depression in a vale extending several miles nearly north and south, bound on each side by ridges of rugged mountains. The water which it now contains is deposited in small, shallow puddles, except where the depression of its surface is greater, whence it extends itself into large sheets from 3 to 6 inches deep. Its bed seems almost impervious to water as the soil 2 inches from the surface was dry enough to crumble. A few hours of warm sunshine would no doubt evaporate its contents at most times.[20]

Between the cañon and the lake we passed through a large patch of pea-vines, which covered the ground for some acres. They were loaded with peas in full maturity. Little or no difference was discernible between them and the English or green pea cultivated in our kitchen gardens, the pods being alike. The taste of the fruit, however, was slightly bitter. The grass near the lake was excellent.

Sept. 11th Many flocks of Gant [gannet?] have this morning been hovering over the lake and at their departure taken a southern course.

At daybreak we received our first depredating visit from Indians. Two Apaches, as appeared from their track, visited the vicinity of our camp, and seizing on two fine horses and two mules, succeeded in carrying them off. On missing the animals their trail was taken and followed by a party of five men for about eight miles. The Indians, contrary to custom, instead of endeavoring to conceal their course, had recourse to many expedients to make it as plain as possible. They first followed up the muddy margin of the lake and on striking for the mountains studiously passed over the most sandy or soft places, as if to leave their trace as plain as possible. The party in pursuit, being small and fearing from all appearances an ambuscade, returned unsuccessful. The Indians had apparently dismounted in places as if for the purpose of showing their numbers, one wearing moccasins and the other being barefoot.

This evening we moved down the lake about 2 miles to an excellent spring near the road. One spring that we passed about ¼ of a mile back was of a most singular character. Its outlet was about 3 feet in diameter, slightly raised above the surrounding level, and its depth about 6 feet. The matter which it voided was of the consistency of honey, of a greyish blue color, as though it held slate or blue clay in solution. The earth around for a circumference of 35 or 40 feet rocked violently up and down, on jumping on it near the orifice. I neglected to taste it, but one gentleman informs me that he could plainly discern a sulphurous odor when within some 40 yards of it. There is another some ½ mile south and nearer the lake to which I could not get.

A ring some 40 feet in diameter had formed around it [the spring] by the trampling of stock. From this it gradually rose to a cone in the centre some 18 to 20 inches above the level ground. Its mouth was circular and filled to the brim with what I conceived to be water, but on throwing a large stone into it a column of black mud was precipitated into the air and from the noise and bubbles which followed the stone's immersion I should judge it to be very deep.

Sept. 12th About 7 miles from the lake we entered a cañon through the mountains which form the western boundary of the valley in which it is situated.[21] On the hill sides I noticed some trees of a different growth from any we have yet seen. They are oaks of good size, very much resembling the "Black Jack" of the Western States, but not so gnarly. I also obtained a beautiful specimen of the cactus tribe some 8 inches long. Its form was oval, divided by spiral lines running perpendicularly into equal divisions about ½ inch wide. These spaces or divisions were indented or ground in the middle, and from their ridges obtruded the thorns or prickles which defended them completely with a coat of impervious mail. The points of each set of thorns described a circle. They sprang from a notch in the ridge, their number from each centre being from 15 to 20, the top ones merely projecting from the rim forming their root, and lengthening as they reached the lower extremity, each set about ½ an inch apart, were partly overshadowed by the long thorns from above. The colors were truly delicate and beautiful, but so imperceptibly blended, and the tints so various, that it would be impossible to describe them. It was encircled by three or four belts of shade, which varied according to position, light on the body itself. Beneath the thorns was a light sea green, the thorns mostly white, running into pink at their points, where crossed by the belts. They were all of deep pink, as were those springing from the top. Altogether it was one of the most beautiful productions of the floral kingdom I ever saw.

After leaving the cañon we descended into a beautiful and extensive vale, along the lower side of which flowed "Quicksand Creek."[22] We crossed two or three hollows and one dry branch leading from the mountains to our left, on the banks of which were a great many Indian wigwams which had been but lately occupied. At the second branch we encamped, at the foot of the mountains. Here were some springs and an abundant supply of running water, altho ½ mile below the creek bore little vestige of ever having formed a conduit.

7

September 14–October 5

*"Along here was the best grass we had on the whole
route, a very good road and excellent water."*
  —*Louisiana Strentzel,*
  1849

Strentzel, member of a Texas train, expressed the opinion
of most of the Forty-Niners about the country from Guadalupe Pass to the village of Santa Cruz. After the rugged
Rio Grande Valley and some arid portions of Cooke's road
through New Mexico, the country appeared to be improving. In fact, the road from the pass to Tucson was the
last good stretch of road Hunter would find on the southern route. Of the twenty-two days covered in this chapter,
Hunter's train traveled 200 miles in nineteen days, a leisurely average of 10 miles per day.

Hunter's company negotiated Guadalupe Pass, near the
junction of the New Mexico, Arizona, and Sonora borders.
While most Forty-Niner accounts concentrated on the difficulties of traversing the rocky pass, Hunter gave rein to his
imagination and recorded vivid descriptions of the majestic
rock formations. Beyond the pass, the road crossed broad
grasslands; it was the end of the summer rainy season and the
grass was high.

At the San Pedro River, most Forty-Niners departed

from Cooke's road, which followed the river to the north, and continued westward to the Santa Cruz Valley. Hunter met Mexicans returning from the California goldfields, and their stories of potential riches spurred the argonauts on.

Beyond the village of Santa Cruz, travelers encountered a series of abandoned ranches and missions as they headed northward through the Santa Cruz Valley to Tucson. The rangeland continued into the upper reaches of the valley, but north of the mission of Tumacacori, in present Arizona, the Santa Cruz River disappeared into the sand and the argonauts began a gradual descent to the desert floor. Their spirits began to ebb at the realization that the worst part of the journey lay just ahead, north of Tucson. A combination of weariness and foreboding, which affected most Forty-Niners by this point, led to dissension in Hunter's group, and the previously stable train divided at the mission of San Xavier.

Hunter devoted considerable attention to describing San Xavier, one of the most beautiful missions in North America. A large Papago village surrounded the mission, and he noted the stark contrast between the stately mission and the primitive habitations of the Indians. Hunter arrived in time to witness the Papago's Scalp Dance, held after the return of an expedition against the Apaches. He was particularly disturbed by their treatment of captured Apache children.

Sept. 14th This morning we were in motion by daybreak. The wolves around were wildly howling their matins, and the crescent moon just imparted sufficient light to render it dubious whether she or the grey eyed morn held preeminence.

Our route for about 1½ miles lay on the Creek bottom,

during which we crossed it twice. One of the fords was desperately bad. Here we ascended a ledge of table land, forming a continuation of the vale traversed by Quicksand Creek. The road was level and excellent, but muddy in spots from the abundance of rain which fell yesterday. In about 5½ miles from the bottom we halted to breakfast at a spring on "Sweetwater Creek." This is a beautiful little pellucid stream running N. and S.[1]

Here from West we turned again a South course. The road was most excellent till we rose a hill at a point where the Janos road enters from the Eastward.[2] Now commenced our traverse of the "Guadalupe Pass," which in contrast with our previous road was terrible indeed, but when compared with some of our Western roads, would merely be termed a "rough route." On descending a hill some [blank] miles from its entrance a wagon tire which had been badly welded parted asunder and compelled us to halt before getting through.[3]

On the plain to our left, before reaching the "Pass," we startled a herd of Antelope from 100 to 150 in number. On being terrified they fell into single file and as they crossed a range of hills in the distance they resembled a large flock of sheep.

Many names were written or carved on the trees by the roadside, mostly emigrants from Texas, some of whom had passed as early as the 10th of June. [Blank] miles from "Sweetwater Creek" the road forked, one taking round the base of a hill to the left and bearing south. This was a new looking trace and from its direction many concluded it turned off and intersected the Janos road, while others contended from its appearance that it had been the track pursued by all recent travelers, and was either the main good road or at least was a cut-off of some advantage. The latter opinion predominated, and we soon found this to be the road discovered by Dr. Foster, while Col. Cook was in a sad dilemma on a hilltop. The other road, much the plainest, ran due W. and was the one followed by Col. Cook.[4]

Sept. 15th   Last night our blacksmith soon put the crippled wagon on its wheels again, and after breakfast this morning we again took the road. We had yet about 4 miles to go before we reached the Western extremity of the Pass.

We shortly came to the foot of a very steep and long hill. There the foremost wagons had to double teams, and it was then a tight pull. Those in the rear were assisted up by the men, who as quick as they could throng pushed from behind and worked at the wheels. We accomplished the ascent without accident and then commenced descending to the ravine through which flows a branch of the Rio Huaqui.[5]

This we reached at the point where Col. Cook's trail intersects it, and on which he certainly must have encountered and overcome obstacles sufficient to have dampened the ardor of any man of less sanguine temperament or less firmness in scrupulously endeavoring to discharge his duty, despite the frowns of fortune or of fate.

Near here a party of men from a train in our rear, who had been round by Col. Cook's route to survey it, report that in many places they found it nearly impracticable for their mules, untrammeled in any way, to descend the rocky and precipitous hills over which the route was effected, and further state that altogether it is probably one of the most desperately bad roads over which a wagon ever passed. From the little we could see of it we rejoiced in having once deviated from the plainest track.

Our route now lay directly down the branch amidst

some of the most wild and rugged scenery imaginable. At every turn of the Creek some new feature was presented tending to add grandeur or sublimity to the vista, while the beautiful green canopy above shielded us from the rays of a sun, which in so confined a spot would otherwise have been insupportable.

The growth in this Pass consisted of Sycamore differing only in the form and color of the leaf from that of the U.S. Ash, Hackberry, and White, Black and Post Oak, Walnut, Laurel, Mezquite of large size and many varieties of shrubs and plants, some extremely beautiful. I noticed a delicate little vine, bearing a flower exactly like that of our Cypress Vine. The leaf was different.

I christened the Pass down the Creek the "Wizard's glow," from its wild and secluded characteristics. Here were caves extending far into the bowels of the Cliffs with walls blackened by the smoke of the Indian's fire, as he sat with impatience watching the preparation of his tardy meal, or stole suspicious glances toward the outlet of his retreat, or perchance calling around him his dusky compatriots, plotted new scenes of theft or devastations on his pusillanimous neighbors, while the fumes from his pipe curled aloft, as if wreathed by fairy fingers into seeming records of his spirit's aspirations.

Here too were dens for the misanthrope, or cells for the hermit of chambers, in the solid rock, whose unroofed walls reached the mountain top. The fissures in their faces tenanted by the bat or the owl, and their floors, shaded by tall sycamores, and covered with dank weeds and grass, afforded secure covert to the most venomous and loathsome reptiles. Here indeed might be the favorite haunts of the evil genii of the glen, as summoned by their superior they hold midnight revel or carried on their diabolic incantations over caldrons of heterogeneous monstrosities such as only Macbeth's witches or professors of the Black art could manufacture or conceive of. Hence the title of "Wizard's glow" seemed appropriate.

One stupendous monument reared itself near the centre of the glen. It consisted of a perpendicular face of rock raised [blank] above the out line of the hills on either side of which sat a dome 80 to 90 feet in height. This was surmounted by a cupola of solid rock some 20 feet high, the whole approaching architectural accuracy so closely as to have a fine effect.

The feature which heightened its grandeur the most remarkably was that the dome and cupola, instead of being seated perpendicularly, seemed from a short distance up the glen to project immediately over the Pass and to threaten instant destruction to all beneath. Without the mathematical precision or straight monotonous outline of "Pia's tower," here was one to which the graces of art could have added but little. One whose grateful and stupendous outline pointed in the clear blue sky above, set at nought all efforts at imitation, and which proudly proclaimed its Architect or Projector Infinite in power, as the rippling stream, the gorgeous flower, and leafy canopy at its base, did His infinity in love and mercy. Many objects beautiful and strange strike the traveler at almost every turn, and I could most pleasurable have spent a week or two in rambling through the recesses of this wild and lonely spot.

Sept. 16th   This morning we emerged from the shades of the "Wizard's glen." In passing through the bottom previous to ascending the table land to the W., I noticed several large patches of wild flax. It was in full bloom and apparently the same in every respect as that cultivated in our fields. The lint was fine, strong and excellent in quality and appearance.

From a day or two before we left the Rio del Norte to the point where we entered the Guadalupe Pass, immense swarms of loathsome looking caterpillars were spread in patches over the country, devouring the grass. In many places every tuft seemed to have its occupant, although I could not discover that their ravages were very devastating. They may, however, have just commenced their work of destruction. On this side of the mountains I have noticed none.

On reaching the summit of the table land, a vast plain covered with grass, mezquite bushes and shrubs extended North, South and West so far as eye could reach, except where a few isolated hills raised themselves. The road was excellent and we arrived at the Deserted Rancho of San Bernardino, distant 9 miles, early in the evening. Here we encamped.

The walls of most of the buildings on this Rancho are yet standing. They form three sides of a square running parallel with the Cardinal Points. It must have once contained from 3 to 400 inhabitants from its size, who were either killed or compelled to abandon their homes from incessant Indian attacks.[6]

From the "pass" we have observed many skeletons of the wild cattle said to abound in this region and to have sprung from the stock left by the inhabitants of these Ranchos at the time of their desertion.

We here found an excellent spring a few yards to the left of the road, W. of the Crossing of the Rio Huaqui. This stream does not deserve the name of "River," with which

Mexican bombast has invested it, as it is invisible, except where a few holes too deep for rushes to thrive in present their surfaces to the sky.

A fine and extensive vale extends E., N. and South from this Rancho, covered with coarse grass in most places taller than a man. Some little distance to the West commences a bench of level land covered with Cedar, Mezquite and Shrubs. At this Rancho there are the remains of an old furnace, which from appearances must have been considerably used for the purpose of smelting ore that no doubt abounds in the neighboring mountains.

Sept. 17th Last night for the first time we heard the bellowing of the wild cattle, and this morning every one was anxious to get a sight at them. About 10 o'clock, as the teams were leisurely wending their way along an excellent road, a young bull 4 years old came dashing up to the foremost wagon until he arrived within some 30 paces, when he came to a halt and stood gazing at the train. Two or three of us who happened to be at the spot flew for our guns, but before they were brought he had turned. One ball was fired into his side and he went off at a sweeping trot, his neck proudly arched and his tail high in the air. A party went in pursuit but did not succeed in killing him.

He was as beautiful an animal as I ever saw, of a light brown color on the back and sides, and verging to a black underneath and over the limbs. His face was dark brown with a beautiful white star. His huge but finely tapered horns sprang in a fine curve from the head and diverged at the points, giving him a very formidable aspect.[7]

Two of our men killed and presented to me a singular looking animal of the lizard genus. Its length from its nose to the insertion of the tail is [blank] inches, and to its extremity

138

[blank] inches. Its color on the back is a rusty black, variegated with irregular lines and figures of pale yellow. Its belly of the same colors, the white or pale yellow predominating and tinged with a shade of pink. Its tail, short and thick, is marked with patches and irregular rings. The lips are jet black, as well as the throat and lower extremities of the legs. These have each five toes armed with talons. The mouth is enormously large, armed with transparent teeth formed like fangs, through which I thought I could distinguish a line of light, denoting them to be tubes, and a thick tongue forked at the point. Its eyes were black. The skin is thick and looks as though it were beaded, the beads touching and raised to half their height.

I conjecture from its appearance that it might be amphibious. It cannot support itself on its legs but crawls somewhat nimbly, its body gliding on the ground. Its food, insects and smaller reptiles. Its internal structure was very curious. Its capacious throat terminated in a very small canal which again distended and formed its stomach, this again contracting formed another small canal to its exit. Its digestive apparatus was uncommonly large, its lungs lay on each side, the back bone apparently disconnected and about 4 inches in length. And, at the lower part of the abdomen, were two elongated masses of bluish looking flesh filled with blood vessels and supplied through the right lobe of the lower by a large artery, which branched and entered at their upper extremity, their orifices I could not discover. Its ribs, 44 in number, extending more than two-thirds the length of the body.[8]

I also saw a centipede, such as are found within the tropics, some few tarantulas and a beautiful snake which all who saw and knew anything about the matter pronounced to be an Anaconda. This was the name also given to it by a

Mexican in our Company. This evening we encamped at a spring at the mouth of the Cañon, in a branch to the left of the road.

Sept. 18th   Last night two of our hunters, more fortunate than the rest, brought us in two quarters of beef which they had succeeded in killing. They saw large numbers of cattle of every color, amongst which was a beautiful cream colored ox, to whom they gave a long run without success. Several were pure white.

   Most of our route today has been through a Cañon between low ridges of hills, and this evening we encamped at a spring near the roadside to the left.

Sept. 19th   Today's travel, 10 miles, had been over an excellent road, and unproductive of much interest. Near our camp, at some ponds by the roadside, a skull, not long since divested of its fleshy appendages, was found, and afforded a great deal of discussion to our Phrenological Amateurs. It was at least decided to have pertained to some adult Mexican, as no one development seemed prominent enough to stamp the individual with any marked characteristics.

Sept. 20th   This evening we reached "Blackwater Creek." This I expected to find from its delineation on the map a bold running stream, but it is as much as one can do to find a hole of water large enough for ordinary cooking purposes.[9] Here we killed another wild ox. The road today has been gravely and bad on our cattle's feet.

Sept. 21st   Today we have been anxiously watching for the "Coyetero trail" (Cook's map) as the southern most part of our journey here is reached. We have not, however, yet reached it. [10]

Our road has been fine. We are now encamped at an excellent spring to the left of the road, near a point of beautiful building rock, which here projects from a hill. This rock, in its texture, is very close and compact, of a dark grey color, and somewhat resembles granite in the disposition and quality of its particles.

Due N. lies a rather singularly shaped mountain. Its form resembles that of the Capitol at Washington, being a vast pile, nearly horizontal along the top, with a pointed eminence shooting up at the centre and forming a dome or pinnacle. This mountain is also remarkable for another feature; it is the first of any magnitude we have yet seen, whose dip was to the West.

Sept. 22nd After breakfast we resumed our march, our horsemen taking the lead in search of game. In about a mile and a half we crossed the "Coyetero trail for plundered mules and cattle," which they steal from the inhabitants of Sonora. This trail crosses the road obliquely, immediately east of a mound to its right.

Here our road turned considerably North of West and commenced a gradual but barely perceptible descent. We were not convinced that we were entering the bottoms of the San Pedro, but the road soon resumed a course due West or sometimes turned to the South of that point, and on comparing with Cook's map, I was convinced that there was either an error there or that we were traversing a road more recently made by the emigrants.

The country through which we are passing is more beautiful than any we have seen for a long time, but it is destitute of timber. The grass is young and tender, and cannot be surpassed in luxuriance by any in the world.

This evening a Mexican who represented himself to be a lieutenant under command of XXX stationed at a mountain within 12 miles of here, came into camp. He spoke English more fluently than any Spaniard I had ever heard, stating that he had received his education in England. He informed us that there are now 800 men in this vicinity on their way into Apache Country. They are forging a war of extermination against these Indians, and during the last six months have been terribly successful.

The wigwams we noticed on the Creek east of Real or Johnson's Creek, had been depopulated by them. At this point they slew 30 warriors at a dash. Their motto is "spare none—take no prisoners." They will shortly proceed to the Dry Lake in hopes of meeting a large band of Apaches, reported to be now there. He states that Cook's old trail is some distance North, this road having been made and traversed only this season.[11]

This morning we caught a scorpion, but he escaped. Mr. Rogers, one of our Company, informs me that while out hunting this morning, he crossed a hill within half a mile of the road. Here he discovered some twenty large stones such as the Mexicans use in grinding their corn, with the rubbers or stones used by the hand in grinding the grain. Some of these were lying apparently in the very positions in which they had been left when last used. There were some mounds resembling Gopher or large Ant hills, but no vestiges of dwellings, nor did he alight to see if any further discoveries could be made.

Sept. 23rd (Sunday)   Today we crossed the "Rio San Pedro," some 30 miles south of Cook's route.[12] We have crossed three prongs or branches, from which we have taken a goodly number of most excellent fish. They somewhat resemble the salmon trout in form and color, but are not spotted. Many average from 18 to 20 inches in length, their flesh firm and close, and their flavor such as would be provokingly tempting to palates more delicate and appetites much less keen than ours.

Some of our Company started and gave chase to a fine American steer, which after a run of 5 or 6 miles they succeeded in capturing. He has been twice shot, one of the wounds not yet being healed. From the stream near us we have taken some excellent fish.

Sept. 24th   Remained encamped on a hill. About a mile West are the ruins of an old town, which must have once been extensive. Near it are the dilapidated remains of an old fort, built of stone. Much broken pottery, &c., lies scattered around. Here are also to be found many beautiful Crystals, some few perfect, but the majority broken or injured.[13]

The country, especially the valleys near here, abound in wild cattle, elk, deer, antelope, rabbits, and some few bears. The grass is most excellent as well as the water, but wood is scarce.

Sept. 25th   Part of our route today was over a fine level road. After traveling some four miles we entered a Cañon, and were at once surrounded by the most romantic and beautiful scenery. The mountains, which rose abruptly from 3 to 600 feet, seemed at one moment to forbid our advance and then at a short distance to retire in modesty by a gentle slope as if to encourage our progress. The timber on their sides was here growing in beautiful clusters, and these are evenly and regularly arranged as a well set orchard.

One basin to the left of this was walled by rugged masses of rock, almost perpendicular, and of a deep red color. Occasionally their caps were of pure white, and wherever the fissures afforded sufficient earth for a root to strike a Cedar with its deep green foliage obtruded, giving diversity and adding a charm to the scent which was truly magnificent.

In a few miles we came to the foot of a rocky and steep ascent, and here commenced the "Pass of Santa Cruz." We had noticed a fresh but dim road some 3 or 4 miles back, which left our road nearly at a right angle to the North. This we should have taken as it is an excellent road, with plenty of wood, water and grass, and is perfectly level, leading round the mountains through which the "Pass" runs. Our road now became very severe on the oxen, especially their feet. The men assisted in pushing the wagons up the steepest points, and supporting them when on the hill sides, where in one or two places there was danger of their oversetting or sliding off down the hills. Altogether it is a Bad pass, and although the road around is somewhat longer, it is by far the most preferable.[14]

The scenery, however, was charming, and to myself and one or two more, amply compensated for the fatigue and obstacles we have overcome. We are now encamped near one of the finest and purest springs I ever saw. It lies at the road side, walled in by huge perpendicular rocks, nearly in a square, its breadth about 12 feet and some 3 or 5 feet deep, its waters so limpid that the objects at its bottom seem scarcely beneath its surfaces.

Sept. 26th The descent of the Pass from the "spring" is tolerably good, except two long and steep hills, which have to be surmounted. The timber, which is large and thrifty, consists of Cotton wood, Sycamore, Laurel, Mezquite (which is a species of our honey locust and resembles it precisely), Oak of two or three varieties, hackberry and Walnut. This last has shed its fruit, which lie by bushels under the trees. The hull is very thin and easily severed by the pressure of the fingers without leaving a stain. The fruit itself is much smaller than that of the U.S., but I think of finer flavor.

At the foot of a hill leading from the Pass we crossed the "Rio Santa Cruz" and entered upon a large tract of rich bottom land, studded with corn fields. The corn is just now in its roasting ear state, and from the piles of ears around the campfires, I should predict that the unfortunate who should attach a "Benjamin's mess" would realize rather pain than pleasure from his repast, especially as we have some venison to add to the feast.[15] We are encamped about a mile and a half above the town, amid a profusion of grass taller than a man, but coarse in quality.

Sept. 27th   This morning we entered the town of "Santa Cruz," which from the best information I could obtain contains about 1,000 inhabitants. Here were some tolerably good peach orchards. The fruit was rather small, but when thoroughly ripe of fine flavor. They had mostly been gathered for the emigrants preceding us. Men, women and children gathered themselves in groups to witness our passage through the town, and one of the gentlemen in the train, having a few cotton goods &c. which he had brought with him to trade with the Indians, and by being eagerly inquired for, he stopped his wagon and a perfect fair was established.[16]

The noise and confusion of tongues amongst the Mexican women as they eagerly thronged around the mart was almost deafening, and I left to take a tour of observation. The first place I entered was the Blacksmith's shop. Here, instead of the improvements of the 19th century, one could imagine that he had retrograded some 3 or four centuries. The forge was without chimney, built under a porch, with a hole in the roof to emit the smoke. The bellows consisted of two circular tubes about 2 feet long, placed horizontally, and were worked alternately by forcing them backwards and forwards, while their emissions, though laboriously effected, were far too weak to be of much service. The work bench was covered with fragments and parts of the terrible Mexican bridle bit. Several old Spanish gunlocks, with the works on the outside, and clumsy enough to have graced the days of Ferdinand and Isabella with the muskets and carbines to which they belonged, seemed to constitute most of the occupation of the proprietors. A room leading from the porch appeared to serve as the Armory of the smithy or for aught I know, of the whole town as the walls were covered with sabres, daggers, and firearms arranged in the most pompous manner.

The people were very loquacious and communicative. Some of the men had just returned from California, and narrated most wonderful stories of the immense riches to be there obtained. They had some 17 ounces and two small calabashes full of the gold, which they showed us and offered to trade. They said that they returned because they were all men of families and had heard of the ravages of the Apaches amongst their villages, and had come back to protect their wives and children. Some of them wore most beautiful blankets figured and dyed in the richest and most glowing colors. We could not, however, prevail on any of them to part with one.

The bottoms below the town were rich [illegible],

many of them fenced in by rows of Cotton wood trees planted equidistant, and wattled with brush and limbs of trees. This fence, though not durable, was substantial and beautiful till the twigs began to decay. The river banks in many places consisted apparently of almost pure beds of mica, which glittered in the sun like gems, studding the pavement of some Houri's palace. The stream, as it lengthens, also increases in size, and where we are now encamped on its bank, it is some 12 or 15 feet wide by 2 or 3 feet deep.[17]

Sept. 28th   Today we have traveled 16 miles down the rim, over a most excellent road from some 2 miles this side of Santa Cruz. We have been constantly passing deserted Ranchos, whose late occupants have sought shelter in the town. Around many of these are orchards of Peach and Quince trees, amongst which we have found a sufficiency of fruit for all culinary and edible uses.

This morning we passed a fine looking edifice which gave rise to a diversity of opinions as to the purpose for which it was built. Its offices and out houses seemed appropriate to various uses. In one was a row of vats, as if for turning. In another, furnaces for smelting, &c., while the main body of the building had evidently been used as a residence, being adorned by a portico in front and a piazza fronting the courtyard. The interior arrangement of the rooms, its baths, cisterns &c. all bespoke the opulence and taste of its late proprietor.

He is now living in Santa Cruz, having left this fine residence some few months since in consequence of the incessant attacks of the Apaches. In one night he had lost over 1,000 head of horses, mules and cattle. The orchards in front of the building was filled with Pear, Quince and Peach trees laid out with much taste, and had borne this year a large crop of fruit, which had been mostly used or wasted by those preceding us. [18]

This evening we encamped near a Rancho where we found an abundance of pumpkins, squashes and potatoes, vegetables which were the finest when cooked that I had ever eaten. [19] Indeed, this whole country, from the banks of the Rio Grande, seems especially well adapted to the culture of all descriptions of the vine family, as both the water and musk melon with various kinds of gourds are strewed in all directions over the surface. The Water melon is scarce, its fruit small but resembling that of the cultivated plant, its taste bitter. The musk melon encounters the traveler at every step, its fruit is small and emits a most offensive odor when opened.

Sept. 29th Today we passed an edifice of large dimensions and imposing appearance, on the Western side of the river. Its Northern end or front consisted of huge square pile, surmounted by a well built dome of burned brick, and white-washed. Its Southern extremity had a large square tower projecting from its eastern angle. This was used as a belfry. Three bells, from 75 to 300 pounds weight, were still suspended and one was lying on the ground. The tone of these bells was highly musical and sonorous, and when struck forcibly, made the whole valley and adjacent mountains echo beautifully with their reverberations.

Its burial ground was large and contained a number of dead, with a circular building over its centre, probably used as a dead house. A small town or village surrounds it, fast going to decay. From the description given me, as I was engaged while near it and I had not visited it, I should imagine it to have once been a Monastery. [20]

At the place where we stopped to noon I noticed some

very large alders and some Poke berry bushes, the only ones of this description I have yet seen. We have lately seen many turkeys and a bird called by the natives "gayata." Its form resembles that of our blue Jay. Its head and neck is as large as those of a turkey. The plumage like that of the Western Pheasant, with two circular bare patches on the back of the head of a vermilion color, lying parallel with the eyes—beak black, 3 inches long, and terminating in a hooked point. Wings very short and disproportionate to the size of the body. Their color black with a shade of invisible green, and striped with three rows of oblong white spots, extending across the fore part of the feather. Tail twice length of the body. Color invisible green tipped with white, and near its insertion overlaid by a coat of short feathers of plum color, fringed around their edges with white. Body the size of a duck, mouse colored on the back, breast and under part fawn colored. Legs very long and of great muscular power. These birds, when running have outstripped in speed our fastest horses and escaped. The wings are only used as propellers, to aid the bird while running, but from an eminence they can sail hours in the air like the flying squirrel to a less elevated spot. [21]

The beautiful Quail also abounds in these regions, as well as deer and antelope, but lately we have seen no wild cattle. We also passed a Fort to the left of the road, in dilapidated condition, its form an oblong square, length 150 feet, breadth 20 feet, with a row of columns down the centre, built of adobes, round a large wooden pillar to support the roof. [22]

A few miles from this we passed through a deserted town called by the Indians "Tomaracacura." Here was a neat looking church with three bells in it. The houses looked as though they had not been long forsaken, and thrifty looking

Peach orchards adorned its eastern side. It must have once contained a population of 800 or 1,000 souls.

The fences which we have for the last two days been passing are made of mezquite poles, driven into the ground and wattled with the branches. They look sound and good as on the day on which they were finished. Their durability is another evidence to me of its being only a variety of locust.[23]

Sept. 30th (Sunday)   Today we remained encamped on the River banks, near a magnificent grove of Cotton wood. In the evening some Mexicans arrived at a Camp below us, one of whom was directly from California. On learning this a large party of us paid them a visit, as we were all anxious to hear news of a recent date. The man informed me that he had been two months on the road, on which he had found grass and water in abundance, and that the road was perfectly level and in excellent order. He had worked on the "Stanislado," a tributary of the "San Joaquin," and had in about 3 months, laboring from 2 to 4 hours per day, gained Eighteen pounds of gold, with which he was now returning to his home.[24]

I asked him why he left so rich a spot? He replied that he had been gone from his family over twelve months, which to him, as well as most Mexicans generally, seemed an age. He said, however, that he should return as soon as possible.

He gave us the prices of almost everything and stated that we should find no poor Americans. Many worked but little, but they were all "Ricos" [rich]. He stated that dissipation of all kinds was shamefully prevalent and that already, dens for the promotion and fulfillment of every vice were in flourishing operation. Many of the Americans, he said, had gold by the "fanega" (144 lbs.) and that one man in the valley where he worked had with his hands dug out 5 quintals and some pounds in a few days, with which he immediately embarked for his home (he was a sensible fellow).[25]

We saw today one of the most extraordinary specimens of the Cactus tribe I have ever seen or heard of. It projects from the side of a bank, near the river, its form that of a column, but with somewhat more bulge, about 10 feet from the ground projected 4 arms, shooting from the main stem gradually towards the ground and then curving abruptly to a perpendicular. Some 15 feet higher projected two others from the opposite sides of the plant. These were similar to the others, and above these the body of the plant shot about 10 feet higher, tapering beautifully to the summit. The surface of the plant and its limbs were regularly grooved in acute angles some 2 inches deep, and from the ridges between the grooves projected bodies of thorns about 2 inches apart. The appearance of the plant, standing isolated from any other, leafless, beautifully symmetrical in form, was singularly striking and picturesque.[26]

Oct. 1st   Today we have traveled 20 miles along the river. The valley over which we have been traversing and through which the river courses is one of great fertility. Its breadth as bounded by mountains on either side varies from 2 to 7 miles, and in the United States it would soon be made to sustain a dense population. I never saw land lie more beautifully. It is covered with a scattering growth of large Mezquite, a seemingly imperishable wood, in sufficient abundance for all farming purposes. The margin of the river is fringed with a fine growth of large Cotton wood, walnut, ash, hackberry, &c., while the mountain sides are covered with Cedar, Mezquite, Laurel, &c., and abound in game. The grass which covers the country as far as eyes can reach is the pure grama, about a foot high, young and tender.

Oct. 2nd   About 6 miles from our last encampment the face of the Country changes, and the land becomes more barren. Here the river loses itself in the sand. Logwood of small size is here also met with, and enormous Cacti from 35 to 40 feet in height, some consisting of a single column, others forming clusters or projecting their massive arms high in the air, looking like the shades of mighty giants ready to challenge the unlucky wight who would intrude on their retirement.

Oct. 3rd   This evening we encamped in a beautiful grove with a fine lawn stretching far to the Eastward, below an Indian or Mexican town called "San Xabier del Bac."[27]

On visiting the place every thing appeared noise and confusion. On inquiring the cause I learned that a war party had just returned triumphantly from an expedition against the Apaches. They had slain ten Coyeteros and brought in with them ten children as prisoners, together with two scalps. These last appeared to give the most general satisfaction.[28]

On an open space in the part occupied by friendly Apaches and Pimos, an old fellow with much ceremony was arranging the scalps on a spear, which being done, a dance of men, women and children commenced around them and the spear which had been signalized as the undoubted conqueror and winner of the bloody trophies suspended near it. The yells and frantic gestures of the performers were truly disgusting and fearful, and after remaining awhile we sought the retirement of the camp.[29]

Oct. 4th   Today we remained encamped. A misunderstanding having arisen amongst the members of our Company, we concluded to separate. Accordingly 11 wagons rolled on whilst 7 remained with 21 men and 2 families.

During the whole of last night the yells and screams of the savages, as they carried on their diabolic orgies, resounded through our camp and prevented many of us from sleeping.[30]

On visiting them this evening they paraded their prisoners, amongst whom was a clean limbed, active little fellow about 10 years old, who had been shot in the back of the neck. In the wound maggots were already ranking, eliciting neither sympathy nor compassion. Indeed, he seemed to be the object of torment and vengeance to an old, fiend-like looking squaw, whose greatest enjoyment seemed to consist in endeavoring to harass and torture him.

The little prisoners, grouped in a circle around the scalp spear, at first evinced some agitation on seeing their prosecutors brandishing their knives, tomahawks, &c., but after the dance had commenced around them, it was surprising to witness their stoical apathy. The squaws would every now and then brandish their knives about their throats, and then rushing furiously upon them, seize them by the hair, and with a stroke which nothing but practice could have rendered so apt, severed a lock of hair from their heads, as near the skin as possible.

The old squaw, aforementioned, would then seize the scalps, and shaking them wildly in the air, with apparent imprecations, thrust them into the faces of the little unfortunates. The boy, however, above alluded to, quailed not. His gaze never once encountered the mementos of the dead, but was steadily and unblanchingly fixed on that of his human tormentor. And never did the lion in all his pride and power cast a more disdainful, withering look of scorn and contempt on his most pusillanimous assailant than that which decked the brow of this stripling of the Desert towards his persecutors.

A magnificent looking Church standing in this place is sufficiently striking to elicit the admiration of the most insensible or least curious traveler upon the earth. Its ground plan is like many of the others we have seen, built in the form of a cross. Two lofty and beautiful towers grace its Southern angles and form part of its front. These towers are three stories high, one yet unplastered. The middle one is used as belfries, in which are suspended two finely toned bells. They were no doubt intended to have been built in the Ionic style, but its purity was lost (like that apparently of almost everything else in this region) amid a superfluity of ornament and gaudy show. Their height, I should think, is about 120 to 130 feet.

The front between the towers was ornamented profusely and looked well. At its top, in a niche, stood the figure of its Patron Saint "San Xabier," while two worthies of lesser note occupied niches less exalted on his right and left.[31] The whole was enclosed within an area of about an acre, surrounded by an adobe wall 15 feet high, plastered, and where perfect, ornamented by small embattled turrets. A small enclosure in its S.W. angle was used probably as a cemetery, and contained a dead house [ie. mortuary chapel] of very neat and chaste appearance. Its walls had niches containing several skulls.

From the stupid Indian who kept the keys and escorted me about, I could learn nothing of interest and so had to make my minutes unaided. The interior of the Church, to those who had never visited a Catholic Church out of the States, was very gorgeous and imposing. From the arms and

head of the cross sprang a fine dome, painted and ornamented in Bas relief in a very tactful manner. The floor was
painted to resemble Mosaic marble, and when untarnished
must have looked well.

The choir was built at its Southern [end], and two
gentlemen from the Peoria train ascended to it and Divine
service, seeming nowadays to be seldom celebrated, sang
two verses of the "Star Spangled Banner," their voices being
fine and blending in delightful harmony, echoed from the
vaulted roof in a flood of melody truly grand.

The cornice running around the Church paralleled
with the foot of the Choir, was a specimen of workmanship
which reflected credit on the architect, but its effect was
tarnished by a stiff, acute angled bay painted on it. The arms
and head of the cross were decorated with images of the
Savior, the Virgin Mary, and many of the apostles and
Saints, all sumptuously gilded, painted and dressed, and
when clean must have looked splendidly. On the railing
enclosing the altar were two figures in the form of which the
artist had studiously avoided infringing on the 3rd Com-
mandment, as they represented almost a little of everything
and a whole of nothing.[32]

A neat pulpit stood at the angle of the Eastern Arm,
commanding a view of the whole atrium, and nearly opposite it stood the Confessional chair, whence many a poor
sinner had stated his tons of penance, or with lightened
pockets rejoiced to think that Romish Dignitaries were civ-
ily accommodated with the use of St. Peter's keys.

The basements of the towers were appropriated, apparently, to the use of the priests. In the Western chamber stood
a font or vase of bronze, on a marble pedestal, used for
preparing holy water, and in an anti-chamber E. of the altar
was the Iron Stamp, for impressing the wafers used at the

administration of the sacrament, with many other implements and things curious and strange.

Around the wall, on the interior, were rooms or cells for the residence of the servants of the Church, now occupied by Mexican families, who are suffering and perhaps helping the Edifice to pass quickly into ruin and decay.

The building and its appurtenances are composed of burned brick, excellently plastered, and compared with the desolation and miserable hovels surrounding it looked like a giant monument of fading beauty, proudly struggling to maintain its grandeur in a place all but it had fled.

A square formed by rows of adobe huts, tenanted by Mexicans, projects from the front of the Church, and beyond this, are the huts of friendly Pimo, Apache and Pueblo Indians.[33] These are built in the form of a beehive, flattened at the top, and are composed of a wicker work of willows overlaid with straw, and daubed over with mud. A conical hole some 2 feet high serves as door, chimney and window, and is entered by the occupant on all fours. A few gourds, an earthen skillet and a skin or two constitute the furniture. The squaws do all the laborious offices of life, and the men lounge about in sunshine or shade as seems to them most inviting, presenting very degraded and most inactive specimens of the "lords of the creation."

East of the village is a mound some 80 to 100 feet high, on which a wooden cross stands [Grotto Hill]. Here a guard is constantly kept to watch for the approach of the Apaches.

Oct. 5th   This morning we started early and passed through the town. Some few wagons had been left here by the emigrants, who had also traded clothing, arms, ammunition &c. to the inhabitants for cattle, mules &c. Large herds of the finest cattle are owned or grazed here. They far surpass in form, size and beauty any I have ever seen, except the wild cattle of South America. They can be bought for about 30 to 40 dollars per yoke.

On leaving town a wagon from another train ran against a carriage belonging to Mr. Williams of Boonville, and broke to pieces one of the hind wheels, retarding our progress till late in the evening, when we proceeded on and encamped near Tucson.

We slew a young beef we had purchased and by night had lightened his weight considerably. Flour cost us $6 per fanega (144 lbs.) with the bran left on it, and $7.50 if sifted. We could get no fruit nor vegetables here except a few pumpkins and some beans.

8

October 6–November 14

*"Until one has crossed a barren desert without food or
water under a burning tropical sun at the rate of three
miles per hour, he can form no conception of what
misery is."*
—John E. Durivage,
May 1849

*"We were now coming to a land of Trouble, where the
bristles of the Hog began to show on the spine of Man."*
—Charles E. Pancoast,
October 1849

Pancoast's metaphor referred to the frustration and despair,
and the demoralization which afflicted most Forty-Niners
after they set out from Tucson. Hunter's journal captures
the change in attitude among his companions. Before Tucson, the journey had been manageable, if at times arduous.
North of Tucson, the deserts and arid valleys of Arizona and
California presented challenges and hardships that quickly
took their toll among the weary travelers.

After the group divided at San Xavier, Hunter remained with the portion of the train under Captain Berry,
which totaled seven wagons, twenty-one men, and two
families. They stopped briefly in Tucson, the last town until
San Diego, California. North of Tucson, the Forty-Niners

confronted the first of the major jornadas of the southern route, the ninety-mile trek to the Gila River.

John E. Durivage, a journalist from New Orleans, made the crossing in the heat of summer, as reflected in his comment above. Hunter's group crossed at a cooler time of the year and made the trip without much difficulty. The stark landscape impressed Hunter more than the weather. His party passed through the Pima Villages, composed of small clusters of huts scattered for twenty miles along the Gila River. The Pimas and neighboring Maricopas were friendly and eager to trade. This was the Forty-Niners' last opportunity to secure fresh supplies and to obtain good grazing for their livestock until they reached Warner's Ranch, more than 300 miles away in California.

Beyond the villages, the argonauts crossed the fifty-mile jornada of the Gila Bend. Though shorter than the Tucson–Gila River jornada, the Gila Bend country caused members of Hunter's company to become discouraged as the cumulative effects of months of fatiguing effort and poor diet began to wear on them. Hunter describes their despair and near panic before they reached the Gila River. The emigrants' spirits did not revive much after they rejoined the river, for ahead lay 150 miles of travel through the barren Gila Valley to Yuma Crossing on the Colorado River.

During the passage down the Gila Valley, the overland journey began to resemble the wake of a retreating army. Abandoned wagons and property littered the road. Dead livestock were to be seen, along with an occasional grave. Hunter's company also discarded baggage to lighten their wagons and for the first time voiced concern over the poor condition of their livestock. Some of Hunter's companions began to consider walking through to California or boating down the Gila River, both desperate alternatives. Problems increased to such a degree that Hunter ceased his journal for a time.

Hunter's train camped for eleven of the twenty-nine days covered in this chapter to conserve the strength of their livestock. With all of their problems the train managed to cover 300 miles for a daily average of 16 miles, still a good rate of travel.

Oct. 6th   Today we passed through Tucson. Here we again intersected Cook's and Kearny's route. This place contains from 800 to 1,000 inhabitants and the town is better laid out than any I have seen since leaving Santa Fe.

Here we heard some awful tales of the route ahead of us, dead animals strewing the road, wagons forsaken, human skeletons, who had famished for want of water, &c., but we could see naught of the Emigrants who were reported to fill the town, unable to proceed further. We were, however, told that there were 800 Americans amongst the Pimos. *Nous verrons.* [1]

The Alcalde, whom I visited, had wondrous tales of California riches. [2] His communications, however, were altogether beyond the reach of credibility. Three or four trains lay encamped near the town, and their men were busily engaged in trading with the natives for cattle, provisions, &c., for which they seemed to be paying tolerably high. This town looks as though it may have once seen better days. [3]

We resumed our journey and continued it for 16 miles over a terribly dusty road till late at night, when we encamped at the point of a range of mountains to our left. Here we found water in some holes to the right of the road, and some scattering grass. The plain at the foot of these mountains as far as the road is covered with broken pottery of ancient make. No other vestige, however, exists indicative of its former occupancy.[4]

Oct. 7th   We started early this morning and traveled 16 miles over a perfect Desert, yielding nothing but dwarf shrubs and weeds, and encamped at night at some small patches of grass, without water.[5]

Oct. 8th   About 2 o'clock this morning we again took the road, the moon shining brightly and the air cool and pleasant. We traveled rapidly till we reached Cook's "holes in the rocks," or rather, the mountains where I suppose it should be. Our horsemen sought diligently for water but could find none. They, however, discovered the remains of an ancient Rancho at the foot of the isolated peak to our left.[6]

So we kept on till 9 o'clock, when we fortunately arrived at some holes and sinks in the prairie full of water from a heavy rain which fell here yesterday. This was truly an unlooked for blessing, and with grateful hearts we availed ourselves of it. There was also some grass, and the cattle, after about two hours of rest, looked very well.

We again pushed on amid occasional showers of rain and encamped to the left of the road after having made 23 miles. Water was in abundance in the sunken spots around us, and some patches of grass about ½ mile to our right afforded us food for our cattle.

Pieces of pottery lay strewn in many places over the surface of this Desert, and it is now wonderful to think what a change must have taken place in the face of this region since it yielded sustenance to a dense population, whose remains at this moment show it once to have contained villages, towns and per chance thickly peopled cities. All is now desolate and forlorn. Spots of many acres are perfectly barren, presenting nothing but a white barren surface covered with saline efflorescence. Not a bird save the buzzard cleaves the thin air, not an animal but the lizard, toad or snake sports over the ground.

Oct. 9th   This evening we reached the "Rain Water Pools" after a journey of 15 miles without grass or water. These pools are sunk in the Prairie or river bottom about 1 mile south of the Rio Gila. The water in them is somewhat muddy but palatable and tolerably cool. Here we found a tall coarse grass, which although the cattle were hungry they did not seem to relish. [7]

Oct. 10th   Today we remained encamped. I visited the Gila, which is a swift running, somewhat muddy stream, about 20 yards across at this place. Its banks are covered with Cotton wood and Willows, and the country for about 2 miles back with Mezquite and weeds. [8]

Oct. 11th   Shortly after midnight we started and by sunrise we who were mounted were in the midst of the first Pimo Village. The Indians were all up and gathered in crowds around us. The villages extended as far as the eye could see. The huts or wigwams, were built like a beehive, flattened on top and daubed with mud.

This roof was sufficiently strong to support the weight of Indians who lazily reclined or sat with elbow or knee on their tops. These villages were seated in the same sandy desert which we had been traversing, nothing but deep sand, with a few thorny shrubs could be seen anywhere near. But on looking towards the river, fences and the deep green blades of maize were plainly visible, showing that altho at this moment they were inactive, yet that they were not always idle or unprofitably employed.[9]

They received us in a very friendly manner. These Indians are well built and of an engaging countenance. Their manners, also, are polite and affable. I observed several very fat old fellows amongst them and one about 30 years of age who would have weighed at least three hundred weight. Such specimens are rare, I believe, amongst the other tribes.

At the time of our arrival they were, I presume, at some kind of devotional exercise. A very old man was sitting in a hut built differently from the rest, its form was an oblong square, its walls and roof consisted of bundles of Willows tied or fastened together. Here the old fellow sat, and in a kind of half chant, uttered a few monosyllabic sentences. When patting his feet, the young men took up a chorus, and with ridiculous motions of the body, raised their heels and by striking them on the ground, beat a kind of time to their doggerel music. Some outside participated, and in about half an hour the assembly broke up.[10]

I then had a long chat with their chief. He is a fine, intelligent looking man, and speaks Spanish fluently. He told me that we could procure from his people whatever we stood in need of, said they had plenty of horses, mules and cattle, but in this he deviated, as I offered him advantageous terms for his animals, which he evaded by telling me that the cattle were grazing on the river, but that he would bring them to our camp. The truth is they possess but little stock of any kind except horses. The samples of wheat they showed us were as fine as any I ever saw and the flour which we bought, had it been properly bolted, would have compared favorably with any in the world.[11]

The road from this point for about [the next] 10 miles is through the midst of their villages, or I might rather call it a continuous village, for there were but few spaces between them extensive enough to amount to a separation. At the road side they [the Pimas] congregated in groups as we passed, while those disposed to trade came toiling along with large baskets, or curiously formed packs filled with water melons, pumpkins &c. These were swung to their backs by a broad bandage which passed around their fore-heads, and thus in a stooping position the squaws (for it was they alone who labored) trudged up to us with loads which some of our stoutest men would have found burdensome.[12]

I noticed amongst the heavy laden one truly beautiful young girl about 16, whose strength seemed proportionate to her beauty [several lines closely written and garbled] They also are not so singularly innocent and "honest" as Cook represents them. They filched several little articles from us.

They were very communicative of the failings of their neighbors and friends the "Marikopos" [Maricopas], whom they denounced as utterly regardless of the precept "Thou shalt not steal." This, however, may have arisen from a desire to screen their own itching propensity for things not strictly theirs in law or justice, and so to throw the obloquy on other shoulders.[13]

Their greatest urging was for white cloth (Domestic). They refused money as a renumeration for almost every-thing, and several times offered in cash which they had gained from previous emigrants from 10 to 20 times the value of such goods. This was also the case, except in points of value, in the towns of Sonora, but we had now none to spare.

Their dress could not well be described without shock to the listener. It was highly amusing to see the ridiculous figure some of them cut in garbs partly American, partly Indian. Vanity could be seen very plainly peeping from the shreds of many a coat. A lady in the train presented some squaws with a part of an old dress. This called for the loudest exultation. They danced, they laughed, and shouted till the air rang again with their glee, and taking their stations in the middle of the road, continued to receive fresh accession to their numbers to admire their prizes and to envy the lucky owners as long as we could see them.

We encamped about 4 miles W. of the village, amid a profusion of coarse salt grass and brackish water, a very poor offering to our weary cattle who had hauled us over a miserably dusty road 28 miles.

Oct. 12th Today we remained encamped, and I had the pleasure of visiting Major McDaniel, who gave me all the information at his command in relation to the route ahead, the sources of both his and mine being much the same and not differing materially in detail.[14] I am afraid little reliance can be placed on anything but our own energy and perseverance.

Our own and the Camps around us have been filling all day with Pimos and Marikopos, from whom we obtained fruit &c. They are in the habit of pulling their melons before they are ripe and burying them, which sensibly destroys their flavor and renders the fruit tough and insipid. This evening at their departure we are minus coats, shoes, hatchets, tin cups and a variety of small articles whose owners were not consulted at the time of transfer.

At this point all those whose teams appear fatigued have been busily engaged in cutting off their wagon beds, denuding their wagons of all surplus iron and fixtures, and throwing away whatever is not absolutely necessary, so that the ground is strewn with chairs, spare axle trees, bolts, bands, &c., &c., and in some cases those who have had cattle lost or stolen have forsaken their own wagons and joined teams with others. [15]

Oct. 13th   Today we removed three miles to somewhat better grass and water. The companies who had rested moved on to try the realities of the unknown region before us.

A party of Mexicans from California called at our camp and were entertained with such fare as we have. From the description given me by their principal [leader] I have drawn a map of the "Jornada" on the other side of the Colorado, which is presented to be some 90 miles across, and nearly destitute of grass and water. They state that hence to the mouth of the Gila we shall find both in abundance. No reliance, however, can with safety be placed in their statements as all the information we have hitherto received from them has ended in barefaced falsehood and deception. [16]

October 14th   This morning we started about 2 o'clock, and from the assertions of the Mexicans were led to believe that we should find grass and water at a distance of nine miles. We soon left the bottom, on which we had been grazing, and struck a sterile, sandy desert. Nothing could be seen ornamenting its surface but high Cacti (Cercus gigantes), Mezquite and the offensive, yet fresh looking Kreosote plant. [17]

We now passed round the point of a ridge of rugged, barren and dark colored mountains between us and the river. [18] Some of us had placed as much confidence in the report of the Mexicans that they had neglected to supply themselves with water, and now that they knew their source from the river to be cut off, vented their rage in no measured terms on the pitiful wretches who would wantonly deceive a traveler to his possible ruin.

After traveling 14 miles we halted to rest our cattle

and to breakfast. A sad and dreary prospect surrounded us, rendered more uncomfortable by the uncertainty which shrouded our advance. In about 3 hours we again took to the road and continued on till we arrived at the mouth of a Cañon running through a range of mountains which here crossed our road. Here we encamped, without a particle of sustenance for our teams or a drop of water, after having traveled 23 miles.

Oct. 15th At midnight we recommenced our journey and entered the Cañon by a very good road. The pass was some 2 miles in length, its sides, dark and broken, seemed almost to meet in the darkness and to increase its density.[19]

The beautiful stars glittered like gems in the deep blue firmament above us, and as they smiled in heaven by radiance seemed to whisper of patience and hope as the anchors on which to rely. Many a heart, though, at this moment brooded over our situation with gloomy forebodings; shrouded in darkness surrounded by an inhospitable desert. Our cattle, manifesting symptoms of weariness and our distance from the river unknown, filled the breasts of many, especially those who had families, with apprehension and dread, and until daylight dawned, scarce a word was spoken, everyone nursing his grief or hope within his own bosom.

Day ameliorated not our condition. A ridge of high mountains, stretching north and south at a distance of 15 or 20 miles, apparently formed a barrier between us and the Gila, and from the mountains north of us, and the general surface of the Country, everyone concluded this to be the case.[20] Shortly afterward some of the loose stock, which were being driven ahead of the train, gave signs that they could proceed but little further, and in a few moments down went one to the earth, incapable of further exertion. This one we left. In less than half an hour down sank another, while two others seemed at the point of exhaustion. Our teams seemed yet to bear up bravely, but evidently nearly choked with dust.

At this time a halt was called and a consultation entered into whether or not we should stop to rest. While talking, down sank a third beast. This seemed to work some of the men to a point of desperation. They quit the conference, and with voices husky with emotion, urged their teams ahead, declaring that our safety depended on reaching the river.

I moved forward some 3 or 400 yards, and stopping accidentally on a little rise by the road side, discovered the Gila at a distance of 5 or 6 miles. I pointed to the water, which was instantly discovered by those in front of the train, and such a joyous shout of "water, water" as instantly rent the still air, I never heard. Each man, from one of the most desponding, seemed at once metamorphosed into the happiest of human beings, the heart cheering tidings reached those still deliberating in the rear. With lightened hearts and smiling faces we eagerly pushed on. Everyone had something pleasant to say to his neighbor, and altho another ox became exhausted and was left, and more were overtaken in a similar condition, it could not dampen the ardor which now buoyed them up.

In the course of a couple of hours we reached the river bank. Here we found plenty of water but no grass, so we drove the cattle to an island in the river to browse on Willows and young Cotton wood which covered its surface.[21]

During the day the other portion of our old company

drove up, with whom was traveling a gentleman of the name of Wood. I saw him at Santa Cruz, where he had purchased two horses of the inhabitants, intending to pack them and so go through to California. They had reached the "Rain Water Pools" [near the Gila River] an hour or two before us, and when we came up he paid us a visit, bringing one of his horses with him. An Indian whom I had first met at San Xabier, and with whom I was then talking, on seeing the animal asked "Where did he get him? What did he pay for him? How long has he owned him?" On satisfying his queries he told me that his owner was a Pimo who resides in the village below us, and shortly after left.

This train encamped near the Village and the Indians, with their chiefs at their head, visited it and demanded the restoration of the horse to its rightful owner. They stated that the Mexican officer whom we met near the head of the San Pedro and an American had stolen two horses from them and that this was one of them. "If you lose anything among my people," said the chief, "I will see it restored, but the horse is ours and I must and will have it." They had to give it up.[22]

Another unfortunate came into our camp late last night. From his dialect I took him to be a Scotchman. He was lame from walking, alone and without food or clothing. A pair of soles were sandaled to his feet, but he seemed so crippled as to be scarce able to stand. He stated that he had started from the lower part of Sonora with the view of overtaking a train to which he was attached, at the Colorado, that he had missed the road wandering about on foot till he reached us and was thus left in his present destitution. Rather an unlikely tale, but his present necessities were relieved and he started with us. He stayed with a train which we passed in the Cañon.

Oct. 16th Today we moved down the river 4 miles. Here, by accident, we had discovered some tolerably good grass about 2 miles south of the road, and gladly drove our cattle to it. The animals which had given out in yesterday's journey were all brought in, so that except being wearied we are again as well off as before.

Oct. 18th Yesterday we remained at our encampment, and this morning moved on down the river. The road was miserably dusty. After traveling about 4 miles we came to a grave, near which was neatly carved on a plank "Reverend Ira M. Allen, New York." Near it was another grave which I did not see.[23]

The whole face of the Country around here appears to be annually inundated, hence the non-appearance of grass on the bottoms. For several miles from the river bank, masses of driftwood, rubbish, &c. are seen amid the branches of trees, and nearer to the stream. Almost every tree and bush show signs of trash deposited by the flood amongst their roots and limbs. It must in some places extend some 20 to 30 miles over the country, whose surface washed into hollows, ravines and fissures, shows the powerful and destructive effects of its turbid visitant.

We again accidentally found a patch of cane grass 2½ miles south of the river, and are encamped ¾ of a mile from the stream, near a range of hills running to the river over which our road passes.[24]

Oct. 19th We remained encamped to rest our cattle and ourselves. The Gila here is some 60 to 70 yards wide, and from 2 to 5 feet deep. Some of our fishermen have for the first time brought in a mess of trout. They are the same as those caught in the San Pedro, delicate and well flavored.

This seems to be rather a dangerous spot for an encampment. Captain Tisdale's train, who have been here two or three days, had fourteen of their cattle driven off, and two of their herders run into Camp by Indians. Two of the cattle were recovered with arrows still sticking in them. The others were lost. A short time afterwards a party of Indians came into their Camp with their arrows still bloody.

Two tall stout fellows of the "Yumas" tribe visited us today, but we started them very quickly. I would rather have their avowed enmity than their masked friendship.[25]

A dreadful affair happened near here on the 5th and 6th of September. Two members of an Arkansas train, which was encamped, had a fracas. The one who was whipped, after he had risen, seized an opportunity, and while his opponent's back was turned, stabbed him between the shoulders, the knife penetrating his heart. He died in 15 minutes.

The members of the train then summoned a jury from other companies near them, tried and convicted the assassin of willful murder and sentenced him to be shot. Accordingly, on the morning of the 6th lots were drawn by the whole company, 12 tickets being numbered, the rest blank to determine who should dispatch the Culprit. 12 guns were then loaded, 6 with blank cartridges and distributed to those whose disagreeable duty it was to execute the sentence. At a signal to fire, four balls passed through the victim's body, and I believe one through his head, causing instant death. The murderer and his victim sleep within 15 paces of each other on the desert bank of the Gila.[26]

Oct. 20th This evening we left our camp to undertake a journey of 24 miles, which from the best information we could obtain, lay between us and the point where we should again strike the river. A Captain of a Company near us told us positively that he had been some ten miles ahead, and that he could see nothing of the river, nor vestige or sign of grass.

We therefore started about 2 p.m., intending to make the longest part of the drive tonight. At the distance of exactly ten miles we struck the river and are encamped on an Island in the middle of the stream, bare, however, as a plank floor of any sign of vegetation.

The drought of this atmosphere, clear, calm and beautiful tho' it be, must certainly tend to evaporate truth from its fountain, or if perchance as many assert, it "lay in the bottom of a well," then has it most certainly slipped through the volcanic fissures, or sunk in the quicksands of this land of dust and desert, and disappeared altogether. All that remains to be done is for natives and sojourners to hold a jubilee, sing its requiem, and give publicity to the world that at or near Mexico there never can or shall be a chance for its resuscitation. This would be but justice, to travelers at least, and candor demands it.

The road on leaving the Camp in about 1½ miles commenced the ascent of a range of black, dreary looking ranges of hills stretching from far to the south to the Gila. On a table at the foot of the higher peaks lay piled on each other dark purple rocks, from the size of a man's fist to that of his head, scattered as regularly and level as tho' an adroit McAdamizer had tried his skill in their arrangement. A Cañon some 2 miles in length, with deep sand bottom, afforded us a convenient and level pass through these hills.

In this Cañon three of our horsemen met two Indians driving a mule and four American oxen. These they were convinced they had stolen and so took possession of them. The fellows readily gave all up except the mule. This they seemed to have a notion of defending, but on a cocked rifle being thrust under one of their noses, they quickly moved off. If they go off and get help we may look out for an attempt at recapture tonight.

On the plain about ½ mile W. of the Cañon stand two peaks some 40 to 50 feet in height, formed of huge masses of rugged rock, resembling the points of two entombed mountains projecting above the surrounding level. Nearly every rock in these pyramids is ornamented with hieroglyphic representations. From their design and execution they are evidently of Indian origin, and of recent date.[27]

From the base of the mountains to the river a light, loose sand covers the plain. This is so fine that the slightest motion given to it instantly fills the air with a cloud so dense that a wagon cannot be discovered in many spots at a distance of six feet. Throughout this plain ancient pieces of pottery lay strewn.

Oct. 21st On leaving the Island in the river and passing some distance down the shallower parts of the bed of the stream, we again landed on its southern side on a bottom enclosed by table land about 100 feet high. Up a Cañon to the south we found some grass and availed ourselves of it by staying to graze. This bottom consists of fine white and black sand, and it evidently inundates at a time of heavy and continued rain. Nothing but weeds grow in it.

This evening we left the bottom by climbing the steep ascent to the table land. This, as well as the level summit, was covered with dark purple rocks of all sizes and had a most dreary appearance. Their texture is nearly that of our wild stone, but coarse in quality. About a mile from the ascent where the road bends to the South there is a plain trail leading off to the right. This leads to a rocky ravine in which are some holes of excellent water. Near here we encamped, without grass or wood.

A beautiful looking mountain stretches East and West on the other side of the river, about 5 miles North of this [point]. Its river face, almost black and mellowed by the distance, looks as smooth and soft as tho' covered with velvet. Its sides are perpendicular and some 300 feet high. Its outline nearly convex, surmounted by a mound in the form of a huge dome.[28]

Oct. 22nd During this morning's travel we had to climb one rocky and tolerably steep hill, and then descend one much worse. In the 4¼ miles we found some tolerable grass about a ¼ of a mile to the right of the road, but no water.

We are now constantly passing wagons that have been abandoned, some entire, others mutilated. Also blacksmith's tools, trunks and articles not indispensably necessary to the further prosecution of the journey. The destruction of property is immense.

The road lies through deep beds of sand, the particles of which are so fine that they rise into the air on the slightest motion, and form dense and suffocating clouds. The days are intensely hot, unrefreshed by any breeze. Hence the dust raised by the teams and wagons remains floating around and above them, causing the cattle, independent of their severe pulling, to suffer greatly. The nights, on the contrary, are very cool, about approaching frost, and are graced by fresh breezes, generally from the North, which die away before daylight.

In the evening, after traveling about a mile, the road forked. The right hand led down to a pond of saltish water, surrounded by Willows and Cotton wood. Here were several wagons that had been forsaken by the early emigrants. The left hand is the one leading down to the river. We encamped about a mile from the fork and found some grass about a mile to the left of the road. We should have proceeded 3 miles further, where we should have struck the river.

Oct. 23rd This morning we reached the river, which here separates into 3 or 4 channels. On the North side of the stream, about ½ miles N.W., there is a hollow in which a salty grass and some cane grows, the latter the cattle appear to relish much. There are several large holes of brackish water in this hollow, from the muddy margins of which we have had to drag our cattle with ropes, as nearly all that approached the water became mired so deeply that without assistance they must soon have died.

Here we found other trains, some resting, others unable to proceed as the Indians had run off their cattle. Three of the oxen we captured Saturday last were here claimed and taken by their owners, which will happily enable them to proceed. Mutilated wagons, clothing, tools and implements of all sorts lie thickly strewn on the beach.

[Break in Narrative]

[Hunter recorded a few comments in the margin of his distance table which cover part of the period in which he ceased keeping a daily journal. On October 27, near present day Aztec, Arizona, he wrote that: "The destruction and loss of property at this camping ground is very great, and many have had their horses, mules, or oxen driven off by the Indians or mired in the sloughs aross the [Gila] river. We have built a boat and intend removing some freight from the wagons and shipping it on her. Her name is TOM MOSELEY."

Many Forty-Niners considered boating on the Gila River and launched numerous boats made from wagon beds or rafts constructed from drift wood. Success was mixed as the shallow river and shifting sand bars made navigation difficult. On October 29, Hunter wrote that "Our boat comes on bravely." No further mention is made and the boat was probably abandoned.

His train continued overland and on November 7, Hunter wrote that "Our uncertainty of the road ahead continues, and our teams [are] daily failing. Some of our men, giving up for lost, either relinquish themselves to desperation or become a tax on the courage of the rest. Many already have the blues badly enough, and no words of comfort can cheer them. Truly a distressing time."]

9

November 15–December 13

"What a Country—I am sure that no sane man will
ever travel this route a second time."
—C. C. Cox,
September 1849

"A Man who has traveled the Gila route may throw
himself upon his knees when reaching [San Diego] and
thank God for preserving him through it."
—John E. Durivage,
July 5, 1849

Hunter's train, which now totaled nine wagons, reached the Colorado River on November 14. The arrival at the long-sought landmark apparently revived his spirits, for he resumed his journal.

Yuma Crossing presented a cosmopolitan scene in November 1849, with Mexican and American argonauts, Yuma Indians, and United States soldiers mingling. It was a transitory scene, however, as the argonauts had to keep moving because of weak livestock and low supplies. Rumors of treachery, robbery, and murder by the local Yumas provided another reason to keep traveling. No grass grew at the Crossing for the emigrant's livestock to graze upon, although vast mesquite groves along the river provided a bountiful harvest of beans which could be used for feed.

Hunter's company crossed the river on November 16 and began the ninety-mile trek across the Colorado Desert, the most formidable jornada on the southern route. Three small, muddy wells provided the only relief travelers could usually expect while crossing the desert. In 1849, however, heavy spring runoffs caused the Colorado River to overflow. One of its ancient channels in the middle of the desert filled with water, and this was christened the New River by grateful Forty-Niners.

During the crossing of the Colorado Desert, Hunter's train shrank to three wagons with several members on foot. They camped five days on the New River, and then made the final push to Carrizo Creek, which marked the end of the desert.

A hard pull of fifty miles up dry, rocky canyons to Warner's Pass lay ahead. Water and forage improved constantly, as the road ascended from near-sea level at the Carrizo to over 3,600 feet at Warner's Pass. The pass marked the summit of the Laguna Mountains and the start of the final leg of the overland journey, down the Pacific slope, amid abundant springs and oak stands. At this point, with San Diego almost in sight, Hunter's narrative ends. His distance table indicated that he reached the town on December 13, almost eight months and 2,200 miles after setting out from Missouri.

On this final phase of the journey, Hunter's group traveled for twenty-nine days, camped for three, and covered over 200 miles. The averate of less than 7 miles per day reflects the difficult conditions of the Colorado Desert and the ascent to Warner's Pass.

Nov. 15th I have postponed my entries of the intermediate distance from the last point to the Rio Colorado as the daily incidents, face of the country &c., were of such a sameness as to render a single notice sufficient. We have trudged on to this point amid discouraging circumstances such as would impress the most buoyant spirit with misgivings for the further successful prosecution of our journey.

Of one thing, however, we felt assured, and that was that if our teams failed, which every probability seemed to warrant, we could pack enough provisions on our backs to foot it through to San Diego. Many men in this situation are and have been for a few days passing us, in this unenviable condition. Most of them seem in good spirits and average sixteen to twenty miles per day.

At this point, "Camp Starvation" (rather an ominous name),[1] we have entrusted our cattle to an Indian Captain who assures us of good pasturage for them. We are to pay him and his subordinates some shirts and I am to furnish him with a recommendation laudatory of his virtues. Such is the contract. What the result will be time will demonstrate— *nous verrons.*[2]

The road till within a few miles back is nothing but deep, heavy sand, and the fatigue of pulling through has caused many of our cattle to fail. These have either lain down to die in the road, or been left at our encampments. The feed we have had has not been sufficiently nutritive to sustain life, especially under severe labor.

One advantage, however, possessed by cattle over horses and mules is that they very soon fill themselves on any kind of food, and then lie down to rest. These latter, on the contrary, require sustenance of a better quality and instead of resting are constantly rambling in search of it, hence they soon become enfeebled and "give out." Their carcasses on and near the road are, compared with cattle, as six to one. This fact goes far to prove the superiority of cattle on this route over other animals.

One fact showing the purity and excessive dryness of the atmosphere here is that most of the carcasses we see are not decomposed as would be the case in a more humid climate, but lie encased in their dry hides as perfect as at the moment of dissolution, the flesh apparently having dried up and shriveled up, leaving a case of shell enveloping nought but the bony structure within.

The day before yesterday the wind blew quite a gale from the South West, and like the Simoon of the Eastern deserts[3] brought with it clouds of fine sand, so dense that had we not been protected by a forest of dead sun flower stalks, we should have probably found it difficult to have breathed. In the evening it clouded up and treated us to a sound drenching, which, though rather too cool to be agreeable, was yet far preferable to the dust of the morning.

About [blank] miles above the mouth of the Gila we passed round the point of a long range of pinnacle topped mountains, and through the gorges of several vast groups of sand hills. Here I had an excellent opportunity of marking the level to which the waters of this stream rises during a freshet.

The water line, clear and well defined, is about 40 feet above the present level of the stream, and when at this height must inundate an immense scope of country on either side, and this leads me to believe that since Lt. Col. Cook passed here an immense and desolating overflow must have occurred and swept with it or buried in sand almost every mark of vegetation, leaving nothing but a wild and dreary waste of sand, except immediately on the river, or around a chain of pools running nearly parallel with it.

The dreary solitude, which through the day would leave its full impress on us all, was broken at night by the wildest music to which human ear ever listened. The wolves along the lower part of the river, either relishing the beauties of solitude, or disdaining the passive state of their human neighbors in this progressive age, were emulous of improving or using to the uppermost the only talent allotted to them, and accordingly about dusk, one whose musical talents possibly entitled him to some preeminence gives a short, sharp key note.

This was answered apparently by other professors on the outposts, the key note was again sounded with a symphony in which the professors join in an instant or two, the tune being arranged and understood. In dusk the concert becomes general, the number of performers, to judge from the wild and fearful notes, would seem to an uninitiated ear to amount to several hundred, but a dozen or two, closely besetting the camp fires, would be amply sufficient to make a school boy's hair "stand erect, like quills upon the fretful porcupine."

These wolves are all of the small species known in the West as the "Prairie Wolf." They must subsist on rabbits, deer &c., as the carcasses of animals that die remain untouched by them.[4]

The Northern bank of the Gila abounds with beaver. Their slides, their dams and the butts of recently dissevered poles and trees show them to be very numerous, and indeed we have seen great numbers of them. Many a time have I, while catching the delicious trout which this stream affords plenty, sat motionless to hear the splash of the beaver as they dropped one after another into the river from the opposite bank, as they gambolled and instructed their young in the merry pastime of the slide. The business of trapping them would no doubt be highly profitable, but extremely dangerous from the Indians.

The road pursued by Cook in crossing the river has

been abandoned, and now continues down the southern bank to its mouth.[5] We have been sadly disappointed in realizing the pictures we had drawn of the ease and comfort we should enjoy on reaching this stream. Instead of rich pasturage for our stock, short drives and abundant leisure and good living for ourselves, we have experienced the very reverse. In most cases we have had to drive our cattle across the stream and either to keep out a strong guard or wade over to look after them several times through the day. This was no pleasant task at daybreak or late in the evening as the nights are really cold. They would also frequently mire in the sloughs and Lagunas, into which they were tempted by the green cane, and had to receive instant help to extricate them. Frequently, while withdrawing one, three or four more would souse in, and thus continue to do so till they were all driven from the place. In short, nowhere have we had less rest or ease, and as to the goodly supply of game with which we had flattered our palates, two unfortunate deer have been all that ever graced our larder, from the Pimo Villages down, no one having time to hunt.

Nov. 16th This morning we crossed the Rio Colorado about ¼ mile below the mouth of the Gila. Lieut. [Couts], U.S.A., in command of a company stationed at this point[6] has started a ferry boat, which to the great convenience of emigrants, the price of ferriage is $3 per wagon and 50 cents per passenger. The mules, horses or cattle are driven above and swim over.[7]

As I stood on the banks musing and tracing the noble stream as it speeded on to mingle its waters with the mighty Pacific, the thought struck me that as I had had no active hand in subduing the territory before me, I ought not at least be under obligation to cross its boundary, but to enter whether for weal or ligation to cross its boundary, but to enter whether for weal or woe fearlessly and independently. Pleased with the idea I sprang at once into the flood and through its cool and refreshing waters soon gained the shore of California.

The River at the junction of the Gila has by some freak forced a passage for itself some 100 yards wide through a chain of hills 120 and 150 feet in height. The walls of the chasm are almost perpendicular, and it looks as though the Gila, whose old bed is very visible south of this ridge and running parallel with it, had left its natural outlet to assist the other in forcing an egress at a point which human ingenuity would have decided to be utterly penetrable. So it is, however, and every sign goes to prove that the gap has been the work of the river itself.[8]

At the crossing the stream is 275 yards wide and widens as it descends. High on a pinnacle, whose base is lined by the confluence of the two streams, were pitched the tents of the soldiers, and at the crossing a mingled crowd of emigrants, soldiers and Indians.

The soldiers were busy with a party of Mexicans en-route from the mines, who were laden with gold. These they were diligently searching, as a great deal of smuggling has been carried on by secreting the precious metal about various parts of the body and clothes. That which is submitted to examination and weighed by the officer is subject to an export duty of five per centum. That which they attempt to conceal and which may afterwards be discovered is declared forfeited and taken from them. A fellow, so I am informed, lost a few days ago twenty pounds weight in this manner. We have not heard yet of the law authorizing this impost, but presume it to be correct as it certainly would be politic.

The Mexicans complain loudly of the duty and would

shun its payment by crossing at Major Graham's ford, 14 miles below, or even swimming the river lower down. From this, however, they are prevented by the Indians (Yumas) who send them all up the river. Most of these Mexicans have large sums with them, the produce of this year's labor, and many are merely returning to take their families back with them to start in February next to a Country in which as American Citizens they may dwell in security and peace.[9]

We are encamped near a large pond, about 1 mile to the right of the road, and 2 ¾ from the ferry. The grazing is poor. The Indians around here manifest an unfriendly disposition towards the emigrants, and have in two or three instances pursued unarmed men with every mark of hostility and vengeance. They even had the impudence to order off the Lieut. and his troops, owing to his having kicked a couple of the rascals for their impertinence.[10] He considered it the more prudent course for the sake of the emigrants to appease them by a few presents as they could in a few hours muster several hundred warriors. Their arms consist of large knives, clubs and but very few bows and arrows. The villains are miserable cowards, and one man with a gun could drive twenty of them. Without firearms no man is safe 100 yards from camp.

Nov. 17th We have been busy today gathering Mezquite beans, as these will be our only resource for a distance of 45 miles after we leave the river. These trees, in many places along the river, resemble orchards regularly set out, and yield a very large crop. We have, however, had some difficulty in gathering enough, as the Indians have been beforehand with us and collected them in heaps, many of them containing from 100 to 150 bushels. These, of course, we hold inviolable, and have to dive amid the thorns and brush for what are left.

Tonight we are encamped on the margin of the River, and one of my messmates has just commenced a profitable sport at fishing. He had already thrown two fine trout close to my feet. They are like those caught in the Gila.

Our road has been sandy all day, and a sand hill directly in our front promises a heavy pull the first thing in the morning. This hill is the eastern terminus of a range of the same character stretching as far as eye can see Westward.

Nov. 18th This morning we entered an Indian settlement where we found large piles of melons, pumpkins, some few beans and a little corn. The last two, however, they refused to spare, having sold all they could to the emigrants ahead. For their melons and pumpkins they asked exorbitantly. Not caring for money they would trade for nothing but clothing, and asked at the rate of a shirt per pumpkin. Our men sold them some useless pistols, blankets, &c., for which they received two or three pieces in cash.

On reaching Graham's ford we supplied ourselves with water, and again turned Westward to encounter the "Jornada." About two miles from the River we entered a large and populous Indian Village. The squaws, who by the bye are the fattest women generally, I ever saw, lined the road on each side while the men and boys, dressed in all kinds of savage and civilized garbs or destitute of any, rushed up to the wagons mimicing the drivers as they spoke to the teams, or with more familiarity than was welcome obtruded their arms around our necks, telling us they were now "Americanos."

There was, however, an impudence, a nonchalance, indicated in their behavior as though they would as soon take a brush with us as shake our hands. Very prudently each man had his gun in good order and bore it with him. This appeared to effect an unmolested transit for the wagons, which from looks and gestures, would have been doubtful had we not been prepared. I seriously fear after the troops leave the crossing, which they will do in a few days, that the later emigrants, most of whom have their families with them, will be insulted or ill treated.[11]

After leaving the village, which we did with some 200 tawny rascals yelling at our heels, we ascended the level of bench land, composed of sand, but covered with Mezquite, Cotton wood and weeds. Our road now lay along the base of a continued ridge of sand hills, their summits forming a high table land stretching northward to the foot of a lofty range of mountains, and westward as far as could be seen. To the South extended a flat desert plain, through which the Colorado flowed toward the Gulf of California.[12]

On ascending a lofty sand hill near the road, a scene of desolation presented itself sufficient to cast a gloom on the most buoyant spirit. Nothing for many miles was to be seen but banks of fine white sand, tossed by the winds into a variety of shapes, and resembling nothing so much as the crested billows of the gulf stream when lashed into fury by a violent North Wester.

We are now encamped near a well dug by Lieut. Col. Cook in 1846. The supply of water is small, and owing to a train having arrived here before us, we shall be occupied most of the night in watering our stock. Two pack trains have passed on, without staying to water. Several wagons and a great many carcasses are strewn along the road.[13]

Nov. 19th   For about four miles after leaving the well, we traversed a good road, running parallel with the bases of the sand hills to our right. Here they make a curve to the south and the road ascends to the level of their summits. The ascent is very laborious. The sand being loose, the wagons sink deeply into it and the animals sink almost to the knee at every step, amid its heavy and non-elastic particles, suffer terribly. The drought of the atmosphere adds greatly to their distress.

On gaining the level of the tableland, sterility and desolation in their widest sense at once greet the traveler. Scattered here and there a solitary and nauseous Kreosote plant may be seen, all else is a barren waste of sand, or gravel thinly strewn over it. This continues for nearly twenty-three miles.

Some two miles before descending again to the Westward the brink of the sandy table is reached, but the descent to the bottom is too steep for wagons to pass. Here are two wells, dug I presume by Cook in 1846. One of these yet contains some water, the other had caved in and partially filled up.[14]

The destruction and waste of property here must amount to several thousand dollars. It is truly painful to witness. Some of the wagons look as though they may have been left by Cook on descending to the bottom. The main road continues to the West, but by turning short to the right and following the base of the sand hills for about half a mile a Laguna or pond is reached, containing very good water. I had, however, arrived within some ten paces before I discovered it, its margin being overgrown around with brush and weeds.

Here we halted and fed away the last of our Mezquite beans. The cattle contentedly lay around the wagons, as if conscious of the sterility surrounding them, and the utter fruitlessness of wandering in search of that which was no where to be found.

About 2 hours before sunset we again set forward, and

from a short distance beyond this point were blessed with an excellent road to the New River, distant 10½ miles. This we reached at about 10 o'clock, and have loosened our stock to roam wherever they please.

Nov. 25th We lay till this morning at New River, improperly so called. The waters designated by this name are contained in holes varying from a few yards to half a mile in length, and from a few feet to a quarter of a mile in breadth. The bed is at present shallow, and if the water ever runs at all, from the observations I have been able to make, I cannot say which course they take. I should, however, imagine that they must find an exit to the South East. The course of the holes is so tortuous that it would take much more time than I could devote to the examination to give an accurate sketch to this region. [15]

We found the grass here mostly dried up, growing in patches amongst dense thickets of large careless weeds. These also have gone to seed and died. Where they have been beaten down by the cattle in search of grass they served as a protection to the growth beneath. Here we found green bunches of very good grass, which we pulled with our hands and cured into hay to last us over a stretch of fifty-one miles of desert said to be ahead of us.

At this place are an American and Mexican encampment in charge of parties under the commissioners for running the boundary lines between the U.S. and Mexico. Col. Fremont is said to be in San Diego. [16]

All the teams that have arrived during our stay at this place are in a miserably broken down condition, parties and individuals afoot, and with their packs on their back have been hourly arriving. Many of these were destitute of provisions, and some had not tasted food for two days.

The officer here in charge of the American troops has, as far as lay in his power, alleviated their distress by giving food to those who had it not, nor the means of procuring it, and by selling to those who had. He yesterday bought a sack of flour containing 100 lbs. from one of my messmates for which he paid him twenty five dollars. There is a rumor current here that the Government has now in transit from San Diego thirty thousand rations for the relief of distressed emigrants.

This evening we reached a branch of New River, distant 8 miles over an excellent road. Here we watered and fed our teams, and after supping, pushed on some 6 miles more, where we encamped on the desert without grass or water. [17]

Nov. 26th   This morning we reached a Laguna, or Lake, of a large size, 4 miles distant, where we halted for breakfast. The water of this lake is good and the last to be had for some 25 miles. [18]

On its bosom sported many water fowl, some of which we shot but did not get, as no one would venture in least he should mire. Here were the fragments of burned wagons and other wasted property, which some miserable looking Indians were collecting. Many of these are now lurking about the road, watching for exhausted oxen, or such as have died, from the carcass of which they speedily cut the flesh, and retire to glut themselves on their unsavory prize, or with it strung across their ponies, make their way to their wigwams to lay up a store for winter use. Some 5 or 6 miles off they have several broken down horses and mules, which I suppose they intend recruiting.

After breakfast we again faced the desert, and proceeded towards a range of mountains running N.W. and S.E. over a route of sand utterly bare in places of many acres, and enlivened only here and there with some nauseous weed or plant.

Early in the evening we ascended a bench of land some 50 or 60 feet above the plain below. At the base of this is the bed of a stream, said to contain some water a mile and a half to the right of the road.[19] At dark we ascended another bench stretching to the foot of the mountain. Here our road turned nearly north.

After about 3 or 4 miles we came to a wagon with two Mexican soldiers. Their team had broken down and they had dispatched the few that could still walk with messengers to Col. Caseco [Carrasco] (one of the Commissioners who is now on the Colorado) for relief. A short distance beyond we encamped.[20]

Nov. 27th   At daybreak we again took the road, and shortly descended a steep and dangerous hill and entered a gorge amid the mountains. Our road now lay down the bed of a dry ravine, which after traversing some 5 or 6 miles, we came to water.[21] This was a little running stream or gutter more properly, some 5 or 10 inches wide, and 3 or 4 deep, which just below sinks in the sand.[22]

Shortly before reaching this we passed among many singularly shaped and colored peaks, a conical one whose northern side being somewhat the lowest displayed a perfect crater. Its depth, from the view I could obtain from the adjacent heights, must be great. I did not visit it as we were all much fatigued. Its diameter is apparently from ¼ to ½ mile wide.

Here we met a party of Americans with a train of mules laden with flour for the use of the emigrants. The person in charge told us that his instructions were to sell to those who could purchase and to give to any who had not the means of so doing. This will be a most seasonable relief to many. Uncle Sam, after all, is not such a niggard, nor so careless of his children as many would represent the old Gentleman to be, and it is flattering to notice the paternal gaze cast westward occasionally. At this crisis particularly, a debt of gratitude from stout and honest hearts will accrue to more than compensate him for his well timed liberality.[23]

In the evening we again moved on up the bed of the stream, which as we ascended augmented in size. We shortly left it when our road again became very heavy. Many carcasses, mostly those of horses and mules, now lined the road, and we continued to plod along, wrapped in woeful meditation and dread. The cattle tottered from weakness and over exertion as they walked, and we knew that many miles of this inhospitable region had yet to be traversed ere we reached grass or water.

Near midnight we came in sight of what a traveler had represented to us as Cabbage trees, where weary and hungry we encamped for the balance of the night.[24] We here fed away the last of our hay and beans, and after sipping a cup of coffee, rolled up in our blankets to obtain a short respite from mental anxiety and bodily fatigue.

Nov. 28th   This morning, at daybreak, I started for the Cabbage trees, which on reaching proved to be "Palmettoes." They are perfectly sheltered from the northern blasts by a range of sand hills near whose bases they grow. There are some twenty to thirty of them, grown nearly in a row, with a small cluster near their eastern extremity.

From the rise in which the cluster stands extrudes many springs of beautifully clear water, strongly impregnated with sulphur. Of these springs I had had no information. Many of the trees had been cut down, no doubt by emigrants to feed their animals, a number of which lay in and about the springs.

In the course of a few miles we commenced a gradual ascent, and much to our satisfaction the road began to grow better. This many of us had predicted from the information we possessed, and our croakers, or green eyed prophets, actually seemed mortified to think that their evil forebodings are not yet realized. They have, however, dodged their position by representing the "Elephant" as yet ahead of us. [25]

After a couple of hours and further fatigue and great anxiety, having left two oxen unable to proceed further, we arrived at "Los Bayacitos," wet to the skin and uncomfortably cold.

Here we found plenty of water in a branch and several springs, but no wood. Mountain and valley were alike bare, and we had to collect Willows about as thick as pipe stems, seeds, weeds or whatever we could lay our hands on.

The bleak winds from the mountains rushed down the valley ahead, and made most of us keenly sensible that chasing cattle through thorny shrubs is very apt to leave a man in neither garments nor exactly suited to a drawing room. [26]

Nov. 29th   Last night it continued to mist, or to pour down rain till daybreak, and our cheerless weed fire only served to aggravate matters, memory incessantly recalling the bright, blazing, joyous and enviable hearths at this season of our friends at home.

Our wagon bed, having been cut off to lighten it, will now admit of but three sleepers. One of my messmates and myself consequently had to sleep under a neighbors, which was broader than ours, and I feel no compunction in classing this night among those things the repetition of which is not to be coveted.

Today we proceeded Westward up a beautiful valley, containing some 2500 to 3000 acres of excellent land. Here we crossed a ridge some 150 feet high, running directly across the vale, and looking like a brace to tie and strengthen the lofty ridges on either side, which here verged to within a few hundred yards of each other. There is, however, a chasm at its Northern end through which a very good road might be made by a few hour's labor, and so avoid the hill which is steep and lengthy.

On descending the opposite side and turning to the Western extremity of the chasm, good water is found. The grass here and at our last camping place has been good and plentiful, but it has been entirely consumed by the earlier emigrants, and our stock, poor things, have yet to chew their cud, not of plenty but of bitter disappointment. The hare is found in this region in great abundance. In about an hour's ramble this evening, near the foot of the mountains, I must have seen at least a dozen.

This place is called "El Puerto," literally "the door." It is appropriate as here used, as it also signifies a gateway or means of egress, I suppose, from the mountains which here apparently completely encircle us.[27]

The Indians, whose wigwams are plentiful through these glens, call themselves "Diegaños" (natives of San Diego), and assume a very pompous way. They answer negatively when asked if they belong to other tribes. They are a filthy, mean looking race, living on carrion, roots, berries, &c.[28]

This morning at sunrise my "Castles in the clouds" assumed one of the most perfect and magnificent illusions I ever witnessed. A ridge of lofty mountains, running nearly North and South lay several miles distant, their crests, crossed with snow, glittered like fairy palaces in the beams of the rising sun, and the clear blue sky above and beyond them seemed but the canvas on which their spires and turrets were beautifully penciled.

Suddenly, a dense and far extended line of clouds, borne on the wings of a Western wind, emerged from the valley beyond and hid their summits from view. The clouds, as they were driven across the height, descended with equal velocity into the intervening valley, and thus after the rain, had descended a few yards, perfect current was formed, as of some mighty river impeded in its course, forcing its restless way over the opposing barrier and wildly bounding and dashing into the abyss below. The light which tinged their surfaces as they boiled in eddying masses rendered the deception complete and was almost horrible to behold, as the advancing traveler seemed journeying into the very jaws of certain destruction. The beautiful phenomenon continued distinct for some 10 or 15 minutes.

Nov. 30th Today, after journeying some 4 miles, we turned abruptly Northward and entered a Cañon, whose sides in many places were almost perpendicular, and so narrow that the projecting rocks on either side had been battered away to admit the passage of wagons. Its length is about a mile when a steep hill is ascended and a gradual descent of some 3 or 4 miles is made nearly East, leading into a vale below. Here another short and steep hill, in the midst of a lofty range, seems to be awesome. On reaching the opposite side [of the pass] the vale of San Felipe is reached. It was late at night when we arrived here and so we encamped a short distance from its base.[29]

Dec. 1st   We pushed on this morning and arrived at San Felipe by about 10 o'clock. Here we had pictured to ourselves a fine, flourishing little town with a busy population surrounded by well tilled fields, with pasture well stocked with good fat cattle, besides a variety of other conveniences, to us very desirable.

This we had anticipated from the pompous talk of the Mexicans, who one and all assured us that we could here obtain whatsoever we stood in need of. How woefully were we deceived. Some 9 or 10 miserable Indian wigwams perched amid rocks on the southern side of the valley constituted its sole edifices. These are inhabited by a poor, degraded set of beings whose food consists of carrion, roots, berries, &c.[30]

There go four of them while I now write, with long strips of flesh swung across their shoulders, cut from the carcass of a poor, exhausted and starved ox that died last night, and for which they have just paid our neighbors, part of the Peoria train, one Dollar.[31]

We have seen within a day or two the skeletons of some three or four oxen who had perished from exhaustion, whose bones had been bared by these gentry as clean as tho' they had bleached there for years.

They leave naught when they obtain a carcass, save the excrement and the bones. Whenever we kill a hare, some of them are sure to be in at the skinning, when greedily seizing the head, entrails, feet and scraps of skin that may be torn off. They carefully fold them in the hide, and with their unsavory prize hasten to their wigwams. The hides they singe on the fire and then eat together with their contents.

A party of Mexicans enroute from the mines to Sonora who are near us killed a beef this morning and sold us part of it. On visiting their camp I found the majority arranged in groups around blankets spread on the ground, and deeply absorbed in gambling. They were playing Monte, their usual game. The betting was moderate.

One or two Mexican women in company with them also joined their play, and it was strange to see the wonderful decorum they preserved even during a run of luck which threatened a heavy inroad on the proceeds of their year's toil. This is, however, a feature seemingly characteristic of this people. I have seen many of them playing for large amounts and after losing a moderate fortune retire with as much placidity of countenance as tho' they had received an invitation to a good dinner.

If our people will gamble, and that too in a country where honest industry is sure of a rich reward, they would certainly lessen the odium in which this practice is justly held by imitating the etiquette of the Mexican gambler.

Dec. 2nd Today we journeyed as far as "Oak Grove," distant 8 miles. Here we found some Indian huts, with patches of ground that had been in cultivation during the summer. These [huts] appear to be much more comfortable than their neighbors to the East. They had raised tobacco, corn, beans, pumpkins, melons, &c. in small quantities, and on gaining a valley south of the village I found several little vineyards.[32]

These [Indians], as well as those we have passed, have wicker work baskets, or stands, somewhat in the form of a beehive, weather-proof, which they stand on a pedestal, and in which they preserve large quantities of acorns. These they roast or pound fine in their unprepared state, and form into a thick paste or mush. This appears to be their main dependence for farinaceous food as they readily part with all others.

I have forgotten to mention a basket used by the Indians in this region. It is composed of splits or willow twig so closely interwoven as to retain water. They are used as drinking vessels, to retain moist substances, or to convey water from the spring.

The mountains South of this are covered with timber and abound with deer. I spoke to a gentleman only this morning who had killed three in about two hours yesterday evening, and had already killed one this morning. A beautiful little rivulet meanders through this dale, and fine springs are found in abundance at the foot of the mountains. The oak, with its dark green foliage, covers both mountain and valley, except in spots near the mountain summits, where a few firs are found in the hollows. These were the first object that for a long time had awakened ideas of the pleasant scenery of home.

Dec. 3rd   This morning we emerged from the valley of the pleasant grove, and after crossing a range of hills running nearly N. and S. [i.e. Warner's Pass], descended gradually by an excellent road into the vale on the opposite side.

After traveling a mile or two we came to several acres of ground that had just been broken up by the plough. It was a rich piece of bottom land, and although the work had been most miserably done, still, the quality of the soil was so excellent that a first rate crop of small grains, for which I presume it was intended, might, with much certainty, be predicted.

From the foot of the mountains to the left stretched a beautiful and extensive valley, covered with a carpet of tender grass from two to four inches high. The old crop had apparently flourished in great luxuriance, but now is dead, and about to be replaced by another.

A little further on a Mr. Warner has erected a store, whether for the purpose of "feeding the stranger," or "taking him in" I cannot exactly determine. His agent vends beef at 8 cents per pound and flour at 37½ cents per pound, other necessaries in proportion.

Whether this process will tend to assist the weary and almost penniless emigrant in the furtherance of his journey, or whether the sight of provision placed before his eyes but rendered unavailable by a light pocket will not rather aggravate his sufferings, the owner's very questionable philanthropy must decide.

We encamped for the night near the store, where we found a range for our stock that had once been good, but was now grazed down to a very scanty picking. Our wood we had to "tote" better than half a mile.[33]

Dec. 4th Our wagon had yesterday morning parted company with those of Dr. Branham and Mr. E. Bush, with whom we had traveled from the States, those gentlemen preferring to proceed via Pueblo de Los Angelos to San Francisco, and the majority of my mess choosing to visit San Diego, and be governed by circumstances on our arrival there. This place is distant 70 miles, and as the two roads have forked, we took that to the left.

We had proceeded but three or four miles, a heavy rain pouring down on us most of the time, when we encamped under the canopy of a huge oak whose widely distended arms offered us a shelter, and whose gigantic trunk, some 6 to 7 feet in diameter, served partly to protect us from a bleak and stormy Westerly wind.

Here we found good grazing for our cattle, and had not the rain continued till near nightfall we should certainly have supped on venison, the hills to our left abounding with black tail deer. One of our party got a shot at a splendid buck, but it was rather too dark and he missed him.

Dec. 5th This day we traveled but little. The road was excellent, but continual showers prevailed and we again sought the shelter of a friendly tree after traveling but a few miles.

Dec. 6th Our road today has been excellent. Shortly after starting this morning we entered a wide and beautiful bottom, covered with a species of wild Rye, from 5 to 6 feet high, which looked like a harvest field ready for the sickle. On the opposite side were several Indian huts, comfortably ensconced under the shelter of a range of mountains.

A mile or two farther brought us to the "Mission de Santa Isabella." This is an old Mission station, the buildings of which are in ruins. The bells that once graced the steeple are now suspended on forks, and are, if ever vocal, used I know not how or when.[34]

There is an Indian village near and around the ruins containing, I should think, from 2 to 300 inhabitants. Here we bought some corn at $1 per almo (about a hat full) of a fierce looking athletic fellow, who was grievously filled with rage at a cursing and perchance a knuckling bestowed on him a short time since by some emigrants.

He seemed almost choked with the vehemence of his choler, which I strove to soothe, by telling him "that he must not take all the Americans to be as bad because some few or probably only one had misbehaved," but sympathy seemed misplaced, and the fellow grew more arrogant, repeatedly striking his breast with his hand and exclaiming vociferously "I am a man," as though he would as soon have taken a "rough and tumble" with us as not.

My companions frequently asked me what he was saying, but I evaded their inquiries, or they would most certainly have accommodated the Gentleman with anything of that nature he could have desired. I deemed it best, however, for the sake of many poor fellows who are behind, many traveling alone on foot, to appease his wrath as well as I could, and we parted seemingly excellent friends.

Notes

Introduction

(1) *Fulton [Mo.] Telegraph*, December 15, 1848, p. 1, col. 3. As an example of the earlier skepticism, the New York *Journal of Commerce* stated in November 1848 that "it appears from all accounts that it costs nearly as much to produce the gold in California, at present, as it is worth." [Reprinted in the Columbia, Missouri *Statesman*, December 22, 1848, p. 1, col. 4.]

(2) *Fulton Telegraph*, March 30, 1849, p. 1, col. 3; *Statesman*, March 30, 1849, p. 2, col. 4.

(3) George R. Stewart, *The California Trail: An Epic with Many Heroes* (Lincoln: University of Nebraska Press, 1983), *passim*.

(4) *Ibid.*, 226.

(5) Harlan Hague, *The Road to California: The Search for a Southern Overland Route, 1540–1848* (Glendale, CA: Arthur H. Clark Co., 1978), *passim*.

(6) *Fulton Telegraph*, April 19, 1850, p. 4, col. 2. The general route of Cooke's road through the southwest was used by subsequent cattle drives and occasional emigrants, but never saw the same extensive use as in 1849. In 1853, Gwinn H. Heap observed several emigrant trains from the southern states using part of the Santa Fe Trail on their way to take the northern route to California. Such a course was out of the way for trains from southern

states but the emigrants thought it was preferable to southern routes "where little or no timber or water are found for long distances." Gwinn Harris Heap, *Central Route to the Pacific . . .* (Philadelphia: Lippincott, Grambo, and Co., 1854), 20.

There was one guidebook published expressly for the southern route, Robert Creuzbaur's *Route From the Gulf of Mexico and the Lower Mississippi Valley to California and the Pacific Oceans* (New York: H. Long & Brother; Austin: Robert Creuzbaur, 1849). He relied on Cooke's and Kearny's official reports and maps, and added little to the knowledge of the route.

(7) Patricia A. Etter (ed.), *An American Odyssey: The Autobiography of a 19th Century Scotsman . . .* (Fayetteville: University of Arkansas Press, 1986), 207; Ralph P. Bieber (ed.), *Southern Trails to California in 1849* (Glendale, CA: Arthur H. Clark Co., 1937), 43. See also John D. Unruh, Jr., *The Plains Across: The Overland Emigrants and the Trans-Mississippi West, 1840–60* (Urbana: University of Illinois Press, 1979), 120.

(8) Merrill J. Mattes, *Platte River Road Narratives: A Descriptive Bibliography of Travel Over the Great Central Overland Route . . . 1812–1866.* (Urbana: University of Illinois Press, 1988), 2. Mattes estimates that as many as 40,000 people may have traveled over the northern routes in 1849. Etter, *An American Odyssey,* 207–20, contains an annotated bibliography of known journals and diaries relating to the southern routes in 1849. A complete citation for Chamberlin's and Powell's works will be found in the bibliography.

(9) *Fulton Telegraph,* May 14, 1852, p. 2, col. 6.

Chapter 1

(1) Arthur T. Maupin settled in Montgomery County in 1838. Almon Rollins (1816–76) was born in Cumberland City, Maine, and moved to Missouri in 1837. Edward W. G. Wingfield (b. 1806) settled in Montgomery County in 1834. William Newlee (b. 1813) emigrated to Missouri in 1837 and served as justice of the peace in Montgomery County from 1845 to 1866.

Rollins and Maupin were related by marriage, as Maupin's sister Patsey was married to William Harris, an uncle of Margaret Harris Rollins. The Newlee, Rollins, and Maupin families were from Albermarle County, Virginia. Hence there were close relations between all four families and this was probably why the members joined together for the journey to California.

The only member not closely related to this group was William W. Hunter. A William Hunter lived in Montgomery County at this time, but according to William H. Hunter, of Grand Island, Nebraska, this Hunter was his fourth great-grandfather and he never went to California. Extensive researching of Missouri historical sources has failed to reveal the background of the author of this journal. He was apparently not a resident of the area and perhaps joined the group while visiting. (I am grateful to William H. Hunter for researching much of the genealogical information in this book. See also William S. Bryan and Robert Rose, *A History of the Pioneer Families of Missouri* (St. Louis: Bryan, Brand & Co., 1876).

(2) Hall's Mill was established on Little Tavern Creek by Henry Hall, an early Callaway County settler. *History of Callaway County* (St. Louis: National Historical Co., 1884), 145.

"Whence the 100 had started" is probably a reference to a group of emigrants from Callaway County. In the April 13, 1849, issue of the *Fulton Telegraph,* under the headline "Off For California," the editor wrote that "this has been a week of great confusion in our little town—of much sorrow and many tears. Quite a number of citizens of Fulton and vicinity have taken leave of their families and friends, and started on the long and wearisome road to California." He estimated that at least 30 men from Fulton and 150 men from Callaway County were involved.

(3) Williamsburg is located in northeast Callaway County. A post office was established there in 1835, and the town platted in 1836. David W. Eaton, "How Missouri Counties, Towns and Streams Were Named," *Missouri Historical Review* 10 (1916), 268; *A History of Callaway County* (Fulton: Kingdom of Callaway Historical Society, 1984), 84.

(4) The Old St. Charles Road (Boone's Lick Road) was the first major east-west route across Missouri. The original road was surveyed in 1814. It connected St. Charles to Boones Lick by way of Williamsburg, Columbia, and Franklin. The road was later bent southward to include Fulton, where Hunter's group entered it. The road was eventually extended to Independence, on the Missouri River. G. C. Broadhead, "Early Missouri Roads," *Missouri Historical Review* 8 (1914), 90–91.

(5) In Hunter's day, the area he was traveling through was heavily forested, and open areas were referred to as "prairies." The term "grand prairie" was applied to several areas in central Missouri. The one that Hunter mentions was located approximately ten miles east of Fulton and was first settled in 1836. *A History of Callaway County* (1984), 84.

(6) Columbia, the seat of Boone County, was platted in 1821 and in 1850 had a population slightly over 650 people. The University of Missouri, the first state university established west of the Mississippi River, was established in the town and in 1850 had 7 instructors and 100 students. Eaton, "How Missouri Counties . . . Were Named," 211.

Not all travelers were disappointed by the town's appearance. James A. Pritchard, a Forty-Niner, described Columbia as "one of the neatest and handsome little Towns that I have seen in my life." Dale L. Morgan (ed.), *The Overland Diary of James A. Pritchard: From Kentucky to California in 1849* (Denver: Old West Publishing Co., 1959), 51.

(7) Rocheport was first settled in 1825. It was a popular place to cross the Missouri River in order to avoid the extra distance imposed when the river turned northward west of the town. Pritchard arrived at the town on April 18 and found so many emigrants waiting to use the ferry that his group would have had to wait three days to cross. Morgan, *Overland Diary*, 52.

(8) The Forty-Niners encountered the second great epidemic of Asiatic cholera. Some historians have estimated that as many as 5,000 Forty-Niners died of the disease, which would amount to almost 12 percent of those starting out. George R.

Stewart argues that this figure is too high and after careful study concludes that perhaps fewer than 1,000 emigrants died from cholera in 1849, about 2 percent of that year's emigration. George R. Stewart, *The California Trail* (University of Nebraska Press, 1983), 225.

Graves of cholera victims dotted the road from Westport to the border of New Mexico. In 1853, Gwinn Harris Heap wrote, "Since our departure from Westport we had seen many graves on each side of the road, and some of the camping-places had the appearance of village graveyards." Gwinn Harris Heap, *Central Route to the Pacific*, 16–17.

(9) St. Joseph, located on the Missouri River, rivaled Independence as a starting point for travelers on the northern route.

(10) Boonville was platted in 1817 and served as the seat of Cooper County. Hunter's group crossed here to avoid the bend northward the Missouri took west of the town. Eaton, "How Missouri Counties . . . Were Named," 280.

(11) The letter of introduction was sometimes necessary as emigrants could be picky about who they traveled with on the long journey. One Forty-Niner wrote proudly that his train had suffered little illness because "we admit no doubtful characters, and have no drinking men; so we are not so much exposed to the scourge [of cholera]." Letter to the St. Louis *Republican*, dated June 9, 1849, at Council Grove; reprinted in the *Kansas Historical Quarterly* 7 (1938), 205.

Augustus M. Heslep traveled with a party organized in Illinois and reported that new members had to "pass the ordeal of a committee inspection before admission, and if found imperfect in character or equipment they cannot obtain admission." Letter to the St. Louis *Daily Missouri Republican*, dated May 24, 1849, reprinted in Bieber, *Southern Trails*, 358.

(12) Warrensburg, the seat of Johnson County, was platted in 1835 and named for John and Martin Warren of Kentucky, early settlers. Eaton, "How Missouri Counties . . . Were Named," *Missouri Historical Review* 11 (1917), 181.

Lone Jack, Jackson County, was named for a lone jack pine

which stood on the townsite when it was platted in 1841. Eaton, "How Missouri Counties . . . Were Named," 11, 178.

(13) Pilot Knob is one of two hills, or knobs, which tower over the generally flat, open terrain. The nearby town of Knob-noster took its name from the Knobs when platted in 1856. Eaton, "How Missouri Counties . . . Were Named," 11, 181–2.

The Shawnee Trace was a road to Shawnee Methodist Episcopal Indian Mission, better known as Shawnee Mission, located just over the Kansas border. The Mission was two miles south of Westport and seven miles south of Kansas City. Founded in 1830 by the Reverend Thomas Johnson, the mission became a thriving settlement and served as the Kansas territorial capital from 1854 to 1855. Franklin G. Adams, "The Capitals of Kansas," *Kansas Historical Collections* 8 (1903–4), 333–4.

(14) N. E. Branham reached California and settled in the Santa Clara area, where he died on December 6, 1856, at the age of 43. His brother Isaac emigrated to California in 1846, and became a prominent citizen in San Jose. *Daily Alta California,* December 17, 1856, p. 2, col. 7.

(15) This is the residence of James B. Yager. Born in Kentucky in 1809, he emigrated to Missouri in 1837 and settled in Callaway County. He later moved to Jackson County, where he was elected to the county court in 1842. In 1835 he married Mary J. Berry, of Callaway County, a relative of Samuel and Frank Berry, in Hunter's train.

Independence, founded as a riverport in 1827, marked the eastern terminus of the Santa Fe Trail. *History of Jackson County* (Kansas City, MO: Historical Publishing Co., 1881), 898.

(16) This crossing of the Big Blue River, located today in the Kansas City suburb of Raytown, Missouri, marked Hunter's entrance to the Santa Fe Trail. There was a second ford a few miles north for travelers using the Westport branch of the trail.

On May 16, 1849, H. M. T. Powell, a gold seeker from Illinois, recorded in his journal: "The waters of the Big Blue came up to our wagon bed. . . . We passed a good many Trains of all kinds today. It would be difficult to say which were the greener, the Teams or the teamsters. They made sad work of it." H. M. T. Powell, *The Santa Fe Trail to California, 1849–1852*, ed. by Douglas S. Watson (San Francisco: The Book Club of California, 1931), 12.

(17) The chief Hunter met was probably Joseph Parks (1793–1859), an influential member of the Shawnee tribe and regarded as their principal chief. A contemporary described him as "a man of culture and of general information." Joab Spencer, "Captain Joseph Parks, Shawnee Indian Chief," *Kansas Historical Collections* 10 (1908), 399–401.

The Shawnees are an Algonquin tribe that consists of numerous subdivisions. Between 1825 and 1845, many Shawnee moved to Kansas and settled near the border with Missouri. In 1846, they began relocating to Oklahoma, then the Indian Territory to join other Shawnee there, and finally ceded their Kansas reservation in 1854. Muriel H. Wright, *A Guide to the Indian Tribes of Oklahoma* (Norman: University of Oklahoma Press 1951), 240–45.

(18) Lone Elm, three miles south of present Olathe, Kansas, was a well-known landmark to early travelers as it marked the separation of the Oregon-California Trail (or northern route) from the Santa Fe Trail (or southern route).

In 1846, Adolphus Wislizenus found it a "rather poor camping place with bad water, scanty grass, and a single elm-tree. . . . How long the venerable elm-tree . . . will yet be respected by the traveler I am unable to say, but I fear that its days are numbered and that the little valley will look then more desolate than ever." Adolphus Wislizenus, *Memoir of a Tour to Northern Mexico* (Washington, D.C.: Tippin & Streeper, 1848), 6.

By 1853, all that remained of the elm was the stump. William W. H. Davis, a member of the party that chopped the stump up for fire wood, noted that "we may be accused of something akin to sacrilege in burning the remains of the old patriarch of the prairie, but with us it was breakfast or no breakfast, and upon such occasions hungry men are not much disposed to give way to romance." William W. H. Davis, *El Gringo: or, New Mexico and Her People* (New York: Harper & Brothers, 1857), 19.

(19) Hunter's group was traveling through an area of Indian settlements, but many of the Indians living near the road fled in fear of cholera. A correspondent wrote, "I noticed at Bull Creek, Kaw River and Willow Springs, among the Delawares and Shawnees, that they had all run off, and left their houses and gardens, with vegetables growing, to the mercy of travelers. . . ." Letter to the St. Louis *Republican*, dated June 9, 1849, Council Grove; reprinted in the *Kansas Historical Quarterly* 7 (1938), 204.

The wolves Hunter refers to throughout his journal were more likely coyotes.

(20) 110 Mile Creek was so named by George Sibley during his exploration in 1825 because it was 110 miles from his starting point at Fort Osage, Missouri. Davis wrote in 1853, "Here flows a small stream of clear water, fringed on either side with cottonwood-trees." In May 1846, Wislizenus found the creek dry. Davis, *El Gringo*, 21; Wislizenus, *Memoir of a Tour*, 6.

(21) The victim's full name was Thomas Hamilton, and he recovered from his wounds. *Fulton Telegraph*, June 15, 1849, p. 2.

(22) The creek was named for John Walker, known as "Big John," a member of Sibley's party. Walker discovered the spring on June 13, 1827. Archer Butler Hulbert, ed., *Southwest on the Turquoise Trail: The First Diaries on the Road to Santa Fe* (Denver: Public Library, 1933), 112.

(23) Possibly a reference to the disaster which struck the firm of Smith, Brown & Company when they attempted to take a train through to Santa Fe late in 1848. They lost one man and 1,600 cattle in a blizzard. A correspondent reported that near 110 Mile Creek he "passed immense numbers of Skeletons of Dead Oxen. . . . Some places thirty would lye in one pile." Louise Barry (comp.), *The Beginning of the West: Annals of the Kansas Gateway to the American West, 1540–1854* (Topeka: Kansas State Historical Society, 1972), 790–91.

(24) The Kansa, or Kaw, were one of the five tribes in the Dhegiha group of the Siouan linguistic family. They depended on

buffalo and crops grown near their semipermanent villages for food. In 1847, a treaty with the Kaw established a twenty square mile tract of land, centering on Council Grove, as their reservation. Between 1859 and 1880, the Kaws sold portions of their land and finally moved to a new reservation in Oklahoma. In 1850 the tribe's population was estimated at 1,700, which declined to 194 by 1889. Wright, *A Guide to the Indian Tribes of Oklahoma*, 160–64.

The Kaws impressed the Forty-Niners. David Brainard, traveling with a Wisconsin train, wrote near Council Grove: "At noon as we stopped, about 30 Indians came among us dressed in regular Indian costume. Their heads were shaven with the exception of a tuft which was braided. Their faces were painted red. Near sunset the chief made his appearance, attended by his interpreter. He was very gaudy with feathers and skins and little bells. He said he was friendly with the whites and liked them. After giving them their supper they left, and a good riddance." David Brainard, "Journal of the Walworth County [Wis.] Mutual Mining Company, Commencing March the 20th, 1849," entry for June 1, 1849. (Transcript on deposit at the Wisconsin Historical Society).

Davis observed the Kaws in 1853 and wrote that the Indians "seem to have learned all the vices but none of the virtues of the white men." Davis, *El Gringo*, 22.

(25) Hunter is referring to Council Grove, located on the banks of the Nesho River. It received its name after Sibley and Osage chiefs met at the site in 1825. Sibley successfully negotiated a treaty with the Osage to allow travelers to pass through their lands along the road. The Grove became a rendezvous where Santa Fe travelers organized their wagon trains. The strip of trees along the river was the last place travelers could obtain hardwood for use as axletrees and other wagon parts until they reached Santa Fe. See Hulbert, *Southwest on the Turquoise Trail*, 111–12, for Sibley's account. See also Josiah Gregg, *Commerce of the Prairies: or, Journal of a Santa Fe Trader* (New York: Henry G. Langley, 1844), Vol. 1, 38–49; Kate L. Gregg, *The Road to Santa*

Fe: The Journal and Diaries of George Champlain Sibley (University of New Mexico Press, 1952), 57–58.

Romanticism surrounded Council Grove after Sibley issued his report. A traveler wrote in 1843 that "the Grove . . . was the largest and most beautiful that we had passed since leaving the frontier of the States. . . . a great variety of shrubs clothed with the sweet foliage of June—a pure stream of water murmuring along a gravely bottom, and the songs of the robin and thrush made Council Grove a source of delights to us." Thomas J. Farnham, *In the Great Western Prairies* . . . (New York: Wiley & Putnam, 1843), 17.

N. K. Grove, a member of Hunter's train, was not impressed and wrote home: "I was a good deal disappointed with the appearance of the 'Grove,' as I expected to find a beautiful piece of woods with no undergrowth, well set in Buffalo grass, and a clear rippling stream coursing its way through its centre. But instead of this I found a strip of timber, nearly half a mile wide, composed of low, heavy topped trees of every kind, with undergrowth of brush . . . at the side of a sluggish stream of muddy water." He added that there was a small village at the site, consisting of two stores, a blacksmith's shop, some cabins and tents. "Take it all in all, it is a dirty, disagreeable looking place." *Fulton Telegraph*, July 13, 1849, p. 2.

(26) At the time of its formation, the Callaway County train consisted of 51 men, 1 woman and 1 girl, 15 wagons, 17 horses, and approximately 100 oxen. Letter from N. K. Grove, *Fulton Telegraph*, July 13, 1849.

(27) Diamond Springs is 16 miles southwest of Council Grove, and was named by Sibley, who wrote in 1827 that "this spring is very large, runs off boldly among the rocks, is perfectly accessible and furnishes the greatest abundance of most excellent, clear, cold sweet water. It may be appropriately called 'The Diamond of the Plains.'" Barry, *Beginning of the West*, 142.

Years later the spring had undergone changes from use by many travelers, and Powell was unimpressed: "There is very little that sparkles about it. It boils up about the size of my arm with some force, bringing with it a considerable quantity of heavy black sand. . . . there was at least a quart of sand settled at the bottom [of a pail] and the water itself is turbid." Powell, *The Santa Fe Trail*, 29.

(28) Samuel H. Berry's family emigrated from Kentucky to Callaway County in 1823. After prospecting in California, he returned home and served as Callaway County sheriff from 1858 to 1862. His brother Frank was also a member of the train.

Freeman S. McKinney's family settled in Missouri in 1818. He had served in Colonel Alexander W. Doniphan's regiment of Missouri Mounted Volunteers during the Mexican War. In California, McKinney became a prominent lawyer in San Jose and was elected to the state legislature on the Know Nothing ticket. In 1857, he joined Henry A. Crabb's ill-fated filibuster expedition to Sonora, Mexico, where he was captured and executed by Mexican soldiers. See Bryan and Rose, *Pioneer Families*, 313, 354; Joseph Allen Stout, *The Liberators: Filibustering Expeditions into Mexico, 1848–1862* (Los Angeles: Westernlore Press, 1973), 163. Anecdotes about McKinney's California legal career may be found in Eugene T. Sawyer, *History of Santa Clara County, California* (Los Angeles: Historical Record Co., 1922), 72–74.

(29) Lost Spring, southwest of Herington, Kansas, received its name for the way it suddenly appeared and then sank into the ground. As a soldier wrote in 1848, the spring rose "suddenly out of the ground, and after rushing over the sand a few yards, as suddenly sinks and is seen no more." William H. Richardson, *William H. Richardson's Journal of Doniphan's Expedition* (Columbia, MO: State Historical Society, 1928), 217.

A Forty-Niner mused that "it might be interesting for us if we could learn just how some of these places along the old Santa Fe Trail got their names. This one for instance, 'Lost Spring.' It is difficult to imagine how a spring of water could ever get lost in an open country like this." Joseph R. Simmons, "Notes of Travel: Adventures of a Party of Missourians Who Traveled Overland from Missouri to California, A.D. 1849," entry for June 17, 1849.

(Journal on deposit at the State Historical Society of Missouri, Columbia.)

The Cottonwood Fork received its name from the trees that lined its banks, the first to be seen west of Diamond Springs. In 1853, Heap described it as "a pretty brook, lined with cottonwood and oak trees, and alive with small fish." Richardson, *Journal,* 217; Heap, *Central Route,* 17.

(30) Gregg wrote of the Little Arkansas that "although endowed with an imposing name, [it] is only a small creek with a current but five or six yards wide." Gregg, *Commerce of the Prairies,* Vol. 1, 56.

(31) When traveling across the treeless plains in 1831, Gregg wrote that "the unthinking traveler might approach almost to [the Arkansas River's] very brink without suspecting its presence." Gregg, *Commerce of the Prairies,* Vol. 1, 58.

(32) Grove was probably reacting to the numerous rumors of hostile Comanche war parties roaming the Kansas plains. A correspondent, commenting on these rumors, found that "on the contrary [we find] that the Comanches are disposed to be very friendly." The friendliness was probably due to the large numbers traveling over the road that year, too many for the Comanches to challenge. Letter to the Philadelphia *Inquirer,* dated June 4, 1849, Council Grove; reprinted in the *Kansas Historical Quarterly* 7 (1938), 205.

Pawnee Fork was on the north bank of the Arkansas River, near present day Larned, Kansas. J. W. Chatham, member of a South Carolina train, wrote: "Here the creek makes a curve and forms a pretty camp ground with sufficient water and wood, but grass is bad." Simmons, *Following the Santa Fe Trail,* 103; J. W. Chatham, "Private Journal," entry for June 9, 1849.

(33) Buffalo chips were the usual source of fuel on the treeless prairies. Chatham commented that the chips were "fine for baking. Makes a very fine fire, but emits an unpleasant smell. Necessity has but one edict." Chatham, "Private Journal," entry for June 11, 1849.

(34) Turkey Fork is near McPherson, Kansas. Stevens de-

scribed it as "a clear stream of water that never goes dry," although it is known today as Dry Turkey Creek. Stevens, "Journal," May 31, 1849; Simmons, *Following the Santa Fe Trail*, 91.

In 1858, a German traveler questioned how the creek received its name, "for as far as I could see I discovered not a tree or a bush," and turkeys preferred wooded areas. H. B. Moellhausen, "Over the Santa Fe Trail Through Kansas in 1858," trans. by John A. Burzle; ed. by Robert Taft, *Kansas Historical Quarterly* 16 (November 1948), 369.

(35) Benjamin Stevens encountered the same band of Cheyennes on June 10, and wrote that the Indians "are friendly and came out to meet us, holding their hands in token of friendship. They were large, fine looking men and women, and were well dressed in their way. Most of them had good horses. Some of them rode two on one horse. They wanted us to trade with them. They were well armed with guns, pistols, and bows and arrows. I gave them some tobacco, and some of our company traded handkerchiefs, etc., for moccasins." Entry for June 10, 1849, journal by Benjamin Stevens, in the John Lewis RoBards Collection, State Historical Society of Missouri, Columbia.

Chapter 2

(1) A group of teamsters led by Daniel P. Mann established Mann's Fort in the spring of 1847. It was located near present day Dodge City, Kansas, approximately twenty miles below the Middle Crossing of the Arkansas River. Intended to serve as a salvage point for wagons abandoned on the Santa Fe road, the post was laid out over an area of sixty square feet, with walls twenty feet high, inside of which were four log cabins. The fort was abandoned the following year. Barry, *Beginning of the West*, 669–70.

History of the fort is sketchy, but apparently soldiers were stationed there during the Mexican War. In 1848, George D. Brewerton found the post "garrisoned by a handful of volunteers, who drank corn whiskey, consumed Uncle Sam's bacon and hard tack, drew their pay with undeviating regularity, and otherwise wore out their lives in the service of the country. . . . these doughty warriors dispelled their *ennui* by chasing buffalo." George Douglas Brewerton, *Overland with Kit Carson: A Narrative of the Old Spanish Trail in '48* (New York: Coward-McCann, Inc., 1930), 258.

Lewis H. Garrard served at the fort in 1848 and describes his activities in *Wah-To-Yah and the Taos Trail* (Cincinnati: H. W. Derby & Co., 1850), 296–306. He described the post as "four log houses, connected by angles of timber framework. . . . In diameter the fort was about sixty feet."

Chatham wrote that the post was "much decayed and torn down by Graders and Emigrants for fuel. Around is scattered vast quantities of Iron taken from waggons broken down. . . . The fort is built of turf and might have stood Savages but not civilized warfare. It is in a plain near the River and commands a view of [a] large plain." Chatham, "Private Journal," entry for June 14, 1849.

(2) Grove, of Hunter's train, wrote home: "There are about one hundred wagons left here to rot in the weather, or be burned [for firewood] by the emigrants. We have burned some, and some of the boys have exchanged their old ones for some of Uncle Sam's new ones. I never could have imagined such a waste of property as I find here. There seems to be plunder enough to supply Missouri." N K. Grove, *Fulton Telegraph*, July 13, 1849, p. 2.

(3) This was probably the train of Ward and Guerrier, on their way back to Independence, Missouri, after hunting for a year along the North and South Platte Rivers. Brainard passed the train near Ash Creek and recorded that it consisted of 9 wagons carrying over 7,000 hides. Barry, *Beginning of the West*, 878; Brainard, "Journal," entry for June 12, 1849.

(4) Hunter's group followed the Cimarron Cut-Off of the Santa Fe road. There were three major fords, or crossings, of the Arkansas River. The Lower Crossing was approximately 18 miles east of Mann's Fort, near present-day Ford, Kansas. Travelers crossed the Arkansas and followed the Mullberry Creek bed southwest to the Cimarron. This route was longer than the Middle Crossing and seldom used.

The Upper Crossing was about seventy miles west of Mann's Fort, near present-day Lakin, Kansas. Travelers crossed the river and traveled due south to the Cimarron River. While shorter, it was a more rugged road than the middle route and only used in wet years. This route was established in 1851 and hence not used by the Forty-Niners.

The Middle Crossing, about twenty miles west of Mann's Fort, near what is now Ingalls, Kansas, lead directly southwest across the Cimarron Desert and involved from fifty to sixty miles of waterless travel. The difference in the distance depended upon whether it was a wet or a dry year. In wet years, water could be found by digging into the bed of Sand Creek, fifty miles south of the crossing. In dry years, travelers had to wait until they reached the Lower Cimarron River before finding water. Hobart E. Stocking, *The Road to Santa Fe* (New York: Hastings House, 1971), *passim*.

(5) Hunter refers to an area more commonly known as the "Battleground," scene of a skirmish between a band of Texans under Colonel Jacob Snively and Mexican soldiers in 1843, one of a number of raids between Mexico and the Republic of Texas from 1836 to 1846. Gregg, *Commerce of the Prairies*, Vol. 2, 169–70.

Wislizenus listed the site at 15 miles south of the Arkansas River and described it as offering "poor, dry grass, but a small waterpool." Powell described the site simply as "some pools on the prairie." Wislizenus, *Memoir of a Tour*, 11; Powell, *Santa Fe Trail*, 51.

South of the Battleground, travelers entered the Cimarron Desert, an arid stretch of prairie. Froebel noted in 1852 that "The further we advanced the more sterile the plateau became and the harder the soil, which as far as the eye reached presented a perfectly level plain." Julius Froebel, *Seven Year's Travel in Central America . . .* (London: Richard Bentley, 1859), 279.

(6) Sand Creek is another name for the North Fork of the Cimarron River. The creek was often dry and travelers had to dig into the sand to find water. Powell reached the area, at a point

southeast of Ulysses, Kansas, on June 20: "[We] descended into a desolate looking valley through which ran 'Sand Creek.' It is worthy of its name. It did not run, however. The water stood in pools." Stocking, *The Road to Santa Fe*, 159; Powell, *The Santa Fe Trail*, 52.

(7) These buffalo hunters, also known as *ciboleros*, were a common sight in the Cimarron Valley. They came from villages in New Mexico on yearly hunts, and the lance was their principal weapon. Gregg wrote that "these hardy devotees of the chase usually wear leathern trousers and jackets, and flat straw hats, while, swung upon the shoulder on each hangs his *carcage* or quiver of bow and arrows and lances." Gregg, *Commerce of the Prairies*, vol. 1, 90; see also Wislizenus, *Memoir of a Tour*, 12.

Taos is located sixty-eight miles north of Santa Fe.

(8) The Cimarron River is an intermittent water course which eventually joins the Arkansas River near Tulsa, Oklahoma. In 1848, Brewerton wrote that "during the mid-summer heats [the Cimarron is] nothing more than a bed of sand, with an occasional pool or buffalo wallow, for that animal frequently spends the hottest portion of the day in these natural bathtubs—a fact which adds nothing to the purity or sweetness of their waters, as our parched lips could but too easily testify. Water of an inferior quality can, however, be generally procured by digging for it in the sand banks." Brewerton, *Overland with Kit Carson*, 242.

Supporting Brewerton's observation on the water found between the Arkansas and the Cimarron, Froebel wrote, "When I use the term *water* it generally designates a brackish mud, and for a long time I have drunk water which was not clean enough to wash my face in." Froebel echoed Hunter's description of the Cimarron: "The river—if I may call it so—formed at the point where we reached it a small stagnant and brackish brook, running amongst reeds and rushes." Froebel, *Seven Year's Travel*, 278, 280.

Travelers depended on three major springs, known as the Lower, Middle, and Upper, for palatable water on the sixty-mile stretch of road through the Cimarron Valley. Marc Simmons, *Following the Santa Fe Trail* (Santa Fe: Ancient City Press, 1986), 146.

(9) The Upper Spring is northwest of Boise City, Oklahoma. Gregg described it as "a small fountain breaking into a ravine that declines towards the Cimarron some three or four miles to the north." Gregg, *Commerce of the Prairies*, vol. 2, 87.

(10) Cold Spring is approximately twelve miles northwest of Boise City, in the Oklahoma panhandle. In 1846, Wislizenus wrote that the Spring "afforded us the best water we have tasted since we left the Arkansas; it breaks out of the sandstone that prevails here, and has a refreshing coolness." Brainard reported, "This is the first good water we have had in many weeks, also [the first] shrub or tree [we have seen] in traveling 150 miles." Wislizenus, *Memoir of a Tour*, 14; Brainard, "Journal," entry for June 28, 1849.

Gibson described the spring as "one of the few pretty places on the road with good water and plenty of grass. The spring gushes out from under a ledge of rocks, cold, clear and refreshing. . . ." Gibson, *Over the Chihuahua and Santa Fe Trails*, 70.

The change in the terrain Hunter noticed is the Cimarron Breaks, which the Santa Fe road followed for twenty miles, from Willow Bar to Cold Spring. Simmons, *Following the Santa Fe Trail*, 148.

(11) The Cold Spring creekbed runs north to south, and the Santa Fe road crossed it at Autograph Cliff, so named because many travelers carved their names in a sandstone outcropping at the site. Hunter walked north along the creekbed to the glen he described.

(12) Whetstone Creek received its name from the sandstone in the area, which contained lime and could be used for coarse whetstones. Wislizenus, *Memoir of a Tour*, 15.

The isolated peaks Hunter noted are probably the Point of the Rocks, a prominent landmark. Simmons, *Following the Santa Fe Trail*, 155.

(13) Gregg described the Canadian River as "a rippling brook, hardly a dozen paces in width," and added, "The bottom being of solid rock, this ford is appropriately called by the Ciboleros el Vado de Piedras," or by American travelers, Rock Cross-

ing. Wislizenus wrote of "a clear mountain stream, with fine grass and good soil; cedars grow on the neighboring hills and further down the creek." Gregg, *Commerce of the Prairies*, vol. 1, 105; Wislizenus, *Memoir of a Tour*, 15; see also Simmons, *Following the Santa Fe Trail*, 156.

(14) The Wagon Mound was a well-known landmark on the plains of northeastern New Mexico, so named because from the far distance the contour resembles an ox-drawn covered wagon. The mound is a basalt outcropping with steep sides, towering over 100 feet above the plain; the town of Wagon Mound is located at the western base. Wislizenus, *Memoir of a Tour*, 16; Simmons, *Following the Santa Fe Trail*, 157–8.

(15) Near the site where Hunter found the skeleton, Powell recorded on July 7: "Some of the party saw some human skeletons to the North, in a ravine." His companions displayed no desire to investigate, leading one to wonder if skeletons were a common discovery in that part of the country. Powell, *The Santa Fe Trail*, 66.

(16) Owl Creek is not mentioned by other Santa Fe diarists. From Hunter's list of distances, it was probably Wolf Creek, a tributary of the Mora River.

(17) The Mora River was considered the boundary between the plains and the New Mexican settlements. Santa Fe caravans usually camped on the river to make final preparations for the return trip to Independence. Wislizenus described the Mora as "a fine mountain stream, and a charming valley." Although it was a good area for farming, he found little settlement there in 1846 because of the threat of Indian raids. The only structure was a large adobe house maintained by two Americans. Wislizenus, *Memoir of a Tour*, 17; see also Simmons, *Following the Santa Fe Trail*, 165–6.

(18) Barclay's Fort was established in 1848 by Alexander Barclay (1810–55). He was active in the fur trade and managed operations at Bent's Fort from 1836 to 1842. In 1848, he established his own trading post, or fort, at the junction of the Mountain and the Cimarron branches of the Santa Fe road, near

present-day Watrous, New Mexico. Simmons, *Following the Santa Fe Trail,* 164–5.

Brainard wrote that the fort was "a strong fortification and will resist all of the attacks that an enemy may make." The post was 300 yards square and built of adobe. Brainard, "Journal," entry for July 9, 1849.

Powell, who like Hunter listed the fort as "Bartley," arrived at the fort the same day as Brainard and described Barclay as "a very sinister looking man" who attempted to swindle the emigrants out of their oxen by telling them that ox teams could not make the trip to California and then offering to trade pack mules for them. Powell, *The Santa Fe Trail,* 67; see also George P. Hammond, *The Adventures of Alexander Barclay, Mountain Man* (Denver: Old West Publishing Company, 1976).

(19) Powell recorded that the settlers were Mexican War veterans: "They have tents and some adobe houses, and it is difficult to say which is the dirtier, the men or the houses." Powell, *The Santa Fe Trail,* 67.

(20) A reference to the town of Rayado, on the creek of the same name, approximately twenty-three miles west of present-day Springer, New Mexico. The settlement was begun in 1848 by Lucien Maxwell, Kit Carson, and others, on the Mountain branch of the Santa Fe road. In 1850, a garrison was stationed there to protect the traffic from Raton Pass to Las Vegas. Lawrence R. Murphy, "Rayado: Pioneer Settlement in Northeastern New Mexico, 1848–1857," *New Mexico Historical Review* 46 (January 1971), 37–56; Simmons, *Following the Santa Fe Trail,* 143.

Stevens' train found fifty soldiers stationed at the small settlement when he arrived there on July 14, "camped on a narrow mountain stream in a pleasant valley about two miles from the ranches of Kit Carson and Maxwell. They are building a fort and have a good deal of stock grazing here." Stevens, "Anonymous Journal," entry for July 14, 1849.

(21) Hunter refers to the campaign of General Stephen W. Kearny's Army of the West in 1846. There were several strong

positions between Las Vegas and Santa Fe which the Mexican forces could have occupied to oppose Kearny on his march to Santa Fe, but they failed to do so. See William A. Keleher, *Turmoil in New Mexico, 1846–1868* (Santa Fe: Rydal Press, 1952).

(22) Las Vegas was a new town; in 1831 Gregg found only "a little hovel at the foot of a cliff" at the site. In 1835, residents from nearby San Miguel began settling in the area. In 1846, Wislizenus saw a village of about a hundred adobe buildings, whose "poor and dirty looking inhabitants" eked out a living by irrigation farming and stock raising. Gregg, *Commerce of the Prairies*, vol. 1, 109; Wislizenus, *Memoir of a Tour*, 17; Simmons, *Following the Santa Fe Trail*, 169.

"Buena Vista" is a reference to a large, broad-brimmed hat worn by many Forty-Niners.

(23) Powell was not as impressed as Hunter by the appearance of the local women and wrote on July 10: "The native women squat down on the ground and lean back against the walls of their dirt houses, dressed in dirty chemise and dirty petticoats, and over their heads wear a light coloured dirty 'rebozo'; each one being the possessor of a very homely and dirty face." Powell, *The Santa Fe Trail*, 68.

(24) Ojo de Vernal, also known as Bernal and as Bernal Springs, was located at the intersection of the Santa Fe and the Fort Smith roads, and in 1846 consisted of about a dozen houses. Powell passed through on July 12, and wrote: "There are a few adobe houses . . . and the corn is fenced in and looks better than any that I have yet seen. . . . Here both the men and the women have their faces daubed. The valley of the Ojo de Verral is very beautiful." Powell, *The Santa Fe Trail*, 69. See also Wislizenus, *Memoirs of a Tour*, 18, and Davis, *El Gringo*, 54.

(25) The term *aguardiente* referred to locally distilled spirits. Gregg described aguardiente as brandy distilled in El Paso from grapes. In New Mexico, it was distilled from wheat and was a type of whiskey. Davis wrote that the beverage was "as barbarous an alcoholic compound was ever was made." Charles E. Pancoast, a Forty-Niner, described aguardiente as "a vile mixture of turpen-

tine, muscat and whiskey." Gregg, *Commerce of the Prairies*, II, 77; Davis, *El Gringo*, 44; Charles Edward Pancoast, *A Quaker Forty-Niner* [ed. by Ann Paschall Hannum] (University of Pennsylvania Press, 1930), 216.

Cap-a-pie means head-to-foot.

(26) Tecolote was settled in 1824, and by 1846 consisted of about thirty dwellings. Davis described the community in 1853 as having "a population of some five hundred, living in miserable mud houses." Powell wrote that it was "a little village in a low valley . . . It put me in mind of the mud houses built by children in a rut in the road." Powell, *The Santa Fe Trail*, 68; Wislizenus, *Memoir of a Tour*, 17; Davis, *El Gringo*, p. 53.

(27) The springs Hunter describes are six miles northwest of Las Vegas, near the present-day town of Montezuma. The Santa Fe Railroad Company developed the area into a resort, as Hunter prophesized, and built the Montezuma Hotel near the springs in 1882. The springs flourished as a resort until 1902, when the railroad closed the hotel in order to develop their Grand Canyon properties. James D. Henderson, "Meals by Fred Harvey," *Arizona and the West*, XLVI, no. 1 (Winter 1966), 37–56.

(28) San Miguel was the main port of entry for the Santa Fe caravans in the Mexican period. It was established in the mid 1790s, and a church was built there in 1805. In 1831 Gregg described it as an "irregular cluster of mud-wall huts, situated in the fertile valley of Rio Pecos, a silvery little river." William H. Chamberlin described the town as "composed of about seventy-five adobe hovels, one story high, all the outbuildings (if they have any) being within the same walls. There are several stores of groceries in the place, their principal business being the sale of inferior liquor, at a 'bit' a glass." Gregg, *Commerce of the Prairies*, I, 109; Lansing B. Bloom (ed.), "From Lewisburg (PA) to California in 1849: Notes from the Diary of William H. Chamberlin," *New Mexico Historical Review*, XX (1945), 51. See also Simmons, *Following the Santa Fe Trail*, 181.

(29) Ruins of the Pecos, near the Pecos River, had been the eastern most Indian pueblo during the days of Spanish domina-

tion. Disease and Apache raids reduced the population and the site was abandoned in 1838. In 1853, Davis wrote that "the church was roofless, and altarless, and fast going to decay . . . Just in the rear of the church, covering the slope of the hill for two or three hundred yards, are the ruins of the village." Extensive ruins may still be seen today. Davis, *El Gringo*, 54–55; Simmons, *Following the Santa Fe Trail*, 183–84.

Chapter 3

(1) Cottonwood Springs was located at the eastern edge of Glorieta Pass. Wislizenus termed it "Cottonwood Branch," "a small valley amidst high mountains." Wislizenus, *Memoir of a Tour*, 19.

(2) Hunter's "great Cañon" is Glorieta Pass, the main passage through the Sangre de Cristo Mountains. It was a strong defensive position and a potentially major obstacle to Stephen W. Kearny's Army of the West (2,700 men) on their approach to Santa Fe in August 1846. Mexican Governor Manuel Armijo had 3,000 men under arms to oppose Kearny, but declined to defend the Pass and abandoned Santa Fe instead. Rumor had it that Armijo was bribed by an American agent not to offer opposition. To many Forty-Niners who passed through the area, it appeared as if the Mexicans had given up a strong position and lacked the will to fight, though Armijo might have simply realized that his ill-equipped militia had little hope of defeating Kearny and bowed to the inevitable to avoid useless bloodshed. Also, there was more than one road to Santa Fe, and Kearny had an alternative plan to march around the Pass by way of Galisteo and outflank the position from the south. See Keleher, *Turmoil in New Mexico*, 11–14 and 114, note 22; and Daniel Tyler, "Governor Armijo's Moment of Truth," *Journal of the West* 11 (April 1972), 307–16.

(3) Benjamin Hayes, traveling with a Texas train, wrote that the people of Galisteo were "pleasant and polite, hospitable and kind." In 1851, a traveler estimated that the town's population was around 600 people. Benjamin Hayes, *Pioneer Notes From*

the Diaries of Judge Benjamin Hayes, 1849–1875 (Los Angeles: privately printed, 1929), 22; Clinton E. Brooks and Frank D. Reeve (eds.), "James A. Bennett: A Dragoon in New Mexico, 1850–1856," *New Mexico Historical Review* 22 (1947), 82.

(4) Monte, also known as Three-Card Monte, was a popular Mexican card game.

(5) The Spanish conqueror founded Santa Fe in 1610 as the capital of New Mexico. The town became a major trading center in 1821 when the Mexican government opened the province to traders from the United States.

Wislizenus described Santa Fe as "that irregular cluster of low, flat roofed, mud built, dirty houses . . . more a prairie dog village than a capital." He estimated the town's population in 1846 at about 3,000 people, with perhaps 6,000 people in the area. Wislizenus, *Memoir of a Tour*, 28.

Chamberlin visited Santa Fe on June 7, and found the town "situated in a narrow valley, on a small stream of water, surrounded by an apparently barren country, and hills of the same nature; in the distance, mountains towering to the clouds, whose snow-clad peaks give nature a chilling appearance . . . The somber appearance of the town . . . inspired us with rather gloomy sensations." Chamberlin, "From Lewisburg," 53.

(6) Construction of Fort Marcy began in August 1846, shortly after Kearny occupied Santa Fe. Initially the fort consisted of a blockhouse erected on a hill 600 yards northeast of the Plaza, which towered over the town. The fort was named in honor of William L. Marcy, Secretary of War at the time. Simmons, *Following the Santa Fe Trail*, 193.

(7) The woman was possibly Doña Gertrudis Barcelo (1800–1850), a well known casino operator in Santa Fe. Popularly known as "La Tules," she amassed a fortune from her gambling activities, and in 1843 invested $10,000 in the Santa Fe trade. Brainard visited Santa Fe in July, and found "Every hotel filled with men, women and children betting at the Monte tables. Madam Goulu [i.e., La Tules] has the most extensive gambling room in the city. She not only attends them herself, but has many

men hired to bet for her." Janet Lecompte, "La Tules and the Americans," *Arizona and the West,* 20 (Autumn 1978): 215–30; Brainard, "Journal," entry for July 27, 1849.

(8) "Placea" does not appear on contemporary maps of New Mexico and Hunter probably referred to Placer, a mining community on the Arroyo Tuerto, north of present day Golden, New Mexico. The road Hunter's party followed led south from Galisteo and then curved westward and passed between the Ortiz and the San Pedro Mountains, along the Arroyo Tuerto. The spring Hunter mentions was probably located along the Arroyo Joya.

(9) Probably L. C. Bostick. His train, composed of Missourians, totaled 27 wagons when they reached Mann's Fort on June 7. Barry, *Beginning of the West,* 855.

An *alcalde* was a Mexican municipal office that combined the functions of a mayor and a justice of the peace.

(10) As stated in Note 8, Hunter means Placer when he uses "Placea." The area Hunter examined was commonly referred to as the "new placers" to distinguish it from earlier gold discoveries on the north side of the Ortiz Mountains.

There are several placer gold deposits in New Mexico, which together produced over 660,000 ounces of gold between 1828 and 1968. Though many of these sites were known to local Indians, gold mining began in New Mexico with the discovery of rich placers on the north side of the Ortiz Mountains in 1828 (the "old placers"). A second discovery was made south of the mountains in 1839, hence the "new placers." Gold in these deposits was found in pockets that were not conducive to large-scale mining operations. Maureen G. Johnson, *Placer Gold Deposits of New Mexico* (Washington, D.C.: Government Printing Office, 1972), *passim.*. [Geological Survey Bulletin 1348]. See also John W. Townley, "El Placer: A New Mexico Mining Boom Before 1846," *Journal of the West* 10 (January 1971): 102–15.

Wislizenus visited the town of Placer (also known as Tuerto) in July 1846, and estimated it to consist of a hundred buildings. Wislizenus, *Memoir of a Tour,* 31.

James W. Abert passed through the town in October 1846,

and recorded it as having a population of 250 people, most of whom were employed in gold mining. The town was pocked with numerous open pit mines and "looked like a village of gigantic prairie dogs."

Windlasses were used to lift ore-bearing gravel up from the pits in leather buckets. The contents were carefully sifted by the men, women, and children of the village. The depressing appearance of the village caused Abert to write: "One cannot but feel pity for these miserable wretches, and congratulate himself that he does not possess a gold mine. Even the life of the poor pastores is much preferable to that of these diggers of gold." James W. Abert, *Report of Lieut. J. W. Abert of His Examination of New Mexico, in the Years 1846–47* (Washington, D.C.: Wendell and Van Benthuysen, 1848) [30th Cong., 1st Sess., Ex. Doc. 41], 451.

Chamberlin noted that many Forty-Niners, running low on funds, worked the placers in hopes of earning enough to continue on to California. Men could reportedly earn from one to five dollars per day at the placer deposits. Chamberlin, "From Lewisburg," 55.

(11) San Pedro was a small mining community south of Golden, New Mexico. Chamberlin described it as a "small rancho containing about a dozen houses [with] about sixty acres of land under cultivation." Chamberlin, "From Lewisburg," 145.

(12) The Ortiz Mountains appeared on some maps as the Placer Mountains.

(13) Santa Antonietta, known also as San Antonito, was approximately four miles north of modern San Antonio, New Mexico. Chamberlin passed through the area on June 19: "We found a spring of water, but no grass . . . there is an American living here, who is very comfortably situated in his adobe house; he raises grain, vegetables, etc." Chamberlin, "From Lewisburg," 145–46.

(14) Lieutenant Colonel John MacRae Washington (d. 1853) served as the governor of New Mexico Territory from October 1848 to October 23, 1849.

(15) San Antonio at that time was a small village on the main road to Albuquerque, and had a population of about 150 people. Chamberlin, "From Lewisburg," 146.

(16) Williams' train probably consisted of seven wagons. Berry's train totaled fifteen wagons when it was organized at Council Grove and twenty-two when it reached Quarai. Powell, *The Santa Fe Trail,* 83.

Chapter 4

(1) Ojo de Cibolo, also known as Buffalo Springs, was six miles southwest of present Moriarty, New Mexico. Powell described the springs as simply "some ponds near the road," surrounded by "a vast meadow, the grass beautiful and the ground perfectly smooth." Powell, *The Santa Fe Trail,* 78.

(2) In the margin of his distance table, Hunter wrote: "The Rio del Norte being very high and the ferriage $2 per wagon, we concluded not to go by way of Albuquerque."

The nearby mountains Hunter mentions are the Manzanos, not the Galisteos.

(3) Hunter's "Veundo" is Ojo Verrendo, or Antelope Springs, located approximately 2.5 miles southwest of McIntosh, New Mexico.

Powell reached the site on July 26, and wrote that "It is a beautiful spring in the vast open Plain, gushing out cold and clear, filling up, just below it, a large hollow forming a pretty round pond around the margin of which snipe and little sandpipers are running." Powell, *The Santa Fe Trail,* 78.

Chatham recorded: "We found an abundance of fine cool water at which we camped for the night." He added that the grass was nearly all consumed by previous trains, a condition that was being found at all of the major camping grounds. Chatham, "Private Journal," entry for July 25, 1849.

To this point the Forty-Niners were following a well-marked road to the salt beds farther south. At Ojo Verrendo, a new road branched off westward towards the mountains and Abo Pass. The Forty-Niners referred to the road from San Antonio to Abo as the "Manzano Route," and it had the advantage of avoiding the sandy roads and irrigation ditches parties encountered if they crossed at Albuquerque. Hayes, *Pioneer Notes*, 23.

(4) Estancia Spring is today the site of the town of Estancia, New Mexico. Southeast of the spring lay a series of salt beds, also known as the *salinas*, from which the people of northern New Mexico obtained most of their salt. Gregg, *Commerce of the Prairies*, vol. 1, 175–76.

(5) La Purísima Concepción de Quarai was a Spanish mission founded in 1629, and abandoned in 1671 because of a drought and frequent Apache raids. Paul A. F. Walter, *The Cities That Died of Fear: The Story of the Saline Pueblos* (Santa Fe: El Palacio Press, 1931), 27.

Some old maps show an Ojo Chico between Manzano and Estancia, and on other maps the southern point of the salt beds is noted as Laguna Chica. Either of these places may have been the "Chico" Hunter refers to.

(6) The emigrants encamped at Quarai while waiting for the desert rainy season to advance and improve the grazing farther south. Powell described the campground, which was located southwest of Eastview, New Mexico, as having "Plenty of wood; large white cedar trees, pine, oak, a tree much resembling black locust and others. Grass plentiful; clover . . . grama [grass], etc., and water from 2 or 3 springs. The best camping ground we have had for many a long day." Powell, *The Santa Fe Trail*, 74, 80.

Chatham echoed this sentiment: " . . . wood, water and the finest grass we have had on the road. It is a perfect Paradise for our ox and horses." Chatham, "Private Journal," entry for July 27, 1849.

The three trains Hunter mentions were the one Powell belonged to (Turner's), Gulley's, and Williams'. Powell, *The Santa Fe Trail*, 79–80, 83.

(7) Hunter's precise citation refers to the edition of Emory's

published report cited in the bibliography. This was probably the edition Branham had in hand when he decided to follow the southern route.

Abert met Jose Lucero in 1846 while examining the Quarai ruins. Lucero claimed that he had discovered rich gold and silver mines near the mission but did not develop them for fear that the properties would be seized by local ranchers. Abert was skeptical and concluded in his report: "I took down Jose Lucero's name, and proceeded on my journey, so that if any one wishes, they yet can go and seek the gold of Quarra [sic]." Lucero had no idea that in two years hundreds of gold seekers would pass through the area and take him up on his offer. Abert, *Report*, 487–88.

New Mexico abounds with legends of lost mines and treasures. In Hunter's area, Quarai and Gran Quivera were rumored to have buried treasure from the Spanish period. Gregg recorded that throughout northern New Mexico there were plenty of local inhabitants willing to lead strangers to lost treasures. These guides were noted for disappearing with the property and livestock of the treasure hunters before the site could be found. Gregg, *Commerce of the Prairies*, I, 163–64; Wislizenus, *Memoir of a Tour*, 25.

(8) Powell recorded meeting Lucero, and found him quite reticent. He told Powell that the mine was six days away in the Sierra Blanca Mountains (also known as the White Mountains) and could only be worked in the winter. Lucero continued his tales, however, and claimed that there was a treasure worth fifteen million dollars buried at Gran Quivera, located southeast of Quarai. "Heard this story before," Powell noted in his journal. Powell, *The Santa Fe Trail*, 80.

(9) Powell recorded the expedition's departure on August 2: "Womenkind are busy cooking bread, etc., for the expedition to the Gold mines . . . After a great deal of fuss and fixing our party started." He estimated that eleven men went on the expedition from his train, twenty-two from Gulley's, five from Berry's, and three from Williams's. Powell, *The Santa Fe Trail*, 83.

(10) Manzano, founded in 1829, was a small village at the

base of Manzano Peak, about four miles northwest of Quarai. Hayes estimated that about one hundred families lived in the village. Hayes, *Pioneer Diary*, 25.

During their long stay at Quarai, many Forty-Niners visited the town and some became quite friendly with the inhabitants, though the degree of fraternization is unrecorded. Chatham noted that "several [of his companions] have gone to the mountains for a bear hunt while others chase another species of game at Manzano. . . . Some of the boys got shot at in robbing the Spaniard's [garden] patches. Look out boys, their seniorities are more easily obtained than their produce." Chatham, "Private Journal," entry for August 7, 1849.

(11) Powell recorded hearing of Roberts's murder on July 28, and his account is similar to Hunter's. Powell added that this was the fourth murder of emigrants by Mexicans his train had heard of since they had entered New Mexico. Powell, *The Santa Fe Trail*, 80.

(12) Nicolas Turner led a small Missouri train. On July 23, Powell's and Chatham's trains voted to combine with Turner's, and Turner was elected captain of the combined train. "He looks tough enough," Powell wrote, "How he will do, I know not, but I am sure I would not have his place on any account." Chatham described Turner as "a man of Energy and action and [one] who does not hold back for his honorable station but lays to."

Chatham mentions Rickets in his journal as early as June 10, near the Arkansas River. He was apparently a member of Lightner's train from Missouri, and he gave a sermon each Sunday. Powell, *The Santa Fe Trail*, 76; Chatham, "Private Journal," entries for June 10, July 23, and July 30, 1849.

(13) Powell attended the same service and summed it up as follows: "In the afternoon we had a meeting and Mr. Rickets preached. The Mexican women attended and laughed outright two or three times; very bad manners. I don't think they thought well of the singing. In truth, it was not the best in the world." Powell, *The Santa Fe Trail*, 86.

Chatham wrote that Rickets "had quite an audience as there are so many camped around. His discourse was feeling to many and several showed it." Chatham, "Private Journal," entry for August 5, 1849.

(14) In Spanish colonial times, several small silver mines were developed at the southern end of the Manzano Mountains, none of which were very productive. Gregg reported a discovery near Manzano, but the ore proved to be too hard for local smelting methods, and the mine was abandoned. Gregg, *Commerce of the Prairies*, vol. 1, 175; Wislizenus, *Memoir of a Tour*, 24.

(15) Congreve Jackson was a colorful character, well known in northeastern Missouri. He served as a lieutenant colonel in the First Regiment of Missouri Mounted Volunteers (Doniphan's regiment) during the Mexican War and had campaigned in New Mexico and the Rio Grande Valley. In 1849, he led a train of gold seekers from Marion County, and later returned to Missouri and served in the Confederate army. Barry, *Beginning of the West*, 856; *History of Marion County, Missouri* (St. Louis: E. F. Perkins, 1884), 55, 211.

(16) Probably Ashley Gulley (sometimes spelled "Gully" in Forty-Niner narratives), who led a train from Marion County, Missouri. He had served as a second lieutenant in Doniphan's regiment during the Mexican War.

(17) Apparently the group's destination was the White Mountain, known today as Sierra Blanca, in the Sacramento Mountains, seven miles northwest of Ruidoso, New Mexico. John Hudgins, a member of the group, claimed that they rode as far south as the site of Fort Stanton, which would have placed them more than eighty miles from Quarai. John Hudgins, "California in 1849," *The Westport Historical Quarterly* 6 (June 1970):8. Hudgins was a member of Gulley's train.

Powell made this evaluation of the expedition: "From all I can hear they have made a miserable business of it; a complete botch. They found no Gold and can scarcely say they have looked for any. A more ill-advised and badly conducted expedition I never heard of." Powell, *The Santa Fe Trail*, 88.

Chapter 5

(1) Hunter mixed several observations into this paragraph. The "immense vale running nearly north to south" alludes to the area between the Manzano Mountains and the Rio Grande, a scene still dramatic to travelers coming west out of Abo Pass.

(2) Founded in 1629, the Mission of San Gregorio de Abo was also the site of a pueblo of 2,000 Indians. A combination of drought and Apache raids caused the mission to be abandoned before 1680. It is located approximately ten miles west of Mountainair, New Mexico. Adolph Bandelier wrote that "the site is quite romantic. Cliffs of red sandstone rise along the little brook, crowned by clusters of pines, cedars, and junipers." Abo is northeast of Scholle, New Mexico. Adolph F. A. Bandelier, *Final Report of Investigations Among the Indians of the Southwest United States, Carried on Mainly in the Years from 1880 to 1885* (Cambridge University Press, 1892), II, 270.

Hayes wrote: "The town was on a hill, at the foot of which flows a rock-bed stream of pure water, lined by the broad-spreading bitter cottonwood, whose branches bend low down and almost hide the stream. One involuntarily remarks, 'a most beautiful spot!'" Hayes, *Pioneer Notes*, 26.

(3) McSwain's train apparently totaled only three wagons since Hunter's train comprised 22 wagons at Quarai (see note 16, Chapter Three). In September, McSwain's group joined with Powell's train. Powell, *The Santa Fe Trail*, 112.

(4) Powell was a member of Turner's train and had been off guard duty about an hour when the stampede occurred: "As my station had been at the mouth of the corral I was well satisfied [that] they [ie. the cattle] did not start an hour or so earlier. With much trouble we succeeded in getting the greatest part back again, but 25 are still out . . ." He killed a large rattlesnake found in the corral the next morning and assumed the presence of the snake had sparked the stampede. Powell, *The Santa Fe Trail*, 89–90.

(5) Hunter was unaware that *salado* is a Spanish word denot-

ing salty or brackish qualities. Froebel described the site in 1852 as "a saltish and alkaline brook . . . called '*Salado*' (the Saltish), designating the quality of its waters." Froebel, *Seven Years' Travel*, 302–303.

The site appears on modern maps as Cañon Salado, northwest of Scholle, New Mexico.

(6) Dripping Springs is located two miles west of Scholle, New Mexico. A Forty-Niner recorded in his journal that the water at Dripping Springs had "a disagreeable sweet taste and the grass is coarse and not good. These dripping springs fall from high rocks in a canon. The scenery here is very grand. The mountains are of such a variety of form and size. This country is beautiful to look at and it is healthy, but with some few exceptions on the little water courses, it is a barren waste." Stevens, "Anonymous Journal," entry for August 16, 1849.

(7) Hudgins, a member of Gulley's train, wrote that the emigrants had feared a stampede because the cattle were well rested and fat from the long stay at Quarai. They found thirty of their cattle the next day "badly used up, many lame from running over the rocks. We yoked and chained them up from this time on and picketed them." Hudgins, "California in 1849," 8–9.

(8) The town is known today as La Joya, located in Socorro County, New Mexico. Although the village appeared as La Joya de Ciboletta on contemporary maps, the proper name was Sevilleta, founded in 1598. The settlement was named New Sevilla, but because of its small size the diminutive "Sevilleta" came into common use. Zebulon Pike described the village in 1806 as "a regular square, appearing like a large mud wall on the outside," with the doors and windows of the apartments facing inward towards a common square. He also thought that the village was "the neatest and most regular village I have yet seen [in New Mexico]." It was an important village on the Camino Real, the last town encountered by parties heading south, or as Pike phrased it, "we now entered the wilderness." Donald Jackson (ed.), *The Journal of Zebulon Montgomery Pike* (Norman: University of Oklahoma Press, 1966), vol. 1, 407.

Cooke had trouble with the name "La Joya de Cibolleta," which he translated literally as the " 'jewel of a little bull' or 'little buffalo'," and added, "I consider it an outlandish name; there must be a little tale to it . . . but perhaps it should be spelled Cebolletta, the little onion!" Philip St. George Cooke, *The Conquest of New Mexico and California* (New York: G. P. Putnam's Sons, 1878), 77; Bandelier, *Final Report*, II, 238–39.

(9) The spelling La Joyita appeared on most maps of the period, and Powell wrote that the village, two miles south of La Joya, looked "quite picturesque, placed on the immediate river bottom, the bluffs encircling it, and interspersed with Cottonwood and fruit trees. Here we got some more grapes and vegetables; corn, peas, beans and onions." Powell, *The Santa Fe Trail*, 93.

Davis estimated that the town had a population of 400 people in 1854. Davis, *El Gringo*, 360–61.

(10) A visitor in 1851 described Lemitar as "a thriving town of some 300 souls . . . This place is situated in a most beautiful portion of the valley." Lansing B. Bloom (ed.), "The Rev. Hiram Walter Read, Baptist Missionary to New Mexico," *New Mexico Historical Review*, 17 (April 1942):134.

(11) Sabino was surrounded by a high adobe wall, hence the "square pile of buildings."

(12) A reference to Manuel Armijo, the last Mexican governor of New Mexico.

(13) Socorro, founded in 1816, was an important trading center and stopping place for caravans traveling the Rio Grande Valley. In 1851 a traveler wrote that "The Whole valley in the vicinity [of Socorro] is very fertile, producing most of the grain and fruits of the country. Grapes and peaches are raised in great abundance. Indeed, this is one of the very best portions of New Mexico." Bloom, "The Rev. Hiram Walter Read," 135.

A detachment of troops garrisoned the town from 1848 to 1851. Robert W. Frazer (ed.), *New Mexico in 1850: A Military View* (Norman: University of Oklahoma Press, 1968), 162.

(14) Powell described San Antonio as a new settlement,

only about three years old, and "a miserable looking place."
Powell, *The Santa Fe Trail*, 96.

San Antonio marked the Forty-Niner's departure from the established route, which crossed the river below the town and followed the Jornada del Muerto, a ninety-mile trek over level land, but one on which water was usually difficult to find. According to Pike, the Jornada del Muerto took two days to cover, while the road along the Rio Grande took five days to reach the point at which the Jornada came out on the river. Jackson, *The Journal of Zebulon Montgomery Pike*, vol. 1, 408.

The road on the west bank of the Rio Grande, which had been used by Kearny and Cooke in 1846, passed over numerous ravines and sandhills, though water could always be obtained. Chamberlin described the road in June 1849 as "nothing but a trail to follow, and it would be impossible for wagons to get along here." By August, continual use must have improved the track somewhat. Chamberlin, "From Lewisburg," 152; see also William H. Emory, *Notes of a Military Reconnaissance from Fort Leavenworth . . . To San Diego, in California* (Washington, D.C.: Wendell and Van Benthuysen, 1848) [30th Cong., 1st Sess., Ex. Doc. No. 41], 52–55.

(15) "Camino Real" is a common term in the Southwest, which refers to a road built with public funds. In New Mexico the term referred to the main caravan route from Santa Fe, New Mexico, to Ciudad Chihuahua and the interior of Mexico. Max L. Moorhead, *New Mexico's Royal Road: Trade and Travel on the Chihuahua Trail* (Norman: University of Oklahoma Press, 1958), 106.

(16) El Paso del Norte, known today as Ciudad Juárez, Mexico, was the center of extensive vineyards and the source of most of the wine consumed in New Mexico. Known locally as "Pass Wine," Gregg described it as "a very pleasant wine, somewhat resembling Malaga." Gregg, *Commerce of the Prairies*, vol. 2, 77.

In 1853, a trade publication estimated that over 200,000 gallons of wine were produced at El Paso. At a price of two dollars per gallon, it constituted a major source of revenue. A traveler wrote that "The El Paso wines are superior in richness and flavor and pleasantness of taste to anything of the kind I ever met with in the United States." J. D. DeBow, *The Industrial Resources, Etc., of the Southern and Western States* (New Orleans: DeBow's Review, 1853), vol. 3, 476.

(17) Hunter's "Table Mountain" was Mesa de La Contadero, located on the east bank of the Rio Grande, across from San Marcial, New Mexico. During the Civil War, Fort Craig was approximately 2.5 miles to the south, and the mesa was on the southern edge of the Valverde battlefield. See David P. Perrine, "The Battle of Valverde, New Mexico Territory, February 21, 1862," *Journal of the West*, 19 (October 1980):26–38.

(18) Hunter's group traveled up Nogal Canyon.

(19) The mound is near the boundary between Socorro and Sierra Counties. Emory mentioned it in his report: "A butte is seen in the distance, close to the river, and surrounded by trees, which was first taken for an adobe house, but the near approached showed it [to be] a conglomerate cemented by lime, which had been left standing when the surrounding earths were washed away." Emory, *Notes of a Reconnaissance*, 55.

(20) The Fra Cristobal mountain range, along the east bank of the Rio Grande, separated the Jornada del Muerto from the river. According to local legend, the range received its name from a peak on the northern end whose weathered lines were said to resemble the profile of a Franciscan friar. Davis, *El Gringo*, 370–71.

(21) Most Forty-Niners found the water of the Rio Grande unappetizing and considered it unhealthful. Chamberlin wrote: "We are forced to use the water of the Rio Grande, which would be excellent if filtered; the current carries a great quantity of sand with it, which makes the water dirty." Powell noted that "The smell of the [river] bottoms is very unpleasant, the water is execrable. I never saw a more unamiable and unpleasant river." Chamberlin, "From Lewisburg," 152; Powell, *The Santa Fe Trail*, 103.

(22) Probably Palomas Creek. Kearny's men left the Rio

Grande at this point and rode westward to the headwaters of the Gila River on his march to California. Emory, *Notes of a Reconnaissance,* 57.

(23) San Diego Peak was a well-known landmark on the east bank of the Rio Grande which marked the southern end of the Jornada de Muerto and also a major river crossing. Gregg, *Commerce of the Prairies,* vol. 2, 72.

(24) Probably Seco Creek, which now empties into Caballo Reservoir.

(25) Probably Las Animas Creek.

(26) Probably Percha Creek, which now empties into the southern end of Caballo Reservoir. Hunter's group was not the only train to name the creek. Brainard's party named it "Amber Creek": "This afternoon we encamped near a beautiful stream, clear as a crystal. It did our eyes good to once more behold a pure stream of water." Brainard, "Journal," entry for September 8, 1849.

(27) The five trains were probably Turner's, Gulley's, Jackson's, Tisdale's, and the Peoria Train. Thus at this point there were in close proximity six trains (including Hunter's), five of which were composed mainly of Missourians. Powell, *The Santa Fe Trail,* 101–104.

Chapter 6

(1) The messenger apparently headed for Turner's train, of which Powell was a member. He wrote that: "We saw a man coming toward us on a mule at full gallop," to inform Wigginton's aunt, a Mrs. Jones, that her nephew had been badly wounded. She and her husband went to Hunter's train to assist. I have used Hunter's spelling of the victim's last name. Powell spells it "Wiginton." Powell, *The Santa Fe Trail,* 105.

(2) On September 3, Powell wrote: "The greater part of Berry's Train passed us. They have left the wounded man, his opponent and 6 wagons [McSwain's train] . . . I found Wiginton, who is a fine looking young man, lying on his back in a tent, in

great distress, senses wandering, and his eyes expressing a deep, wild anxiety. He seems to suffer acutely . . . Gadson was lying in the sun near the tent, where he could hear every groan of his victim. He had a large log chain round his legs, and seemed very indifferent. He has a bad countenance; in fact, he is a truculent, ill-looking fellow."

Powell recorded a version of the incident told him by several people: "Wiginton's waggon, being the head one, was ordered to stop by the Captain at a certain time; the order was obeyed. Gadson wanted to move on, I believe. This led to some words. Finally Gadson jumped into his waggon and got out his gun, stepping out on the other side. Wiginton jumped over the tongue, wrestled the gun from him, struck him with it and nearly knocked him down. Gadson ran along the line of waggons calling for another gun. Then Gadson's brother went up to Wiginton and took hold of the gun, on which Wiginton asked him if he intended to take up the quarrel. He replied no, but said something about Wiginton paying for the gun if he broke it, upon which Wiginton gave up the gun and told Gadson's brother to put it away. At this moment Gadson himself rushed up behind and stabbed Wiginton in the back with his bowie knife." Powell, *The Santa Fe Trail*, 106–107.

(3) Wigginton died that evening and was buried. Brainard's train came upon the grave on September 9: "It was on an eminence overlooking the Rio Grande on the left, and the road on the right. A plain board was his tombstone. . . . He was about 25 years of age, of robust constitution. By the blood on some of the bedding which had been left, we came to the conclusion that he had died of some wound." Brainard, "Journal," entry for September 9, 1849.

(4) Hunter's group turned westward between Garfield and Hatch, New Mexico, and ascended a bench to pick up Cooke's road. Most Forty-Niners were glad to leave the Rio Grande as the route south of Socorro had been difficult and exhausting, punctuated by bad roads and bad water. Simmons wrote that "The last hundred miles of our road down the river brought us through a barren, desolate looking section of country which we were all glad

to escape from, and while we are confident that we can have nothing worse ahead of us, we will hope for something better." Simmons, "Notes of Travel," entry for September 3, 1849.

(5) San Diego Peak, approximately ten miles southeast of Hatch, New Mexico, marked a major ford on the Rio Grande (see Note 23, Chapter Five). Travelers proceeding northward crossed the river at the base of the peak and then continued up the west bank for twenty miles before turning westward onto Cooke's road. John Russell Bartlett, *Personal Narrative of Explorations and Incidents in Texas, New Mexico, California, Sonora, and Chihuahua* (New York: Appleton & Co., 1854), vol. 1, 215–17.

(6) Cooke named the spring in honor of Dr. George B. Foster, a member of his staff, and wrote that "The water is about 100 feet lower than the camp, in a rocky chasm, difficult of descent for the animals. The chief supply is a natural rock-bound well, thirty feet in diameter, and twenty-four feet deep. It contains 55,000 gallons. Many feet below it are two smaller holes, which the animals can get at two or three at a time." Philip St. George Cooke, *Journal of the March of the Mormon Battalion* (Washington, D.C.: Senate Document, Special Session, 1849), 16.

Hayes described the spring as simply: "a little cove to the right of the road." Hayes, *Pioneer Notes*, 39.

The "Proposed Road" is a reference to a notation on Cooke's map. His command traveled around the southern edge of Cooke's Peak, and he speculated that a pass north of the peak might be practical for a shorter road. Cooke's Peak is eighteen miles northeast of Deming, New Mexico.

(7) This is Cooke's Spring, near the entrance of Cooke's Canyon, six miles northwest of Florida, New Mexico. He probably called it "Mud Springs" because the emigrant's livestock often stirred up the loose dark soil around the springs and polluted the water. Frobel, *Seven Years Travel*, 478.

Cornelius C. Cox, a Texas argonaut, wrote that "The spring is situated in a low marshy place, and the water is bad. There is no wood here of any kind and the grass is more indifferent than we have had since leaving the River." He added that the road from the Rio Grande to the spring was "the finest I ever saw. Water plenty and at convenient distances." Cornelius C. Cox, "From Texas to California in 1849: Diary of C. C. Cox," [edited by Mabelle Eppard Martin], *Southwestern Historical Quarterly,* 29 (1925–26), 135.

A Butterfield Overland Mail stage station was later built near the spring. In 1862, Fort Cummings was established at the site. Margaret B. and Roscoe P. Conkling, *The Butterfield Overland Mail, 1857–1869* (Glendale, CA: Arthur H. Clark Company, 1947), vol. 2, 113–16.

(8) Powell wrote on September 5: "Mr. McSwain went from here with the prisoner Gadson to take him on to Berry's Train and see what was best to be done with him. Their train [i.e., McSwain's] is so small that they do not like to take [the] responsibility of punishing him, and we do not choose to be mixed with it in any way." Powell, *The Santa Fe Trail,* 110.

(9) The Mimbres River flows south out of the Black Range and across the plain for about forty miles in present-day Luna County, New Mexico, before sinking into the sand. Cooke described it as "a fine, clear, bold stream, and is in places fringed with trees . . . a pleasant campground." Cooke, *Journal,* 19.

Bartlett wrote in 1852: "Great was our disappointment, after the anticipation we had indulged in, at finding nothing but a diminutive stream from ten to twenty feet in width, and in some places even less. . . ." The watercourse was a welcome sight nevertheless: "Its water was soft and delightful to the taste, surpassing that of the Rio Grande." Bartlett, *Personal Narrative,* vol. 1, 222.

Hunter's train reached the Mimbres at a point approximately twenty miles northwest of Deming, New Mexico.

(10) Hunter did not state what the punishment was, but a description was included in Powell's account of the affair: "In the evening Berry's Train . . . empaneled a Jury, chose a Judge and Sheriff, appointed Counsel, etc., and tried William Gadson for killing William Wiginton. The testimony modified the affair

some from what I had heard it was. It was, however, still sufficiently atrocious to have subjected him in any State in the Union, I think, to the Penitentiary for life. The Jury sentenced him to have 50 lashes and to be expelled from the Train. This was all the penalty they deemed necessary for stabbing a man in the back. Comment is needless." Powell, *The Santa Fe Trail*, 113.

Powell had stated (see Note 8) that his train did not want anything to do with the matter. The emigrants probably feared being held accountable for murder if they executed Gadson, as they had no legal authority to enforce death sentences.

(11) Powell witnessed the punishment: "I saw a little knot of men a short distance down the Mimbres. On enquiring I learnt it was on [account] of putting the sentence in execution against Gadson. Was somewhat surprised at the privacy of the concern, publicity being a part of the punishment as I had understood, but I suppose they wished to save the poor lamb's feelings as much as possible. The punishment was inflicted by a sick man, or rather a very weak one just recovering from sickness. The instrument was a willow switch. Said the poor sufferer, 'Hit me a little lower!' or 'Hit me a little higher!' and again, 'Stop now! And let us rest at that awhile!' The so-called Sheriff accommodated himself to the request of the amiable and much abused man in every instance; for which kindness and lenity the prisoner threatened to shoot him as soon as he was cast loose. Who can hear this and not—but no, as I said before, comment is needless." Powell, *The Santa Fe Trail*, 113.

The murderer disappears from the historical record at this point and his ultimate fate is unknown. Two vague mentions, however, offer a tantalizing suggestion as to what may have followed after Gadson was expelled from the train. Pancoast was in the area at the time and in his memoirs mentions a man he terms the "Missouri Homicide" following his train, camping near it at night. The man offered to pay for someone in the train to carry his baggage to California, but when local Mexicans informed the emigrants that he had been expelled from another train for murder, the train members refused to allow him to join. They warned the man not to follow them, though apparently he did. Pancoast, *Quaker Forty-Niner*, 226–7.

The next mention is a floating item in the *Fulton Telegraph* the following year which notes that a "William Gatson," charged with the murder of "William Wiginton [while] crossing the plains of New Mexico," was being turned over to authorities in San Francisco. Given the phonetic spelling of proper names common in the diaries and journals, it is possible that this Gatson is the same person Hunter lists as Gadson. If so, Gadson apparently followed along with other trains to California, news of his crime accompanied him, and he was arrested. *Fulton Telegraph*, May 24, 1850, p. 1, col. 3.

(12) "Rock Creek" does not appear on modern maps and was probably a branch of West Antelope Draw.

(13) Hunter refers to Ojo de Vaca, a prominent landmark on Cooke's map, located in Luna County, three miles east of the Grant County line. Powell was not impressed by the spring and called it "a second edition of mud springs [i.e. Cooke's Spring]; a little better perhaps, but not much." Another Forty-Niner wrote on September 6: "Here we find good grass and water middling to drink but, with difficulty, we get enough for our stock. Here is a swamp around the spring. The mud is black and the water in the swamp has a bad smell." A few years later, Bartlett wrote: "This spring is but a depression in the plain surrounded by a couple of acres of grass, resembling an oasis in a desert." Powell, *The Santa Fe Trail*, 114; Stevens, "Anonymous Diary," entry for September 6, 1849; Bartlett, *Personal Narrative*, vol. 2, 243.

The "copper mines north of us" refers to the open-pit mines at Santa Rita, twelve miles east of Silver City, New Mexico.

(14) Ben Moore is located at the southern end of the Burro Mountains, between Lordsburg and Deming, New Mexico. It marked the point at which Cooke's road turned southwest towards Guadalupe Pass. Emory described the point as "a formidable bluff of trap, running northwest and southeast." He named it in honor of Ben Moore, a captain in the First Dragoons and a member of Kearny's army, who later died at the battle of San Pasqual in

California. The hill's name changed to Soldier's Farewell in 1856, supposedly in reference to a detachment of soldiers on their way to garrison Arizona. From the look of the wild, empty land, it appeared as if they were going into exile. Emory, *Notes of a Reconnaissance,* 58; Conkling, *Butterfield Overland Mail,* vol. 2, 124–5.

Cox reached the site on August 6, termed it "Cluster Springs," and wrote that "there are twenty or thirty springs here within an area of one or two acres—the water has a slightly sulphury smell but is clear, very cold and good tasted." Cox, "From Texas," 136.

The springs in the area were often dry, which is why Hunter's party was unable to find water. The one member of his party who located water at the north end of the hill probably happened upon Hawk Spring, renamed Ojo de Ynez by Bartlett.

(15) Hunter describes an ocotillo, a thorny plant common in the Southwestern desert.

(16) A reference to Cooke's map which shows a dotted line from Ben Moore directly westward to the San Pedro River, with the notation: "Believed by Mr. [Antoine] Leroux [one of Cooke's guides] to be an open prairie & a good route if water is sufficient." At least one Forty-Niner company, that of Robert Eccleston, took this route. It later became the major road through this area, known variously as the Stein's Pass or Apache Pass route.

(17) Apparently Hunter meant that their train resumed travel without having resupplied with water because the person who discovered the spring at Ben Moore returned too late for them to take advantage of it.

(18) Powell's party considered this stretch of road to be a jornada of forty miles. Like Hunter's group, they had failed to fill their water kegs before starting out. "This was a bad business," Powell wrote. "And turn back is a thing never ever hinted on a journey like ours." Fortunately it rained in the afternoon, and both groups were able to water their livestock from rainwater pools. Powell, *The Santa Fe Trail,* 115.

(19) Hunter refers to a pass through the Coyote Hills, in

Grant County, New Mexico. Another Forty-Niner described it as "a small mountain pass where we find a small hole of muddy water. Some few buckets full were obtained, but none to give our stock, save one or two head." Stevens, "Anonymous Diary," entry for September 8, 1849.

(20) Playas Lake, a prominent landmark on Cooke's map, is about fourteen miles long and a mile or so wide. Bartlett described the playas as "a long white streak," and added, "the surface of this dry bed was an indurated clay, so hard that the wheels of our wagons scarcely made an impression." Bartlett, *Personal Narrative*, vol. 1, 246.

Another Forty-Niner described the lake bed as "a level surface like a brick yard floor, with here and there a shallow pond of very muddy water, almost as thick as common paint. Tho' in the distance it looked like beautiful ponds or small lakes of clear water." Stevens, "Anonymous Diary," entry for September 8, 1849.

(21) Probably Whitmire Canyon, a pass through the Animas Mountains, located twenty miles northwest of Cloverdale, New Mexico.

(22) "Quicksand Creek" is known today as Animas Creek, in Hidalgo County, New Mexico.

Chapter 7

(1) Possibly Cloverdale Creek, in Hidalgo County, New Mexico.

(2) The Janos road connected the copper mines at Santa Rita, in the Gila Mountains, with the presidio of Janos in northwestern Chihuahua, Mexico. Max L. Moorehead, *The Presidio: Bastion of the Spanish Borderlands* (Norman: University of Oklahoma Press, 1975), 21. See also Note 13, Chapter 6.

(3) Guadalupe Pass is a rugged descent of 1,400 feet from the Animas Valley westward to the San Bernardino Valley. It was the only practical point for wagons to pass through the mountains for fifty miles to the north or south. The pass is located near the

junction of New Mexico, Arizona, and Mexico. There is some confusion in the overland literature as to the pass's exact location. According to the USGS topographic maps, the eastern approach to the pass begins in New Mexico three miles from the Arizona border and, once the descent is made, continues for several miles as Guadalupe Canyon until the San Bernardino River is reached just south of the Arizona-Sonora border. The Guadalupe Pass area is described in the *Report of the Boundary Commission Upon the Survey and Re-Marking of the Boundary Between the United States and Mexico West of the Rio Grande, 1891–1896* (Washington, D.C.; Government Printing Office, 1898), vol. 1, 18, 187.

While Hunter was enamored with the scenery, most Forty-Niners found the pass and canyon rough going. Louisiana Strentzel, member of a Texas train, described the route through the pass as a "tremendous bad road," sixteen miles long, and recalled: "We had to back our wagons seventy times in going six miles." Asa B. Clarke, member of a different Texas train, wrote: "I never once dreamed that an eight mule team, with a large wagon, could be got over such mountains, and across such difficult ravines. I do not believe that Hannibal carried his baggage into Italy by a more difficult mountain passage." "The Letter of Louisiana Strentzel," dated December 10, 1849, in Kenneth L. Holmes (ed.), *Covered Wagon Women* (Glendale, CA: Arthur H. Clark Co., 1983), vol. 1, 255; Asa B. Clarke, *Travels in Mexico and California* (Boston: Wright & Hasty's Steam Press, 1852), 74.

(4) A reference to Cooke's account of his difficulties in finding a route through the mountains. Cooke and his main group followed a narrow path and found themselves in difficult country, while Dr. Foster discovered an old wagon road to Guadalupe Pass. Cooke retraced his steps and followed Foster's route. Cooke, *The Conquest,* 136–7.

(5) The "Rio Huaqui" is more commonly spelled Rio Yaqui. Hunter's party probably crossed the Rio San Bernardino, a tributary of the Yaqui. He used the latter name as it was the only one that appeared on Cooke's map for that section of the road.

(6) The San Bernardino Ranch was on a mesa that over-

looked the surrounding countryside for many miles. The Spanish government maintained a presidio there from 1775 to 1780, and in 1821 a large cattle ranch was founded upon the site. The area was subject to numerous Apache raids and the settlers abandoned the ranch in the early 1830s, reportedly leaving behind 80,000 head of cattle. A member of the 1891 border survey commission described the area as "flat and marshy, covered with grass, and has several springs of good water, also a number of quite large pools." Moorhead, *The Presidio*, 71, 81; *Report of the Boundary Commission*, vol. 1, 187.

Cooke described the site in 1846 as "a ruined ranch, with buildings enclosed by a wall, with regular bastions. It overlooks a wide, flat and rich valley, watered by a noble spring, which runs into one of the upper branches of the Huaqui River." Bartlett reported that the adobe walls enclosed two acres of land. Philip St. George Cooke, "Report of Lieut. Col. P. St. George Cooke of His March From Santa Fe . . . [to] Upper California," in Emory, *Notes of a Military Reconnaissance, From Fort Leavenworth . . . to San Diego . . .* (Washington, D.C.: Wendell and Van Benthuysen, 1848) [30th Cong., 1st Sess., Ex Doc No 41], 555; Bartlett, *Personal Narrative*, vol. 1, 255–56.

The site is approximately eighteen miles east of Douglas, Arizona.

(7) The wild cattle were descended from the stock left behind when the ranches in the area were abandoned in the 1830s. Cooke's description of the cattle made them a sought after attraction on the southern route, both for sport and for food. Bartlett reported that "these herds were small, not more than six each, led by a stately bull." Over-hunting by Mexicans, Indians and emigrants led to the extinction of the herds by 1854. Bartlett, *Personal Narrative*, vol. 2, 256; Larry D. Christiansen, "The Extinction of Wild Cattle in Southern Arizona," *Journal of Arizona History* 29 (Spring 1988): 89–100.

(8) Hunter apparently obtained a gila monster, a large lizard common in the southwestern deserts.

(9) "Blackwater Creek" is known today by its Spanish equiv-

alent, Rio Agua Prieta, which denoted the dark muddy water which surges through it after rainstorms. It is an intermittent watercourse; in May 1851, Bartlett reached the creek and "found only a dry ravine without a drop of water. . . . Not a tree was near us, and every thing around had a most forbidding aspect." When he returned to the area in August 1852, he found the ravine filled with water from recent rains. Bartlett, *Personal Narrative*, vol. 1, 257; vol. 2, 326.

(10) The term "Coyetero Trail" appears on Cooke's map and is named after the Coyotero Apaches of the Western Apache group.

(11) The Mexican soldiers were part of an expedition commanded by José María Elías, Commandant General of Sonora. On September 22, 1849, Elías's main force was at Fronteras, Sonora, approximately fifty miles southeast of Hunter's position on the San Pedro River. Hunter's party probably encountered the detachment from the Tucson presidio, under the command of Captain Antonio Comaduran, which totaled sixty soldiers and twenty packers. The well-educated officer they spoke with was probably Lieutenant Colonel Jose Ignacio Terán y Tato.

Pancoast's train also saw the Mexican column and wrote: "There came over the Mountain a Company of Mexican cavalry, armed with long Swords, wearing sugar-loaf caps of leather adorned with Crow or Rooster feathers or old Revolutionary cockades, blue coats with brass buttons (many of which were missing) and Pants too short for them, and riding miserable Bronco Horses; altogether bearing much resemblance to Don Quixote's Company." Pancoast, *Quaker Forty-Niner*, 233.

Elías's column rendezvoused with Comaduran's on the San Pedro River, and the combined force rode north and swept the San Pedro Valley. Finding no Indians, Elías's force turned south and marched through the Guadalupe Pass and on up the road towards Ben Moore Peak. The Mexicans fought several skirmishes with Indian bands on October 13–15, killing in all eleven Apaches and suffering a loss of four soldiers and one Indian scout. Elías's force also captured four Indians and freed four female captives. John Nugent, member of a Texas train, witnessed the return of the soldiers after the skirmish and wrote that the former captives "were absolutely idiotic from the blows, starvation, and brutality to which they had been subjected." He noted nine pairs of ears, taken from the Apache dead, nailed to an artillery carriage. John Nugent, "Scrapes of Early History," *The Argonaut* (San Francisco) vol. 2, no. 11 (March 23, 1878), 11.

After the skirmishes, Elías's force returned to the main road and met a train led by Jack Hays, of Texas. Elías provided the travelers with guides to show them a direct route to Tucson, which avoided the longer road by way of Guadalupe Pass. The soldiers then marched south to Janos and later returned to Sonora. In all Elías's force totaled 440 soldiers. (From *The Campaign Diary of the Commanding General of Sonora, Don Jose Maria Elias Gonzales While Pursuing Wild Indians, September and October 1849,* compiled by Teodoro Lopez de Aros (microfilm copy on file at the Arizona Historical Society, Tucson). Translation courtesy of Diana Hadley and Dr. James Officer, University of Arizona).

The adventures of Jack Hay's party are recounted by Robert Eccleston in *Overland to California on the Southwestern Trail, 1849* [ed. by George P. Hammond and Edward H. Howes], Berkeley and Los Angeles: University of California Press, 1950 (see also note 16, chapter 6).

(12) The San Pedro River flows northward from Sonora to the Gila River. In 1892 the Boundary Commission described the river in the area of the Arizona-Sonora border as "a stream of about 15 feet in width and 6 or 8 inches in depth, fringed by a fine growth of cottonwood and willow." *Report of the Boundary Commission,* vol. 1, 19.

Forty-Niner perceptions of the San Pedro, as with any other geographical feature, varied. Brainard's and Simmons's trains both reached the river on October 3, and each man recorded a different impression. Simmons described the San Pedro as "a pretty stream of clear, sparkling water, with pebbly bottoms." Brainard wrote that "We were disappointed in finding it nothing but a small creek with an extensive marsh." Simmons, "Notes of

Travel," and Brainard, "Journal," both entries for October 3, 1849.

(13) Possibly the site of Terrenate, a Spanish presidio established in 1741 on the Rio Terrenate, a tributary of the San Pedro. In 1774 the presidio was moved to Las Nutrias, a nearby village, and in 1787 it was relocated on the San Pedro in modern Arizona. Paul M. Roca, *Paths of the Padres Through Sonora*, Tucson: University of Arizona Press, 1967, 81; see also John L. Kessell, "The Puzzling Presidio San Phelipe de Guevavi, Alias Terrenate," *New Mexico Historical Review*, 41 (January 1966): 21–46.

(14) The previous year a battalion of the First U.S. Dragoons, under the command of Major Lawrence P. Graham, left Cooke's road at the San Pedro River and struck westward for the Santa Cruz Valley. This route was shorter than Cooke's to Tucson, and brought travelers into contact with a line of villages in the valley from which they could obtain fresh food supplies.

Graham encountered difficulties in blazing the new trail through the mountains and had to make several attempts before a practical path was found. First Lieutenant Cave Johnson Couts, a discontented subordinate, wrote that Graham was "scorning to follow Cook's trail, Cook's wagon route! We must have a 'Major Graham's wagon route'! . . . winding our way up a Cañada we suddenly butted against an old *he mountain* almost impassable for man or beast. Here the Major was out done." Graham sent ahead to the village of Santa Cruz for guides to show him the proper route. The route to the Santa Cruz was often referred to as Graham's Route, and the pass as Graham's Pass. Cave Johnson Couts, *Hepah, California!* [ed. by Henry F. Dobyns] (Tucson: Arizona Pioneer's Historical Society, 1961), 53.

(15) A Benjamin's Mess refers to the largest portion of a meal.

(16) The village of Santa Cruz was established in the mid-seventeenth century on a mesa on the west bank of the Santa Cruz River. In 1787 it was expanded into a presidio. Powell recorded that "The first view of the town is very beautiful. It is on a rise of land in the centre of the valley," though the town itself "is

an old looking place, very dilapidated; the grama grass growing on the tops of the houses. Two churches, one quite large and ornamented, the other smaller, are quarters for the soldiers." Powell, *The Santa Fe Trail*, 135–36; see also Roca, *Paths of the Padres*, 78.

Clark wrote that the village "is a small, compactly built place; some parts of it in ruins. On each side of the town there is beautiful fertile valley." The village's population was estimated by different travelers to total between three hundred and five hundred people; Hunter's estimate of one thousand is incorrect. Clarke, *Travels in Mexico*, 81.

Santa Cruz experienced a boom in trading with the multitude of passing emigrants. Strentzel noted that "we bought of them peaches, apples, quince, pomegranates, tender green corn, onions and coarse unbolted flour. They had no meat of any kind to sell. The articles that traded best with them were calicos and white domestic. *Covered Wagon Women*, vol. 1, 255.

The town was 5,000 feet above sea level and experienced cool temperatures all year. For most of the Forty-Niners this was their last contact with cool temperatures as they gradually descended to the desert floor. Frank C. Lockwood, *Story of the Spanish Missions of the Middle Southwest* (Santa Ana, CA: Fine Arts Press, 1934), 20–21.

(17) The Santa Cruz River rises in the San Rafael Valley of Santa Cruz County, Arizona, flows south into Sonora, gradually curves around the southern end of the Patagonia Mountains and then flows north, crossing the Arizona border eight miles east of Nogales, and follows the western base of the Santa Rita Mountains. Although the ancient riverbed continues to the Gila River, the Santa Cruz as we know it sinks into the sand well before the Gila, usually between Tubac and Tucson.

The upper reaches of the valley were considered good cattle country, and by 1750 there were approximately one hundred Spanish settlers on ranches west of the village of Santa Cruz. A series of Apache raids in January 1849 drove most of the settlers away and the Forty-Niners recorded several abandoned ranches and missions. Clarke described the Santa Cruz as "one of the most beautiful and fertile valleys in the world, once inhabited by the Mexicans, but now representing a melancholy spectacle of deserted ranchos and fields running to waste. . . . This valley is well adapted for grazing, and is capable of supporting large herds of cattle." Another Forty-Niner wrote that the Santa Cruz was "a very respectable stream for . . . Sonora but which we [would] class no higher than a creek in the U.S." Kieran McCarty, *Desert Documentary: The Spanish Years, 1767–1821* (Tucson: Arizona Historical Society, 1976), 73–74; Clarke, *Travels in Mexico,* 84; Carlo M. De Ferrari (ed.), "The Journal of the La Grange Company," *The Quarterly of the Tuolumne County (Calif.) Historical Society,* 6 (Jan–Mar 1967): 198.

(18) Probably San Lazaro, an early cattle ranch. A church was built at the site in 1706, and the ranch was abandoned in 1845 after Apache raids. Bartlett saw the site in 1851 "The buildings were beautifully situated in the valley, amid a grove of large cotton-woods, in an extensive orchard of peach and quince trees . . ." Roca, *Paths of the Padres,* 77; Bartlett, *Personal Narrative,* vol. 1, 412.

(19) Probably Santa Barbara, an early cattle ranch.

(20) Probably Buenavista, an early cattle ranch also known as San Luis Bacoancos, located two miles south of the present Arizona-Sonora border. The ranch was founded in 1697 and a church built at the site in 1706. The ranch flourished until Apache raids began to discourage the settlers, who left the area between 1765 and 1768. Roca, *Paths of the Padres,* 76; John L. Kessell, *Friars, Soldiers and Reformers: Hispanic Arizona and the Sonoran Mission Frontier, 1767–1856* (Tucson: University of Arizona Press, 1976), 34–35.

Brainard described Buenavista as a "ranch and mining establishment," and noted that the house "was somewhat dilapidated, but still [retained] some of its former grandeur." Brainard, "Journal," entry for October 11, 1849.

(21) Better known as a roadrunner.

(22) Probably Calabassas, site of an Indian village, a church, and a cattle ranch, located near the junction of the Santa

Cruz River and Sonoita Creek, in Arizona. Indian raids caused the abandonment of the settlement. See Bernard L. Fontana, "Calabazas of the Rio Rico," *The Smoke Signal* (Tucson), 24 (Fall 1971):66–87.

(23) San Jose de Tumacacori was established in 1692 and served as the center of Spanish missionary activity in the Santa Cruz Valley. A new church was built in 1822, but after repeated Apache raids little remained when the Forty-Niners passed by. Bartlett wrote that Tumacacori was a "beautiful and picturesque church [which] showed finely among the thick grove of trees by which it was enclosed." Bartlett, *Personal Narrative*, vol. 2, 308; Earle R. Forrest, *Missions and Pueblos of the Old Southwest* (Cleveland, O.: Arthur H. Clark Co., 1929), 247.

(24) A reference to the Stanislaus River, southeast of Stockton, California, a center of gold mining activity.

(25) A *fanega* is a dry measure equal to 1.6 bushels; a *quintal* is a dry measure equal to 200 pounds.

(26) The saguaro cactus, a distinctive plant of the Sonoran desert environment.

(27) More properly known as San Xavier del Bac. Construction of the church may have begun as early as 1776, and was completed in 1797. It was surrounded by a large Papago Indian village. Bartlett described it as a "truly miserable place, consisting of from eighty to one hundred huts, or wigwams, made of mud or straw . . . In the midst of these hovels stands the largest and most beautiful church in the State of Sonora." A Texas Forty-Niner wrote that "This [church] would be considered a pretty building in any part of the world. . . . The town itself is but a poor affair, containing about 6 or 700 inhabitants." McCarty, *Desert Documentary*, 65; Bartlett, *Personal Narrative*, vol. 2, 298; see also Bernard L. Fontana, "Biography of a Desert Church: The Story of Mission San Xavier Del Bac," *The Smoke Signal* (Tucson), 3 (1961); De Ferrari, "The Journal of the La Grange Company," *The Quarterly* 6 (Jan–Mar 1967):198.

(28) An expedition against the Apaches had just returned from a successful sweep of the Arivaipai Valley, sixty miles

northeast of San Xavier. Captain Guadalupe Lunque, of the *Guardia Nacional,* commanded the expedition, which was composed of 130 Papago Indians. Lunque's force attacked three Apache camps, killing twelve Indians and taking twelve children prisoners. (From the "Apache" column of *El Sonorense* (Ures), November 16, 1849. An official report of the expedition is found in Luis Burrell, Justice of the Peace at Tucson, to José de Aguilar y Escoboza, Governor of Sonora, dated Tucson, October 9, 1849. Photocopies of *El Sonorense* courtesy of Dr. James Officer, and of the official report courtesy of Dr. Kieran R. McCarty, University of Arizona.)

The Indians who lived at San Xavier were Papagos, related to the Pimas. Both groups speak the Piman language and inhabit the arid regions of southwest Arizona and northwest Sonora. The Papagos came under the influence of Spanish missionaries, while the Pimas, because of their relative isolation in the Gila Valley, successfully resisted Spanish domination. Both the Pimas and the Papagos depended upon a combination of foraging and irrigation farming for their livelihoods, and considered the Apaches enemies. Alfonson Ortiz (vol. ed.), *Handbook of North American Indians* (Washington, D.C.: Smithsonian Institution, 1983), vol. 10, *passim.*

(29) Hunter described the Papago Scalp Dance. The Papagos took no booty in their retaliatory raids; their only trophies were scalps. The slain enemy's scalp was thought to contain the warrior's magic power, which might be passed on to the victorious Papago warrior. The returning Papago war party timed its march to arrive home at dawn. The Apache trophies (scalps, ears, and occasionally a shirt, moccasin or belt) were tied to a long pole and sent ahead. This pole became the center of their victory celebrations, which lasted sixteen days and were highlighted by nightly dances around the pole. Ruth M. Underhill, *Papago Indian Religion* (Columbia University Press, 1946), 166, 185–87.

These particular celebrations were still in progress on October 13, when Lorenzo D. Aldrich, member of a New York train, reached San Xavier. "Some of our company attended at a war dance they [the Papagos] held last evening over some Apache Indians they had taken prisoner," he recorded in his journal. "I could hear their constant 'pow-wow' all the evening." Lorenzo D. Aldrich, A *Journal of the Overland Route to California & the Gold Mines* [with notes by Glen Dawson] (Los Angeles: Dawson's Book Shop, 1950), 51.

Pancoast also witnessed the scalp dance and identified the wounded child as a girl. His companions offered to trade for her but the Papagos refused. They assured the emigrants that the children would not be killed, as the Papagos intended to make slaves of them. Pancoast, *Quaker Forty-Niner*, 238–39.

Another Forty-Niner recorded that the child was a boy of about 12 or 13 years of age: "[The Papagos] gathered around him and danced and jumped and gave the most hideous yells and fiendish expressions of joy at the capture of their enemies. They jumped the poor child up and down and pressed him. Everyone would catch a lock of his hair as he was jumped up and down, and hold on to it until they cut it off with a butcher knife. Then they would throw it up in the air and yell the louder." Stevens, "Anonymous Journal," entry for October 3, 1849.

(30) Hunter's group arrived in time for the Papagos' annual religious celebration of the Feast of Saint Francis of Assisi (observed October 4). The return of the warriors and their prisoners added to the planned festivities.

(31) There are four niches, each with the plaster statue of a female saint.

(32) The figures were lions.

(33) Although it might appear contradictory for Hunter to state that there were Apaches living with the Papagos at San Xavier, Spanish pacification policy for the preceding fifty years had resulted in a large number of Apaches settling peacefully in villages with other Indian tribes and local settlers. They were known as *Apaches mansos* (tame Apaches). The 1835 *census* listed nearly 500 Apaches mansos living near Tucson. James E. Officer, *Hispanic Arizona* (Tucson: University of Arizona Press, 1987), 130, 133.

Hunter is in error as to the presence of Pueblo Indians; the nearest Pueblo tribe was the Hopis, in northern Arizona.

Chapter 8

(1) Tucson was the northernmost settlement in Sonora. Spanish settlers came to the area in 1772, and the site was designated a presidio in 1775. The village's population fluctuated over the years. In 1804, a total of 1,015 soldiers, settlers and Indians were listed in the community; the 1848 census reported 760 inhabitants. McCarty, *Desert Documentary,* 86; Officer, *Hispanic Arizona,* 214.

The town experienced a brisk business in 1849 as most emigrants sought fresh food supplies and replacements for lost livestock. Strentzel recorded that the people of Tucson had for sale "mules, oxen, cows and calves, sheep, green corn, unbolted flour, cheese, grapes and dried beans." *Covered Wagon Women,* I, 256.

Hunter is in error when he states that "Kearny's route" passed through Tucson. Kearny followed the Gila River, far to the north. Cooke's route, which most Forty-Niners departed from at the San Pedro River, entered Tucson from the east.

Nous verrons is French for "we shall see."

(2) The office of *alcalde,* as mentioned earlier, corresponds roughly to the combined functions of a mayor and justice of the peace. By tradition, however, alcaldes were appointed in large communities. In a small village such as Tucson, the head administrative position was *juez de paz* (justice of the peace), which in 1849 was held by Luis Burruel. Officer, *Hispanic Arizona,* 118.

(3) Brainard made a similar observation: "This place [is] not worthy of note." Bartlett provided a more detailed description when he visited in 1852: "The houses of Tucson are all of adobe, and the majority are in a state of ruin. No attention seems to be given to repair . . . as soon as a dwelling becomes uninhabitable, it is deserted." Brainard, "Journal," entry for October 17, 1849; Bartlett, *Personal Narrative,* vol. 2, 296.

(4) The campsite was at the northern edge of the Tucson Mountains, south of Rillito, Arizona. From this point, travelers left the Santa Cruz riverbed and headed towards Picacho Peak, forty miles to the northwest.

(5) The campsite was south of Red Rock, Arizona.

(6) "Holes in the Rocks" was Cooke's notation for the location, and referred to numerous clefts in the rocks at the base of Picacho Peak, which filled with water during heavy rains. The road passed through a two-mile-wide gap between Picacho Peak and the Picacho Mountains; once through the pass, travelers turned northward towards the Gila River.

(7) "Rain Water Pools" was Cooke's notation for the site, located along the eastern slope of the Sacaton Mountains, seven miles northwest of Coolidge, Arizona.

The countryside stood in stark contrast to the green, rolling hills of Callaway County, Missouri, which Hunter's train had left a few months previously. In the margin of his Distance Table, Hunter wrote that "one vast sterile plain, with an occasional isolated peak or short ridge obtruding, stretches from Tucson NW to the Gila. It is a perfectly unbroken level as far as the eye can scan, and its surface is composed of finely pulverized volcanic remains, yielding nothing but a scattered growth of dwarf mezquite and weeds, with an occasional patch of coarse grass. In places of many acres not a vestige of vegetation appears."

(8) Brainard's party reached the Gila River two weeks later, and he wrote that "The width of the river is about fifty yards, with fine, hard banks. It has quite a rapid current, which tends to make the water riley. It has a strong mineral taste, and is not very palatable, but better than the mud pools [previously encountered]." Brainard, "Journal," entry for October 23, 1849.

(9) Pima Indians inhabited the middle Gila Valley, with villages spread out along the banks of the river for twenty miles, to its confluence with the Salt River. The Pimas, and their neighbors to the west, the Maricopas, farmed by means of irrigation. Bartlett reported that: "The villages consist of groups of from twenty to fifty habitations, surrounded by gardens and cultivated

fields." Thomas Antisell, a government geologist, reported in 1854 that "The cultivated ground . . . is fenced around, each field being small, scarcely 150 feet each way." Corn, cotton, pumpkins, melons, and squash were the Pimas' main crops. Bartlett, *Personal Narrative*, vol. 2, 232–33; Thomas Antisell, "Geological Report," in *Reports of Explorations and Surveys to Ascertain the Most Practicable and Economical Route for a Railroad from the Mississippi River to the Pacific Ocean* (Washington, D.C.: Beverly Tucker, 1857), vol. 7, 137.

In the margin of his distance table, Hunter wrote that "The grass tastes strongly of salt and the water in the lagunas about here is very brackish. The Pimos and Marikopas are both desperate thieves. Travelers should keep a sharp look out for their property."

A flourishing trade developed between the Indians and the Forty-Niners. Clarke wrote that the Indians had "for sale frijolas, or beans, flour, penole, salt, tortillas, and molasses, from the fruit of the pitahaya. They would not take money for any thing near its value, but preferred beads, shirts, especially red flannel, pieces of old cloth, &c." Clarke, *Travels in Mexico*, 89.

The Forty-Niners gave varying estimates of the population of the villages. In 1858, there were officially reported to be 4,177 Pimas and 518 Maricopas on their newly established reservation. *Handbook of North American Indians*, vol. 10, 170.

(10) Hunter probably witnessed a curing ceremony.

(11) Travelers recorded various names of the supposed principal chief of the Pimas. Cooke listed Juan Antonio as chief, and Emory credited Juan Antonio Llunas with the honor. The principal Pima chief in 1849 was Culo Azul. Llunas was apparently a Maricopa. Frank Russell, *The Pima Indians*, 26th Annual Report of the Bureau of American Ethnology (Washington, D.C.: G.P.O., 1908) 196.

(12) These baskets are described by Clara Lee Tanner in "Papago Burden Baskets in the Arizona State Museum," *The Kiva*, 30, no. 3 (February 1965), 57–76.

(13) The Maricopas were a Yuman-speaking tribe related to Quechan tribes inhabiting the lower Colorado River Valley. Al-

though the Pimas considered the Yuma Indians enemies, they coexisted peaceably with the Maricopas, who lived in the western portion of the Pima Villages. See Leslie Spier, *Yuma Tribes of the Gila River* (University of Chicago Press, 1933).

(14) Probably William McDaniel, from Hannibal, Missouri, who was traveling with Congreve Jackson's train. McDaniel was active in Missouri politics, had held several elected offices, and served a term in the U.S. House of Representatives. *History of Marion County, Missouri*, 252–3.

Cave Johnson Couts met McDaniel on October 30, 1849, at Yuma Crossing and described him as "a remarkably clever man. . . . He says that he hardly knows himself, that when he left home he was large and fleshy; that now, although he had enjoyed fine health, he is poor and lean, weighing only 240 pounds and that by measurement he had fallen away exactly two feet." William McPherson (ed.), *From San Diego to the Colorado in 1849: The Journal and Maps of Cave J. Couts* (Los Angeles: Arthur M. Ellis, 1932), 53.

(15) The campsite is probably at Maricopa Wells, eight miles north of Maricopa, Arizona. Cooke's troops dug several wells at the site in 1846, and it constituted the last reliable source of water before setting out on the Gila Bend jornada. Bartlett reported that "The water here is found in several holes, from four to six feet below the surface. . . . In some of these holes the water is brackish, in others very pure."

Bartlett camped at the site in June 1852, as he traveled eastward and noted that the grass there was the best his party had encountered since they left a camp at San Isabel, 56 miles from San Diego, California. Thus Hunter's train had passed the last good pasturage for 300 miles, another factor which contributed to the emigrant's demoralization on this portion of the journey. Bartlett, *Personal Narrative*, vol. 2, 211; see also Conkling, *Butterfield Overland Mail*, vol. 2, 170.

(16) The "jornada" here is a reference to the Colorado Desert. The Mexicans were not generally regarded as reliable informants, though some trains gave considerable credence to

such reports. Members of Strentzel's train talked to a group of Mexicans returning from California, in the Gila Bend area. "They gave awful accounts of the road before us," she wrote, "that the way was strewn with dead animals, and that wagons and property of every kind were left on the road all the way through the desert. This news created great alarm amongst the emigrants. We immediately unpacked our wagons and threw out all heavy articles we could possibly dispense with to lighten the load." *Covered Wagon Women*, vol. 1, 256.

(17) The plants Hunter lists are: saguaro (*cereus gigantea*), mesquite (*prosopis juliflora*), and creosote (*larrea divaricata*).

(18) Cooke's road led southwest from Maricopa Wells to a pass between the Sierra Estrella and the Palo Verde Mountains. The Gila Bend jornada was also known as the Forty Mile Desert. Although a difficult stretch of road, particularly with weak livestock, travelers could save at least sixty miles by taking this route rather than following the Gila River as it curved to the northwest.

Chamberlin's party, because of the poor condition of their pack mules, followed the Gila River the whole way and required four days to reach Cooke's road on the other side of the jornada, while some travelers crossed the Gila Bend in twelve hours. Although the travel time might not appear to be significant, most Forty-Niners' livestock were in such poor condition by this point that any way to reduce travel time and conserve their animals' strength was eagerly adopted. Chamberlin, "From Lewisburg," 176.

(19) Hunter refers to the pass between the Sierra Estrella and the Palo Verde Mountains.

(20) The Maricopa Mountains appeared impenetrable to many travelers at first. Bartlett described them as "a mountain range which had long loomed up before us and seemed to present an impassable barrier to our progress; but as we drew near, what appeared at a distance to be continuous now showed many passages through, of easy access, and with an ascent so gradual as to be scarcely apparent. The great mountain chain . . . was in reality a collection of detached ridges and isolated mountains rising

abruptly from the desert. . . . The road was excellent through all the defiles." Bartlett, *Personal Narrative*, vol. 2, 209.

(21) The emigrants rejoined the Gila River north of what is now Gila Bend, Arizona.

(22) Another Forty-Niner wrote an extended account of this incident. On October 10, he wrote that Woods, who was from New York and traveled with Berry's train, traded his wagon for two horses at the village of Santa Cruz. Several Pima Indians recognized one of the horses when Woods visited Stevens' train, headed by Archibald S. RoBards, of Hannibal, Missouri.

Soon more Indians arrived and the emigrants feared an attack. The train numbered about thirty men and they readied their firearms. Finally, RoBards gave the chief a letter to Samuel Berry which summarized the situation and requested that he persuade Woods to surrender the horse. Although the train had divided at San Xavier, the separate groups were apparently still known as "Berry's Train."

The Indians held a dance that night which the emigrants interpreted as a war dance. The next morning, word was received that Woods agreed to surrender the horse, and the crisis passed. The members of RoBards's train never doubted their ability to defend themselves, but they did not want to fight and perhaps kill for a horse they figured was worth only about $45. Stevens, "Journal," entry for October 10, 1849.

(23) Reverend Ira M. Allen was from New York City, and had been a member of the Knickerbocker Company. Grant Foreman, *Marcy and the Gold Seekers* (University of Oklahoma Press, 1939), 329.

(24) A reference to the Painted Rock Mountains. The area is today Painted Rock State Park.

(25) The Yuma (or Quechan) Indians inhabited the lower Colorado River Valley.

Stevens reached the site on October 16, and wrote: "We have passed today good wagons deserted by their owners, excellent trunks, boxes, lead, new ox shoes, coats, vests, pants, sacks, cotton, wool, and hair which had been used for mattresses, in fact, almost everything an emigrant carries except provisions; all done to lighten them, as their oxen and mules are getting poorer and weaker and there is but a poor prospect of ever getting them through." Stevens, "Journal," entry for October 16, 1849.

By October 20, the trains of Moore, Tisdale, Hubbard, Berry, and RoBards were camped in the area. They were all from Missouri and had camped together at Quarai, New Mexico.

(26) A note was posted at the site from which Hunter acquired his information of the incident. The note is reprinted in Eccleston, *Overland to California*, 217.

Hunter discreetly avoids making a comparison between the way the Arkansas train handled the murder and how his own train handled the Wigginton-Gadson affair (chapter 6).

(27) This area is now enclosed in the Painted Rocks State Park. Bartlett visited the spot in 1852, and wrote that it "consisted of a pile of large boulders, heaped up some forty or fifty feet above the plain, and standing entirely alone. Such of these rocks as present smooth sides are covered with sculptures, rudely pecked in, of animals and men, as well as of various figures, apparently without meaning." Bartlett, *Personal Narrative*, vol. 2, 206.

(28) Probably the Agua Caliente Mountains, which today are bisected north to south by the boundary between Maricopa and Yuma counties.

Chapter 9

(1) Camp Starvation was a popular campsite, located about three miles from the confluence of the Gila and the Colorado Rivers. The name appears on Couts' hand-drawn map of the area in 1848, and was retained by later travelers as it described the condition of many emigrants by the time they reached the Colorado River. Couts, *Hepah, California!*, section of maps between pages 46 and 47.

Chamberlin's comments on reaching the Colorado River summed up the feelings of most Forty-Niners after the exhausting trek down the Gila Valley: "we could turn our backs upon the Gila now, with as much pleasure as we first beheld [it], drank and bathed in its cool and limpid waters, which have since gradually changed into a broad, heated, turbid and brackish stream." Chamberlin, "From Lewisburg," 241.

(2) Several tribes speaking Yuman languages inhabited the lower Colorado River Valley and southern California. By the middle of the nineteenth century, the Yuman tribes on the Colorado were the Mohave, the Quechan (Yuma), and the Cocopa. Travelers came into contact with the Quechans at Yuma Crossing. They numbered approximately 3,000 men, women and children. *Handbook of North American Indians*, vol. 10, 1–3.

"Captain" was a term used to denote local Yuma chiefs.

(3) An allusion to the monsoon storms of northern Africa, a popular image among Forty-Niners crossing the southwestern deserts. Chamberlin wrote of a storm his group encountered on the Gila River: "The sand flew in all directions, blinding and almost suffocating us for a time. It must almost have equaled the 'monsoons' of the deserts of Africa." Chamberlin, "From Lewisburg," 175.

(4) Hunter refers to coyotes.

(5) Hunter means that the road continued to the mouth of the Gila River. Kearny, Cooke and Graham crossed the Colorado at a point twelve miles south of the junction of the Colorado and the Gila Rivers. This ford was known to Forty-Niners variously as Kearny's, Graham's, and/or the Lower Crossing. Most Forty-Niners crossed at a point just south of the river junction known as the Upper Crossing. The river was about a quarter of a mile wide and twelve feet deep in the Yuma Crossing area.

The road left the river opposite the Lower Crossing. After crossing the river, the Forty-Niners traveled down the west bank until they reached the Lower Crossing, where they turned west for the Colorado Desert. The crossing sites and the shifting nature of the Colorado River in the Yuma area is illustrated in Don Bufkin, "Geographic Changes at Yuma Crossing, 1849–1966," *Arizona and the West* 26 (Summer 1986), 155–60.

(6) A reference to Cave Johnson Couts, First Lieutenant,

First U.S. Dragoons. He had traveled to California in 1848 with Graham's battalion, and in 1849 commanded the escort for the U.S.-Mexican Boundary Commission surveying party that operated in the Yuma Crossing area.

Many Forty-Niners were pleased to find the troops there. Strentzel wrote: "We had dreaded this river [the Colorado] the whole way for we had heard that several Americans had been killed by the Indians, and that it was [a] dangerous crossing, but gratitude to our Government, a company of soldiers were here for the protection of the emigrants." *Covered Wagon Women*, vol. 1, 258.

The soldiers were there to protect the survey group; they withdrew in December.

(7) Aldrich crossed the river four days earlier, on November 12, and wrote: "Arrived at the river [where] we found about thirty American soldiers stationed, who had a ferry over which they transported emigrants at the following rates: Waggons $4, mules $1, and men $4 . . . It is crossed by means of a rope suspended from either bank, a mode of travel very disagreeable and somewhat dangerous." Aldrich, *A Journal of the Overland*, 58–59.

Not everyone viewed the effort of crossing with dread. A Texas argonaut recorded that their crossing operation "was an exciting time. The bustle & business were very pleasant to mix in after so lone & monotonous a journey, besides which many old acquaintances were met & notes of our travels [and] accidents compared." De Ferrari, "The Journal of the La Grange Company," *The Quarterly* 7 (July–Sept 1967):217.

The ferry was located approximately half a mile south of the confluence of the two rivers.

(8) Clark recorded this description of the area: "Below the junction [of the Gila and the Colorado the river] pass[ed] through a canon about one fourth of a mile long, with walls 50 feet high. On the north side, the mountains rise with several remarkable looking prominences, one of which resembles a round tower. There is a thick growth of willows and cottonwoods, filled up with

canes, vines, and weeds along the bank, through which it is difficult to penetrate." Clarke, *Travels in Mexico,* 105.

(9) Pancoast wrote that the commander at Yuma Crossing, whom he declined to name but who was undoubtedly Couts, claimed that Congress had enacted a tax of 10 percent on all gold being taken out of the United States. It would appear that Couts had no such authority and that his actions amounted to theft and fraud. Couts says little of his "tax-collecting" activities. In an entry for October 24, he mentions the arrival of James Collier, the newly appointed port collector for California. Couts wrote that Collier "directed me to make all the Sonorans passing out of California with gold pay a duty on the same, and for my trouble to put the whole of it in my pocket. Certainly!" Pancoast, *Quaker Forty-Niner,* 255; Couts, *From San Diego,* 47–48.

(10) Couts found the Yumas' "impudence and insolence almost intolerable." Couts, *From San Diego,* 38, 51–53.

(11) A Texas company experienced a similar farewell from the Yumas, their diarist recording on September 2 that, as they passed the last village, "At least 200 men, women & children came out on the road, following us, importuning & annoying us dreadfully." De Ferrari, "The Journal of the La Grange Company," *Quarterly* 7 (July–Sept 1967):218.

(12) A reference to the Algodones Sand Dunes. Travelers headed southwest and then northwest to get around the dunes, which later inhibited construction of highways and railroads through the area.

(13) This was the first well on the jornada, better known as Cooke's Well, located approximately six miles south of the present international border. Mexican soldiers established the well in 1826. Kearny found it a shallow, dry hole in December 1846, and had to dig down farther to find water. Cooke reached the site six weeks later and dug two more wells. Conkling, *Butterfield Overland Mail,* vol. 2, 217.

When Simmons's group arrived they "Found the well nearly dry but by shoveling out a large quantity of sand and waiting some time we got enough to water all the animals with buckets." Simmons, "Notes of Travel," entry for November 25, 1849.

In 1854, William P. Blake, a geologist, recorded that the well "was dug in the clay under a bank or terrace, about thirty feet high. . . . It was also nothing more than a hole scooped out in the clay, and the water was small in quantity and slightly brackish." William P. Blake, "Geological Report," *Reports of Explorations and Surveys,* vol. 5, 111.

Clarke's group was greatly depressed by the desert and after reaching the well he wrote that "[these] are times to try men's souls. Some [of our members] broke out in the most extravagant expressions, declaring that we had lost the way—should never find water—all perish, &c. Others said nothing, but jogged steadily on with a fixed determination to preserve." Clarke, *Travels in Mexico,* 111.

(14) This is the second well, better known as Alamo Mocho, so named after a gnarled cottonwood tree which stood nearby ("mocho" translates from the Spanish as deformed or maimed).

The well was located in the bed of the ancient Alamo River, which flowed only after rainstorms. Once many cottonwoods stood along its banks, but by 1849 only the deformed tree remained and it disappeared by 1858. The well was located approximately six miles south of the international border. Conkling, *Butterfield Overland Mail,* vol. 2, 221–23.

Blake wrote that the well was "dug at the foot of [a] bank, in one of the lowest places, and appears to be in the dry bed of [a] watercourse. . . . The well was about eighteen feet deep, and lined with boards and protected by a low curb. . . . This water was found to be turbid and slightly brackish." He described the surrounding countryside as "peculiarly dreary and desert-like. Quantities of skeletons of cattle and mules, with loose bones and skulls, were lying about in confusion." Blake, "Geological Report," *Reports of Explorations and Surveys,* vol. 5, 109–10.

Simmons wrote after his arrival at the well that "This has been a wearisome day for men and for animals. No firm road any part of the way. Nothing but loose sand into which the feet sink at every step." Simmons, "Notes of Travel," entry for November 26, 1849.

(15) The New River had been a dry ravine when Kearny, Cooke, and Graham passed through the area in 1846 and 1848, and its presence greatly assisted the emigration of 1849. Couts established a base on the river, which he named Camp Salvation, and wrote: "This particular place of the river [in the middle of a desert], favored with such luxuriant grass, can only be the work of an Invisible Hand to aid the thousands of distressed emigrants." Couts, *From San Diego*, 20.

Strentzel concluded that "had it not been for this water [at the New River], the muskite beans [at Yuma Crossing], and the corn at the Pimose village, not one wagon could have come through." *Covered Wagon Women*, vol. 1, 259.

In 1852, a dry year, Bartlett's party found only a ravine "some twenty or thirty feet wide, and about ten feet [deep] that forms the bed of what is known as the 'New River'." Bartlett, *Personal Narrative*, vol. 2, 135.

Augustus M. Helsep happened to be at the New River when Hunter's train arrived. He reported that Hunter's party had suffered "the loss of two wagons between this point and the [Colorado] river, and they abandoned all but three of seven wagons at this point. A portion of the company proceeded through on foot, while the other portion will make an effort to get through on the teams retained." Helsep's letter was reprinted in the St. Louis *Missouri Republican*, January 28, 1850, p. 2.

Thus Hunter's train apparently divided again, this time under the strain of the desert crossing. Hunter traveled with the group which retained the wagons.

(16) A reference to the joint United States–Mexican Boundary Commission, established after the Mexican War to survey the new border between the two nations. Various detachments of the commission, based in San Diego, operated in southern California in 1849. John B. Weller was the American commissioner, appointed by President James K. Polk. While Weller

was in the field Zachary Taylor's administration took office and replaced Weller with John Charles Fremont. William H. Goetzman, *Army Explorations in the American West, 1803–1863* (New Haven: Yale University Press, 1959), 153–67.

(17) By November, the New River consisted of two large lagoons, referred to by the Forty-Niners as the Big and the Little lagoons. Hunter had reached Little Lagoon, located just north of the present international border and west of Calexico, California. Simmons wrote that "The water in all these lakes [lagoons] is alkaline, so much so that we suppose if the animals drink much of it there would be danger of its killing them. We do not drink it." Simmons, "Notes of Travel," entry for December 2, 1849.

The two lagoons were approximately ten miles apart. In dry years, travelers obtained water by digging into the channel between them. This site, about twelve miles north of the international border, was known as Indian Wells, and apparently was where Hunter's party camped on the 25th. Charles H. Poole, a civil engineer, described Indian Wells in 1855: "The water is at a depth of about 30 feet, and is of tolerable quality." Charles H. Poole, "Report Upon the Route," *Report of Explorations and Surveys*, vol. 7, Appendix B, 23.

(18) Hunter breakfasted at Big Lagoon, located near modern Sunbeam Lake, south of Seeley, California.

(19) Hunter refers to the third well, which was located approximately three miles northwest of Plaster City, California, in the streambed of Coyote Wash.

Chamberlin visited the well in August: "It is situated in a large, deep ravine, but the supply of water was so scanty that we could get but a quart apiece for our animals, and none for ourselves. This place is a perfect Golgotha—bones of thousands of animals lie strewed about in every direction; and a great number of carcasses of horses and mules that have died lately pollute the atmosphere. Deserted wagons, harness, saddles, etc., add to this destructive and sickening scene." Chamberlin, "From Lewisburg," 245.

In later years the site became known alternately as Hall's

Well and Sackett's Well, named after two of the managers of a nearby stage station. Conkling, *Butterfield Overland Mail*, vol. 2, 226.

(20) This would be Colonel José María Carrasco. Powell encountered the Mexican column on November 24, and recorded that "We passed Colonel Carrasco's Command and Baggage Train about 2 leagues before we arrived at Rio Nuevo. The mules were very heavy laden . . . many of the poor animals groaned aloud." Powell, *The Santa Fe Trail*, 180.

(21) Nine miles northwest of the third well the road entered a pass between the Fish Creek and the Coyote Mountains, near the boundaries of San Diego and Imperial Counties.

(22) This is Carrizo Creek, an intermittent stream that marked the end of the Colorado Desert. Bartlett wrote that the creek "rises in the very centre of barrenness, flows for about a mile, and is again absorbed by the desert. It has worn for itself a bed about fifteen feet below the plain." Bartlett, *Personal Narrative*, vol. 2, 126–27.

Clarke reached the creek on June 30, and wrote that along the road from the Colorado River to Carrizo they passed numerous carcasses of mules and horses, sometimes thirty or forty a day. Clarke, *Travels in Mexico*, 113.

(23) Powell was in the same area: "we met a Government Train of mules with 3,000 rations under charge of a Mr. Boone going out for the relief of Emigrants." Simmons's train met the relief party at the New River, and recorded that Boone's instructions were to issue half regular army rations "of flour and beef to all the emigrants he meets who are in need of them, enough to last them until they can get to San Diego or Los Angeles." Simmons's group drew half rations for six days and purchased 100 pounds of flour for $25. Powell, *The Santa Fe Trail*, 181; Simmons, "Notes of Travel," entry for November 30, 1849.

Though many Forty-Niners were in bad straits by the time they crossed the Colorado Desert, some could be difficult to aid. Couts records meeting an emigrant who claimed that he and his brother were nearly starved to death and out of food. Couts ordered his cook to give the emigrant four pounds of flour, which the emigrant examined closely and then returned as not good enough. Such experiences were not uncommon and led Couts to exclaim: "The emigrants! Ah! 'Still they come.' I never was in my life so annoyed. To sit and tell them of California . . . is only a pleasure. But then follows begging for sugar, flour, molasses, pork, a little fresh beef, rice, coffee, etc. and God only knows how they have the face to push such entreaties as they do." Couts, *From San Diego*, 13, 22–23.

(24) Hunter is at Palm Springs, described by Cooke as a grove of twenty to thirty palm trees. By 1858 vandals had cut all the palms down and none exist today. "Cabbage Tree" was a common term for palm trees. Cooke, *The Conquest*, 185; E. I. Edwards, *Lost Oases Along the Carrizo* (Los Angeles: The Westernlore Press, 1961), 46.

Blake described the road from Carrizo Creek to Vallecito as "entirely dry and sandy, and almost as forbidding as the [Colorado] Desert. The monotony is broken by a clump of palm trees on the north [side] of the trail, and a green bank from which springs issue, known as the 'Palm Springs'." Blake, "Geological Report," *Reports of Explorations and Surveys*, vol. 5, 122.

(25) Hunter uses contemporary derogatory terms to describe some of his companions. "Green eyed prophets" referred to envious people; "croakers" were chronic complainers. "Seeing the Elephant" was a common expression at the time which implied meeting with defeat, encountering a setback, or becoming disillusioned.

It is interesting that dejection appeared at this point, for Cooke considered the fifteen miles from Carrizo Creek to Palm Springs the worst stretch of road between San Diego and the Rio Grande.

(26) Hunter's "Los Bayacitos" is Vallecito, located midway between Yuma Crossing and San Diego. Cooke listed the site as "Bajiocito," and described it as "a wet swampy valley, with willow bushes, bad rank grass and no fuel." Cooke, *The Conquest*, 185.

Blake wrote that, for people coming from the east, Vallecito was "the first place where grass and vegetation greet the eyes of the traveler who has crossed the dreary Desert. It is a narrow valley between the granite ridges, and is well supplied with springs that are surrounded with grass and willows." Blake, "Geological Report," *Reports of Explorations and Surveys,* vol. 5, 123.

Froebel described Vallecito as "a small green oasis, surrounded on all sides by barren mountains." Froebel, *Seven Year's Travel,* 540.

(27) El Puerto is a narrow pass between the Vallecito and Mason valleys. Couts described the pass as "about 12 or 14 feet wide, perpendicular on either side, and about 2½ miles long." Couts, *From San Diego,* 9.

(28) The Diegueño Indians speak a Yuman language and are related to the Yuma tribes along the Colorado River. The Indians made a poor impression on travelers. Bartlett described the Dieguéños he met in 1852 as a "filthy looking set, half clad and apparently half starved." He added that "They cultivate beans and pumpkins, and pick up an occasional mule, which serves them for food, though their main reliance is upon acorns, which they collect and store up in large baskets for winter use." Bartlett, *Personal Narrative,* vol. 2, 122, 125.

(29) This is the Box Canyon, which Cooke's men widened with shovels and axes for their wagons in 1846. Prior to 1846 the pass was negotiable only by horses and mules. Some of the wagons in Froebel's train barely fit through the narrow defiles and he considered this the worst stretch of road on the southern route since Guadalupe Pass. Bartlett, *Personal Narrative,* vol. 2, 123–24; Froebel, *Seven Years' Travel,* 541.

(30) Bartlett wrote in 1852 that the village of San Felipe consisted of "twenty-three miserable old huts or wigwams built of straw and rushes. Some were covered with raw hides of various colors. A few small patches of ground were cultivated, not exceeding altogether a couple of acres." Bartlett, *Personal Narrative,* vol. 2, 122.

As to the water resources, Simmons wrote: "camped near some fine springs of good, pure water. There is no alkali in this!, and we know now to appreciate such water now if we never did before!" Simmons, "Notes of Travel," entry for December 12, 1849.

(31) The Peoria Train started out from Peoria, Illinois, and underwent several reorganizations as it made its way west. The rigors of the Gila Bend jornada and a growing sense of desperation caused several members to leave the train. Pancoast, a member of the train, wrote that "twelve of our best-equipped Teams (including that of our Leader, Capt. Rogers) started down the River with no explanation to us . . . leaving us all the 'Crippled Ducks' to take care of." Apparently it was Rogers's party that passed Hunter as Pancoast's group did not arrive at San Felipe until mid-December. Pancoast, *Quaker Forty-Niner*, 249.

(32) Oak Grove was a belt of trees near the head of the San Felipe Valley, at the entrance to Warner's Pass (elevation 3,629 feet). Poole, "Report Upon the Route," *Reports of Explorations and Surveys*, vol. 7, Appendix B, 21.

(33) John Trumball Warner (1807–95), was also known in California as Juan José Warner, and as "Juan Largo" in recognition of his height (six feet, three inches). He emigrated to California from Connecticut in 1831, worked as a fur trapper, merchant and rancher, and was active in local politics. In 1844, he received a land grant in the San Jose Valley from the Mexican government, totaling over 44,000 acres. His ranch was in a strategic location on the main road across the Laguna Mountains, and he established a trading post to take advantage of the traffic.

Chamberlin wrote that Warner's Ranch consisted of "a few old adobe buildings and Indian huts, situated at one end of a broad, beautiful valley covered with a fine growth of green grass and timber." Chamberlin, "From Lewisburg," 251–52; see also Joseph J. Hill, *The History of Warner's Ranch and Its Environs* (Los Angeles: Privately Printed, 1927).

Many Forty-Niners were critical of Warner's business practices. Clarke wrote that "Provisions are exorbitantly high, it being the first ranch in California, and travelers arriving from a long distance, and where there is but little opportunity for purchasing food, are sometimes scandalously imposed upon. For beef they asked as high as 20 or 25 cents; horses nearly as high as in the States." Clarke, *Travels in Mexico,* 116.

Cox noted that "Warner has established a grocery & Butchery for the accommodation of the emigrants—and this being the first place at which supplies can be obtained, the emigrant has been subjected to the severest extortion, it being the motto of this semi-savage to 'size the pile' of all who come along." Cox, "From Texas," 207.

Warner, of course, was a businessman and did not establish his ranch to dispense aid and assistance. Couts also expressed frustration in dealing with the demands of the harassed emigrants (see note 22).

(34) Blake wrote that Santa Isabel was "a beautiful valley among the mountains, well watered, and bordered by groves of oak and other timber. . . . Adobe buildings of great size were erected here in the time of the Padres, but are now partly in ruins. They were, however, in part occupied as dwellings and storehouses, the valley being used as a cattle rancho." Bartlett noted that it was once the site of a substantial mission, though a "roofless church and a few miserable huts are now all that remain. Nevertheless, the inhabitants cultivate the soil, and by means of irrigations . . . raise wheat, maize, pumpkins and beans." Blake, "Geological Report," *Reports of Explorations and Surveys,* vol. 5, 126; Bartlett, *Personal Narrative,* vol. 2, 119.

Appendix

William W. Hunter's Distance Table

"Table of Distances as measured by a roadometer attached to a wagon on Dr. N. E. Branham, from Williamsburg, Callaway County, Missouri, via Santa Fe, New Mexico, to California."

Date	Location	Distance (miles)	Cumulative (miles)	Day
April 24	Fulton	16½		I
	Millersburg	11	27½	
	Columbia	12½	40	
	Rockport	13¾	53¾	
	Boonville	10¾	64½	
	Georgetown	35¼	99¾	
	Warrensburg	30	129¾	
	Independence	50	179¾	
	Judge Yager's	19¾	199½	
	Big Blue Creek	2	201½	
	Lone Elm	14	215½	
	Bull Creek	9½	225	
	Willow Spring	19½	244½	
	Rock Creek	12¾	257¼	
	110 Creek	10¾	268	
	Switzler's Creek	7	275	

Appendix

William W. Hunter's Distance Table *(cont.)*

Date	Location	Distance (miles)	Cumulative (miles)	Day
April 24	Wald's Creek	4¼	279¼	1
	142 Creek	11½	290¾	
	Big Walnut Creek	2	292¾	
	Bluff Creek	8½	301¼	
	Big John Creek	11	312¼	
May 21	Council Grove	2½	314¾	28
May 22	Diamond Spring	16	330¾	29
May 23	Lost Spring	15¾	346	30
May 24	Cottonwood Fork	16¾	362¾	31
May 25	Encampment	—	—	32
May 26	Turkey Fork	19	381¾	33
May 27	Little Arkansas	25½	407¼	34
May 28	Little Cow Creek	17½	424¼	35
May 29	Big Cow Creek	2¾	427½	36
May 30	Plumb Buttes	10¾	438¼	37
May 31	Walnut Creek	14	452¼	38
June 1	Ash Creek	20½	472¾	39
June 2	Pawnee Fork	6½	479½	40
June 3	Banks of the Arkansas	18½	497¾	41
June 4	-do-	19	516¾	42
June 5	Big Island	18	534¾	43
June 6	Mann's Fort	15	549¾	44
June 7	Encampment	—	—	45
June 8	-do-	—	—	46
June 9	-do-	—	—	47
June 10	Crossing of Arkansas	25¾	575½	48
June 11	Battle Creek	16¾	591¼	49
June 12	Sand Creek	32	624¼	50
June 13	Cimarron, Lower Spring	11½	635¼	51
June 14	-do-	9	644¼	52
June 15	-do-	22	666¼	53
June 16	-do- , Middle Sprg.	7½	674¼	54
June 17	-do- , Upper Sprg.	28	702¼	55

Appendix

Date	Location	Distance (miles)	Cumulative (miles)	Day
June 18	Cold Spring	18	720¼	56
June 19	Encamped	—	—	57
June 20	Cedar Spring	16¼	736½	58
June 21	Cottonwood Creek	21¾	758¼	59
June 22	Rabbit Ear Creek	13	771¼	60
June 23	Rock Creek	19	790¼	61
June 24	Point of Rocks	21	811¼	62
June 25	Saltpeter Creek	17	828¼	63
June 26	Ocota Creek	10½	838¼	64
June 27	Wagon Mound	19	857¾	65
June 28	Encampment	—	—	66
June 29	-do-	—	—	67
June 30	Branch of Rio Moro	26½	884¼	68
July 1	Encamped	—	—	69
July 2	Las Vegas	19	903¼	70
July 3	Ojo Vernal	17½	920¾	71
July 4	Encamped	—	—	72
July 5	San Miguel	7½	928¼	73
July 6	Ruins of the Pecos	20½	948¾	74
July 7	Encamped	—	—	75
July 8	-do-	—	—	76
July 9	Cottonwood Spring	5	953¾	77
July 10	Great Cañon	6½	960¼	78
July 11	Forks of the Road	6	966¼	79

"The distance computed to Santa Fe is 12 miles, making the distance from Williamsburg to Santa Fe 978¼ miles, and from Independence 798½ miles."

Date	Location	Distance (miles)	Cumulative (miles)	Day
July 11	Galisteo	23½		79
July 12	Encamped	—		80
July 13	-do-	—		81
July 14	-do-	—		82
July 15	Encamped	—	23½	83
July 16	-do-	—	—	84
July 17	Spring on Placea Road	8	31½	85
July 18	San Pedro	22	53½	86

William W. Hunter's Distance Table *(cont.)*

Date	Location	Distance (miles)	Cumulative (miles)	Day
July 19	San Antonitta	3½	57	87
July 20	Encamped	—	—	88
July 21	-do-	—	—	89
July 22	-do-	—	—	90
July 23	-do-	—	—	91
July 24	-do-	—	—	92
July 25	-do-	—	—	93
July 26	-do-	—	—	94
July 27	-do-	—	—	95
July 28	-do-	—	—	96
July 29	Cibolo Springs	22	79	97
July 30	Ojo La Estancia	14	93	98
July 31	Pueblo Quarrá	18	111	99
August 1	Encamped	—	—	100
August 2	-do-	—	—	101
August 3	-do-	—	—	102
August 4	-do-	—	—	103
August 5	-do-	—	—	104
August 6	-do-	—	—	105
August 7	-do-	—	—	106
August 8	-do-	—	—	107
August 9	-do-	—	—	108
August 10	-do-	—	—	109
August 11	-do-	—	—	110
August 12	Ruins of Pueblo Abó	15	126	111
August 13	Dripping Spring	7	133	112
August 14	La Joya de Cibolita	26	159	113
August 15	Joyeta	6	165	114
August 16	Sabino	8	173	115
August 17	Limitar	2	175	116
August 18	Encamped	—	—	117
August 19	Socorro	9	184	118
August 20	Lopez	5	189	119

Appendix

Date	Location	Distance (miles)	Cumulative (miles)	Day
August 21	San Antonio	16	205	120
August 22	River bottom	17	222	121
August 23	Table land west of River	17½	239½	122
August 24	Bank of river	8½	248	123
August 25	Bank of river	4	252	124
August 26	Near the river	12	264	125
August 27	Near the river	10½	274½	126
August 28	Near the river	10½	285	127
August 29	Encamped	—	—	128
August 30	"Berry Creek"	1	286	129
August 31	Near the river	8	294	130
September 1	Encamped	—	—	131
September 2	-do-	—	—	132
September 3	Foster's Hole	11½	311¼	133
September 4	Sulphur Spring	9¼	321	134
September 5	Rio Mimbres	31½	352½	135
September 6	Encamped	—	—	136
September 7	-do-	—	—	137
September 8	Ben Moore Mountain	27½	380	138
September 9	Sink in the prairie	17	397	139
September 10	Las Playas	19	416	140
September 11	Encamped	—	—	141
September 12	Johnson's Creek	20	436	142
September 13	Quicksand Creek	15½	451½	143
September 14	Janos Road, near the commencement of Guadalupe Pass	13½	465	144
September 15	Rio Huaqui	2	467	145
September 16	Western egress of Guadalupe Pass	13	480	146
September 17	San Bernardino	9	489	147
September 18	Center of cañon	9½	498½	148
September 19	Ponds near the road	10	508½	149
September 20	Blackwater Creek	10¼	518½	150
September 21	Spring left of road	13½	532¼	151
September 22	Branch	20¼	552½	152

William W. Hunter's Distance Table *(cont.)*

Date	Location	Distance (miles)	Cumulative (miles)	Day
September 23	Rio San Pedro	8¾	561¼	153
September 24	Encamped	—	—	154
September 25	Santa Cruz Pass	12¼	573½	155
September 26	Santa Cruz	7¾	581¼	156
September 27	Bank of Rio Santa Cruz	8¾	590	157
September 28	" " " " "	16	606	158
September 29	" " " " "	17½	623½	159
September 30	Encamped	—	—	160
October 1	River bank	20	643½	161
October 2	" "	10	653½	162
October 3	San Xabier del Bac	16½	670	163
October 4	Encamped	—	—	164
October 5	Tucson	8	678	165
October 6	Near road	16	694	166
October 7	" "	16	710	167
October 8	Near the road	23	733	168
October 9	Rain water pools	15	748	169
October 10	Encamped	—	—	170
October 11	Pimo Villages	28	776	171
October 12	Encamped	—	—	172
October 13	To better grass	3	779	173
October 14	" " "	23	802	174
October 15	Rio Gila	15	817	175
October 16	Bank of Gila	4	821	176
October 17	Encamped	—	—	177
October 18	Bank of Gila	14	835	178
October 19	Encamped	—	—	179
October 20	Island in the river	10½	845½	180
October 21	Near the road	3¼	848¾	181
October 22	" " "	6¼	855	182
October 23	River bank	3	858	183
October 24	Encamped	—	—	184
October 25	-do-	—	—	185

Appendix

Date	Location	Distance (miles)	Cumulative (miles)	Day
October 26	River bank	7	865	186
October 27	Slough 1 mile from river	8	873	187
October 28	Encamped	—	—	188
October 29	River bank	9	882	189
October 30	" "	8	890	190
October 31	Encamped	—	—	191
November 1	Ponds of water and grass	10	900	192
November 2	Encamped	—	—	193
November 3	-do-	—	—	194
November 4	River bank	8	908	195
November 5	" "	3	911	196
November 6	Encamped	—	—	197
November 7	"From this point we descended the river to its mouth by occasional short drives in order to rest and to recruit the strength of our cattle."			
November 15	Rio Colorado	41	952	206
" "	Laguna 1½ miles on W side of river	2	954	"
November 16	River bank	7	961	207
November 17	Graham's Ford	5	967	208
November 18	Alamo Mucho	34¼	1001¼	209
November 19	El Rio Nuevo	10½	1011¾	210
November 20	Encamped	—	—	211
November 21	-do-	—	—	212
November 22	-do-	—	—	213
November 23	-do-	—	—	214
November 24	-do-	—	—	215
November 25	Bend of New River	8	1019¾	216
November 26	Laguna	10	1029¾	217
" "	Mouth of cañon	16	1045¾	"
November 27	Palmetto Spring	19	1064¾	218
November 28	Las Bayacitos	6¼	1071	219
November 29	El Puerto	4½	1075½	220
November 30	Western extremity of cañon	7½	1083	221

Appendix

William W. Hunter's Distance Table *(cont.)*

Date	Location	Distance (miles)	Cumulative (miles)	Day
December 1	San Felipe	6½	1089½	222
December 2	Oak Grove	8	1097½	223
December 3	Warner's Ranch			224
December 4	Roadside			225
December 5	Near Santa Isabella			226
December 6	Santa Isabella			227
December 7	Santa Maria Rancho			228
December 8	Cañon			229
December 9	Western extremity of Pass			230
December 10	Encamped			231
December 11	Roadside			232
December 12	Mission de San Diego			233
December 13	San Diego	60		234

1157½ miles from Santa Fe
966¼   "   " Williamsburg
2123¼ miles

Selected Bibliography

I. Primary Sources

A. Published Overland Journals

Aldrich, Lorenzo D. *A Journal of the Overland Route to California and the Gold Mines.* Edited by Glen Dawson. Los Angeles: Dawson's Book Shop, 1950. First published in 1852, this was one of the earliest accounts of the Southern Route to appear in print. Includes Dawson's bibliography of other southern route accounts.

Audubon, John Woodhouse. *Audubon's Western Journal, 1849–1850.* Edited by Maria R. Audubon. Tucson: University of Arizona Press, 1984. Audubon traveled most of the way through northern Mexico and joined the southern route at the Pima Villages.

Bieber, Ralph P., editor. *Southern Trails to California in 1849.* Glendale, CA: Arthur H. Clarke, 1937. Early scholarly study of the southern route; includes newspaper accounts and several brief journals.

Brownlee, Robert. *An American Odyssey: The Autobiography of Robert Brownlee.* Edited by Patricia Etter. Fayetteville: University of Arkansas Press, 1986. A third of his account is devoted to reminiscences of the trip over the southern route in 1849; appendix contains Etter's extensive bibliography of Southern Route diaries and journals.

Chamberlin, William H. "From Lewisburg (PA) to California in 1849: Notes From the Diary of William H. Chamberlin." Edited by Lansing B. Bloom. *New Mexico Historical Review* 20 (1945). The edited diary appeared in all four issues for 1945. After Powell's narrative (see below) this is the best published account of the Southern Route. Chamberlin traveled with a mule pack train from Fort Smith, Arkansas to California.

Clarke, Asa B. *Travels in Mexico and California.* Boston: Wright & Hasty's Steam Press, 1852. Clarke traveled through northern Mexico and joined the southern route at Guadalupe Pass.

Cox, Cornelius C. "From Texas to California in 1849: Diary of C. C. Cox." Edited by Mabelle Eppard Martin. *Southwestern Historical Quarterly* 29 (1925–26). The diary appeared in all four issues.

De Ferrari, Carlo M., editor. "The Journal of the La Grange Company: Being the Record of a Journey From Texas to California in 1849." *The Quarterly of the Tuolumne County [CA] Historical Society* 6 (Oct–Dec 1966): 182–84; 6 (Jan–Mar 1967):193–200; 6 (Apr–June 1967):206–12; 7 (July–Sept 1967):217–20; 7 (Oct–Dec 1967):224–28; 7 (Jan–Mar 1968):236–40. The journal was kept at different times by three members of the train: John Murchison, Samuel Pearce Birt, and J. B. Cameron.

Dillon, Richard H., editor. *Texas Argonauts: Isaac H. Duval and the California Gold Rush.* San Francisco: Book Club of California, 1987. Duval traveled across Texas and joined the Cooke's road at Guadalupe Pass.

Foreman, Grant. *March and the Gold Seekers.* Norman: University of Oklahoma Press, 1939. Detailed study of the Fort Smith-Santa Fe route; includes excerpts from diaries and newspapers.

Green, Robert B. *On the Arkansas Route to California in 1849: The*

Journal of Robert B. Green, of Lewisburg, Penn. Edited by J. Orlin Oliphant. Lewisburg, PA: Bucknell University Press, 1955. Green was a member of Chamberlin's party.

Hammond, George P. and Howes, Edward H., editors. *Overland to California on the Southwest Trail, 1849.* Berkeley and Los Angeles: University of California Press, 1950.

Harris, Benjamin Butler. *The Gila Trail: The Texas Argonauts and the California Gold Rush.* Edited by Richard H. Dillon. Norman: University of Oklahoma Press, 1960.

Hayes, Benjamin. *Pioneer Notes.* Los Angeles: Privately Printed, 1929.

Pancoast, Charles Edward. *A Quaker Forty-Niner.* Edited by Ann Paschall Hannum. Philadelphia: University of Pennsylvania Press, 1930.

Powell, H. M. T. *The Santa Fe Trail to California, 1849–1852.* Edited by Douglas Watson. San Francisco: Book Club of California, 1931. The most descriptive and entertaining of the southern route accounts.

B. Unpublished Manuscripts

Brainard, David. "Journal of the Walworth County Mutual Mining Company, Commencing March the 20th, 1849." Manuscript, State Historical Society of Wisconsin.

Chatham, J. W. *Overland Journal.* Manuscript, Center for Southwest Research, Special Collections, University of New Mexico General Library. Chatham's account from South Carolina to Quarai, New Mexico.

Simmons, Joseph R. "Notes of Travel: Adventures of a Party of Missourians Who Traveled Overland from Missouri to California, A.D. 1849." Manuscript, State Historical Society of Missouri, Columbia, Missouri.

Stevens, Benjamin. Untitled account of a journey from Hannibal, Missouri, to California in 1849. Manuscript in the John Lewis RoBards Papers, State Historical Society of Missouri, Columbia, Missouri. The journal is anonymous, but internal evidence indicates that it was kept by Benjamin Stevens (1801–96), a Baptist minister from Hannibal, Missouri.

C. *Other Primary Sources*

1. *Reports*

Abert, James W. *Report of Lieut. J. W. Abert of His Examination of New Mexico, in the Years 1846–47* [30th Cong., 1st Sess., Ex. Doc. 41] (Washington, D.C.: Wendell and Van Benthuysen, 1848.

Bandelier, Adolph F. A. *Final Report of Investigations Among the Indians of the Southwest United States: Carried on Mainly in the Years from 1880 to 1885*. Cambridge University Press, 1892. Includes information and description of the former missions and other sites visited by the Forty-Niners.

Bartlett, John Russell. *Personal Narrative of Explorations and Incidents in Texas, New Mexico, California, Sonora, and Chihuahua*. New York: Appleton & Co., 1854. Bartlett headed the U.S. Boundary Commission, and his account is valuable for descriptions of areas in New Mexico, Arizona and California traversed by the Forty-Niners.

Cooke, Philip St. George. *Journal of the March of the Mormon Battalion*. Washington, D.C.: Senate Document, Special Session, 1849. Cooke blazed the road from the Rio Grande to the Gila River which was followed by the majority of American Forty-Niners on the southern route.

Emory, William H. *Notes of a Military Reconnoissance from Fort Leavenworth . . . to San Diego, in California* [30th Cong., 1st Sess. House Doc. 41] Washington, D.C.: Wendell and Van Benthuysen, 1848. This edition also included Abert's and Cooke's reports.

Report of the Boundary Commission Upon the Survey and Remarking of the Boundary Between the United States and Mexico West of the Rio Grande, 1891–1896. Washington, D.C.: Government Printing Office, 1898.

Reports of Explorations and Surveys. 1855–61. Included in this massive compilation are the following reports relevant to the areas crossed by the Forty-Niners:

In vol. 2:

> Parke, John G. *Report of Explorations . . . Near the Thirty-Second Parallel . . . Between Dona Ana, on the Rio Grande, and [the] Pimas Villages, on the Gila.*

In vol. 7:

> Antisell, Thomas. "Geological Report."
>
> Campbell, Albert H. "Remarks on Meteorology." (Appendix A)
>
> Poole, Charles H. "Report Upon the Route from San Diego to Fort Yuma." (Appendix B)

Whipple, Amel W. *The Whipple Report: Journal of an Expedition From San Diego, Calif., to the Rio Colorado, From September 11 to December 11, 1849.* Los Angeles: Westernlore Press, 1961. Whipple was at Yuma Crossing when the Forty-Niners were passing through, and his report describes the conditions they encountered.

2. Travel Accounts

Barry, Louise, comp. *The Beginning of the West: Annals of the Kansas Gateway to the American West, 1540–1854.* Topeka: Kansas State Historical Society, 1972. A chronological compilation of newspaper reports and articles. The chapter for 1849 is extremely valuable for information about groups setting out over the Santa Fe Trail portion of the southern route.

Brewerton, George Douglas. *Overland With Kit Carson: A Narrative of the Old Spanish Trail in '48.* New York: Coward-McCann, Inc., 1930.

Carleton, James Henry. *Diary of an Excursion to the Ruins of Abo, Quarra and Gran Quivira in New Mexico in 1853.* Santa Fe: Stagecoach Press, 1965.

Cooke, Philip St. George. *The Conquest of New Mexico and California.* New York: G. P. Putnam's Sons, 1878. A rewritten and expanded account of the Mormon Battalion's operations and the opening of the road from the Rio Grande to San Diego.

Couts, Cave Johnson. *From San Diego to the Colorado in 1849: The Journal and Maps of Cave J. Couts.* Edited by Arthur Woodward. Los Angeles: Westernlore Press, 1956. Couts commanded the escort for Whipple's surveying party (see above) to the Yuma Crossing, and his account includes descriptions of the Forty-Niners.

————. *Hepah, California!* Edited by Henry F. Dobyns. Tucson: Arizona Pioneer's Historical Society, 1961. Couts' account of his journey from Mexico to San Diego by way of the Gila Valley in 1848 with a battalion of Dragoons.

Davis, William W. H. *El Gringo: or, New Mexico and Her People.* New York: Harper & Brothers, 1857.

Froebel, Julius. *Seven Years' Travel in Central America, Northern Mexico, and the Far West of the United States.* London: Richard Bentley, 1859. Froebel traveled the Santa Fe Trail in 1852, and took Cooke's route from Mexico to California in 1854.

Garrard, Lewis H. *Wah-To-Yah and the Taos Trail.* Cincinnati: H. W. Derby & Co., 1850.

Gregg, Josiah. *Commerce of the Prairies: or, Journal of a Santa Fe Trader.* New York: Henry G. Langley, 1844.

Gregg, Kate L., editor. *The Road to Santa Fe: The Journal and Diaries of George Champlain Sibley.* Albuquerque: University of New Mexico Press, 1952.

Heap, Gwinn Harris. *Central Route to the Pacific . . . Missouri to California, in 1853.* Philadelphia: Lippincott, Grambo, and Co., 1854. Heap traveled a portion of the Santa Fe Trail.

Hulbert, Archer Butler, editor. *Southwest on the Turquoise Trail: The First Diaries on the Road to Santa Fe.* Denver: Public Library, 1933.

Wislizenus, Adolphus. *Memoir of a Tour to Northern Mexico.* Washington, D.C.: Tippin & Streeper, 1848. The author traveled over the Santa Fe Trail.

II. Secondary Sources

A. General Histories

Forrest, Earle R. *Missions and Pueblos of the Old Southwest.* Cleveland: Arthur H. Clark Co., 1929.

Frazer, Robert W., editor. *New Mexico in 1850: A Military View.* Norman: University of Oklahoma Press, 1968.

Hague, Harlan. *The Road to California: The Search for a Southern Overland Route, 1540–1848.* Glendale, CA: Arthur H. Clark Co., 1978. A good review and summary of the various expeditions and attempts to establish a viable road.

Keleher, William A. *Turmoil in New Mexico, 1846–1868.* Santa Fe: Rydal Press, 1952.

Kessell, John L. *Friars, Soldiers and Reformers: Hispanic Arizona and the Sonoran Mission Frontier, 1767–1856.* Tucson: University of Arizona Press, 1976.

McCarty, Kieran. *Desert Documentary: The Spanish Years, 1767–1821.* Tucson: Arizona Historical Society, 1976. Historical Monograph No. 4. An excellent source for the history of the Santa Cruz Valley prior to the coming of the Forty-Niners.

Moorhead, Max L. *New Mexico's Royal Road: Trade and Travel on the Chihuahua Trail.* Norman: University of Oklahoma Press, 1958.

———. *The Presidio: Bastion of the Spanish Borderlands.* Norman: University of Oklahoma Press, 1975.

Officer, James E. *Hispanic Arizona, 1536–1856.* Tucson: University of Arizona Press, 1987. Includes sections that provide Mexican views of the passage of the Forty-Niners through southern Arizona.

Roca, Paul M. *Paths of the Padres Through Sonora.* Tucson: University of Arizona Press, 1967. Contains information on various sites in northern Sonora and southern Arizona passed by the Forty-Niners.

Unruh, John D. *The Plains Across: The Overland Emigrants and the Trans-Mississippi West, 1840–60.* Urbana: University of Illinois Press, 1979. Scholarly study of overland emigration on the northern routes.

Walter, Paul A. F. *The Cities That Died of Fear: The Story of the Saline Pueblos.* Santa Fe: El Palacio Press, 1931. A history of the Quarai and Abo areas.

B. Guides, Gazetteers, and so forth

Broadhead, G. C. "Early Missouri Roads." *Missouri Historical Review* 8 (1914) issue no. 2.

Conkling, Margaret B. and Roscoe P. *The Butterfield Overland Mail, 1857–1869.* Glendale, CA: Arthur H. Clark Co., 1947. A classic study of the overland route; includes descriptions of the route through the southwest followed by the Forty-Niners.

Eaton, David W. "How Missouri Counties, Towns and Streams Were Named." *Missouri Historical Review* 10 (1916), nos. 3 and 4; 11 (1917), nos. 2 and 3.

Edwards, E. I. *Lost Oases Along the Carrizo.* Los Angeles: Westernlore Press, 1961. A detailed study of the final portion of the southern overland route, from Yuma Crossing to Warner's Pass.

Franzwa, Gregory M. *Maps of the Santa Fe Trail.* St. Louis, Mo.: Patrice Press, 1989.

Granger, Byrd Howell. *Arizona's Names.* Tucson: Falconer Publishing Co., 1983.

Gudde, Erwin G. *California Place Names.* Berkeley: University of California Press, 1949.

Pearce, Thomas M. *New Mexico Place Names: A Geographical Dictionary.* Albuquerque: University of New Mexico Press, 1965.

Peterson, Charles S. [and others] *Mormon Battalion Trail Guide.* Salt Lake City: Utah State Historical Society, 1972. Utah State Historical Society Western Trail Guide Series No. 1. Includes a series of topographic maps which trace the unit's route from Fort Leavenworth to San Diego, California.

Selected Bibliography

Much of the route was the same as followed by Hunter's train.

Simmons, Marc. *Following the Santa Fe Trail: A Guide for Modern Travelers.* 2nd ed. Santa Fe: Ancient City Press, 1986. The standard guide for finding trail landmarks.

Stocking, Hobart E. *The Road to Santa Fe.* New York: Hastings House, 1971. Includes numerous maps showing the Santa Fe Trail in relation to modern landmarks.

Williams, Jerry L., editor. *New Mexico in Maps.* 2nd ed. Albuquerque: University of New Mexico Press, 1986. Good coverage on historical topics.

Index